For Laci

For Laci

A Mother's Story of Love, Loss, and Justice

Sharon Rocha

THREE RIVERS PRESS

NEW YORK

Published in the United States by Three Rivers Press, an imprint of the
Crown Publishing Group, a division of Random House, Inc., New York.
www.crownpublishing.com

THREE RIVERS PRESS and the Tugboat design are registered trademarks
of Random House, Inc.

Grateful acknowledgment is made to the following for permission to reprint
previously published and unpublished material:
Carole Bruzzano: "Mom Share 'Our' Smile with the World," by Carole Bruzzano.
Copyright © 2004 by Carole Bruzzano. Reprinted by permission of Carole Bruzzano.
Dianne Collins: "Laci's Baby" by Diana Garrison. Copyright © 2003 by Diana
Garrison (D. Collins, Dothan, Alabama). Reprinted by permission of Dianne Collins.

Originally published in hardcover in the United States by Crown Publishers,
an imprint of the Crown Publishing Group, a division of Random House, Inc.,
New York, in 2006.

Library of Congress Cataloging-in-Publication Data is available on request.

ISBN-13: 978-0-307-33829-7
ISBN-10: 0-307-33829-0

Printed in the United States of America

Design by Lauren Dong

10 9 8 7 6 5 4 3 2 1

First Paperback Edition

For Laci and Conner

Contents

Mom, Share "Our" Smile with the World

I am embraced in love and light,
And my baby is embraced by me
God's loving arms, they hold us now
For all eternity

Remember the laughter we shared
Please keep laughing,
I still laugh with you

No more sleepless nights, Mom
Please rest for me

In the morning I'll be there
Rising with the sun

I am in your soul
I am your sunlight
I am the rays that break through
Mom, please understand
I do this now for you

My smile, he could not take from me
My smile that graces the screen
It's your smile, Mom . . .
It's your smile now they see

For all I've become
It's because of you
You've allowed the world to see
Your hope, your tears,
And now,
My spirit soaring free

It's in our smile, Mom
It's yours, it's mine

Please, keep smiling for me

Adapted from a poem by Carole Bruzzano and read by
Sandy Rickard at Laci's memorial service,
on her twenty-eighth birthday, May 4, 2003

Author's Note

You wake up from most nightmares and they're over. Mine was different. I was awake when it started, and I've barely slept since. It was December 24, 2002, a date when life as I'd always known it stopped forever. We were expecting my daughter, Laci, and her husband, Scott, for dinner. But about forty-five minutes before they were supposed to arrive, the phone rang and Scott asked if Laci was with me. When I said no, he said she was missing.

Missing? Laci, *missing?* The word was so wrong in terms of Laci. She was twenty-seven years old, seven and a half months pregnant, and happy and healthy. She was reliable, punctual, and responsible. She and I were on the phone all the time and she was in constant touch with her girlfriends. We called her JJ—a childhood nickname for Jabber Jaws—because she talked nonstop. She didn't wander off without telling someone. She didn't go missing.

When Laci and her son, Conner, were found on April 13 and 14, 2003, everything just got worse. Instead of hoping we'd get Laci back, we had to come to terms with the permanence of her death. She'd been murdered, and the person who murdered her was the man she loved most in the world, her husband. It shouldn't have happened, and yet I don't know how we could have prevented it.

This has been an intensely personal tragedy played out in public. At the core, my family and I have experienced new depths of anger, pain, fear, confusion, frustration, and grief. We saw Scott convicted for murder, but we were never getting Laci back. This ordeal continues to feel like a horrible sickness for which there's no cure. Laci was my daughter, my best friend, a wonderful person. She added to the world in a positive way. You knew everything you ever needed to know about her the instant she smiled.

I needed to be convinced it was okay to write this book, and that wasn't a quick or easy process. I did a lot of soul searching. I worried it was inappropriate and fretted I was betraying Laci. I had many conversations with her about these issues. Then, one day I recalled a conversation I'd had with Det. Craig Grogan during the trial. I'd asked him if the dog handlers who were involved in the original search for Laci were still looking for her. He said no, and explained that the handlers' expenses are covered through donations or out of their own pockets and basically the police department was out of money.

Recalling that conversation became my deciding factor; I'd use money from this book to start a fund for search and rescue in memory of Laci and Conner.

I knew Laci would approve.

In this book, I've tried to recall some of those everyday moments that will help people know Laci the way her family and friends did. She deserves to be remembered for her life, not her death. I've also described to the best of my ability what I went through from that first unsuspecting moment when I picked up the phone on December 24, 2002, to the tears I cried when Scott was convicted of murdering Laci and Conner and was sentenced to death.

For the past couple years, I have filled Laci's old bedroom with everything I have from her life and her death. You can't get into the room anymore. Whenever I received a box of letters, I put them in there. When a San Luis Obispo businessman sent me two paintings he found that she'd done in high school, I leaned them against her old bed. I saved every newspaper article and put them in boxes. And in the back corner is a cedar chest containing her cheerleader outfits, school awards, letters, and albums, all things I struggled to retrieve from her old house after she was murdered. I saved her belongings so I wouldn't lose her.

On the day I started this book, I opened my cedar chest and some of the boxes for the first time. I found papers she'd written in grade school. I reread the holiday cards she made as a child, each one ending with "Love, Laci." I watched her wedding video again and cried at how beautiful and happy she was that day. I also went to the house where she lived with Scott, and I walked through the park where we'd looked for her in the cold the night Scott called and said she was missing, the night our lives changed forever.

I wanted to put it all in this book, and I tried. By going through all this again, this time on my terms, I hoped to start the healing process and repair some of my hurt and heartbreak. Thus far, that has proved to be unrealistic. I still cry every day. I've moved forward, but not very far. My wound has remained large and fresh. I don't know if I'll ever heal. I think you learn to live with the pain.

I still talk to Laci. There are so many things I still want to say to her. I tell her that I am so sorry this happened. I'm sorry I wasn't there to protect her when she needed to be protected. I'm sorry I didn't see Scott for who he really is and get her away from him before he could hurt her. I tell her how much I miss her, how much I wish she was still here, able to stop by or call, and how much I love her.

I can't recall a single day since she disappeared when I haven't thought about her and cried. I'll hear a certain song, catch a particular scent, see a sunflower, a ladybug, or a dragonfly—her favorites—or pass her junior high school, and I'll be reminded of her.

For a moment, I'll forget she's gone. Then it hits me, cruelly and hard.

About a year after Laci was murdered, I was on my way out of the house, and I'd just closed the door behind me when I heard the phone ring. I hurried back inside, thinking it might be Laci because I hadn't spoken to her for a long time. Of course it wasn't Laci. It won't ever be Laci.

These are still tough times. I get by one day at a time. I feel better when I'm helping others. I speak out on behalf of victims' rights. I am eternally grateful to my family and friends—my circle of love, as I refer to them—who have been with us from day one of this nightmare.

In times of despair, they offered hope. During times of weakness, they provided strength. In moments of hate, they gave love.

As always, I want to express my unending gratitude to the Stanislaus County District Attorney's Office and the Modesto Police Department, and to every person and organization that helped search for Laci and Conner and sought justice for their murders. I also want to acknowledge everyone who sent e-mails, cards, photos, flowers, and gifts; who posted messages in our online guest book; and who kept us in their prayers.

I may have often felt alone, but I know I was never by myself. All of you sustained me through the worst times.

I believe there is more love in the world than there is pain, and when I'm feeling doubtful about that or down, I remind myself of it by looking at the cards and letters I received, such as this one:

Dear Sharon,

I know it's not the same as if you were getting the card from Laci, but I hope this eases some of the pain on Mother's Day. My mother won't talk to me and never loved me. My baby doesn't have a grandmother. I wish I could bring Laci back for you. I don't have a mother, so I hope you don't mind if I make you my mom today . . .

I've never been able to fully understand why Laci's disappearance and murder captivated so many people, but I have my own theory. I believe that Laci wasn't going to allow Scott to get away with murder, so she kept the spotlight shining down on him until he was convicted. She was determined to see him punished. At the same time, I know Laci wouldn't have believed all the attention. The outpouring of love and concern would have amazed her. Whenever she was surprised about something, she said, "Nah-ah," and I can hear her saying that about all the attention her story generated around the world.

"Nah-ah, Mom."

She wasn't perfect, but there was something special about Laci. She couldn't wait to be a mom. When she smiled, every one of her five feet one inches lit up. You felt her enthusiasm. She made an impression. She was a real person, not a face in a magazine, and I will always remember her as someone who truly lived life, who savored each moment of her life.

I'd give anything to go back in time for one more minute with her. She loved Scott. All of us did. Not only did I lose Laci and Conner, I also lost my son-in-law. The Scott Peterson the world came to know is not the Scott Peterson we knew before December 24, 2002. We learned about that person through police investigations and in court, in the papers and on television, the same as everyone else. Prior to that, he was different. All of us were.

Part One

Her Mother's Daughter

She'd want us to laugh and recall all of

the good times we had with her.

Brent Rocha, Laci's brother

Chapter One

It was spring 2005, and I heard a sound at home that had been absent for a long time—laughter.

Two of Laci's longtime girlfriends, Stacey Boyers and Lori Ellsworth, were at my dining room table. Both were in their late twenties, the same age Laci would have been. They were dressed casually, they looked nice, and they radiated a youthful glow. I marveled at how much life they had in them. I pictured them as little girls at that table doing homework, snacking on cookies, and giggling at which boys liked which girls. Now they were reminiscing about Laci.

I gave Lori a cold beer, put a glass of Chardonnay in front of Stacey, and took one myself. Soon they were telling Laci stories that made them laugh, especially the latest one. Stacey started to describe what they'd done at the cemetery but abruptly cut herself off.

Seeming alarmed, she looked at Lori and, while trying not to laugh, asked, "Should I tell her what we said today?"

"Oh my God," Lori said. "You can't."

I looked around the table. There were four chairs and three of us. If Laci were in that fourth chair, she'd be the one most eager to hear what was making them laugh. I said exactly what Laci would've said to Stacey: "Go ahead. Tell me."

Stacey—whom I've known since she was eight—didn't require much coaxing, and neither did Lori, once they got started.

"Lori and I went to visit Laci today," Stacey said. "We were standing there, talking to her, like we always do, catching her up with all the gossip.

"Then we were quiet for a minute and I said to Lori, 'I know what's going on with her. I can hear Laci now, knocking on her neighbors' caskets, saying, *Hello! Anybody in there? Who's there? I need to talk to somebody.*'"

As she said this, Lori was turning red from embarrassment. She was probably thinking, Oh my gosh, how's Sharon going to take this? Here's what I did: I laughed. I couldn't help it. It had been so long since I heard the sound of laughter at home. At one time, it had been common. Laci had a terrific sense of humor. She laughed a lot. Listening to Lori and Stacey, I was reminded of all the times the girls had sat around the table, talking and laughing.

"You know she's down there talking nonstop," Lori said, laughing. "She's down there going, *Hey, excuse me! Pardon me! We haven't met. I'm Laci . . .*

"*I want to tell you about my little boy,*" Stacey said in a Laci-like voice. "*I want to tell you what I'm cooking today . . .*"

Lori pretended to be Laci's neighbors.

"*Who put her here?*" she said in a deep voice. "*Can somebody please move her! She doesn't stop talking.*"

They were right. That was Laci.

And I missed it. I missed her so much.

Without her, a part of me was gone forever, too.

I grew up in Escalon, a small agricultural town of about 2,000 people adjacent to Modesto in central California. I remember Escalon as a picture-postcard of rural small-town life: cattle ranches, farms, dairies, and orchards. The Sierras rose in the distance.

I was the second of four children. My father, Cliff Anderson, was a foreman on a peach and almond ranch, and my mother, Elta, was a full-time homemaker. In high school, I was an A-student, a cheerleader, and Homecoming princess. I don't know where I got the nerve to be a cheerleader. Unlike Laci, I was always shy, self-conscious, and easily intimidated.

During my freshman year, I started dating Dennis Rocha, the son of a dairyman whose Portuguese family had deep roots in Escalon. Dennis was already attending Modesto Junior College when a mutual friend introduced us at a dance in Turlock. We became serious very quickly. After I graduated from high school in 1969, Dennis and I married in a traditional ceremony at St. Patrick's Church attended by four hundred people, most of them Dennis's relatives, or so it seemed. We moved into a new three-bedroom home on the north end of his family's 365-acre ranch.

I started Modesto Junior College but left by the end of the year, feeling pressure to be a wife, not a student. My first child, Brent, arrived in 1971. As much as he became the center of my world, I sensed that I had married and left school too young. I couldn't articulate it then, but I felt I might have cheated myself from life experiences.

So much was going on in the world, so much was happening up the highway in the hippie-populated San Francisco, and I was curious about life beyond the small California town I knew way too well. I was just nineteen, a child myself, and I had barely started to live my own life. I wondered what opportunities I might be missing.

But I kept those thoughts to myself. Besides, my life wasn't terrible.

Nearly four years later, I got pregnant again, this time with Laci. I wish I could remember more about carrying her for those nine months, but I'm afraid the pregnancy was uneventful other than the time I got sick eating a bowl of banana-nut ice cream, which, in reality, I didn't even like. I also craved hot fudge sundaes and See's candy, and ate my fair share.

"No wonder I'm chubby," Laci said when she was twelve years old and I told her about the significant amounts of chocolate I'd consumed while pregnant with her. "I didn't stand a chance because of all the chocolate you ate while you carried me."

True to form, Laci arrived right on time, on her due date of May 4, 1975, and she was in a hurry. It felt as if I had just checked into Doctors Medical Center when I complained to the nurse, "I think the baby's coming."

"The doctor's not here," the nurse snapped. "That baby can't come yet."

I said, "Oh yes it can," and we went back and forth like that for what seemed to me a cruel number of hours.

In reality, I was at the hospital only two hours before I gave birth. When the doctor said I had a baby girl, I was ecstatic. Then, as I've always joked, I saw her. Laci was wrinkly, with a mess of dark hair, and my first impression was that she looked like my grandmother on my father's side, not exactly the personification of beauty. But as time passed, Laci got much cuter. She was all smiles and spunk. And no one ever thought of my grandma when they saw her.

I named Laci after a pretty girl I had met when I was in high school. I'd done the same with Brent, his namesake being one of Dennis's college buddies who I thought was very handsome.

Having felt so good through my pregnancy, I sensed Laci was going to be an easy baby, and I was right. It took just two weeks until she slept through the night, and she almost always woke up in the best mood. On most mornings, I found her sitting in her green spindle crib with a smile on her face, staring at the yellow-and-orange elephant quilt on the wall. She amused herself and smiled all the time. I hate to boast, but she was so cute. I still look at those pictures and want to squeeze her.

Just after Laci turned one, I split from Dennis—proof that I spoke from experience when I later declared to Scott that *divorce is always an option, not murder!* At the time we split, I thought the reasons were complicated, but I now know that I was simply facing what I felt in my gut. I'd married too young. Except for my children, nearly everything in my life was left over from high school, and it didn't feel right. I was still in my early twenties, and I craved more.

I've read that Dennis is the one who left, but I'm the one who moved out, and it wasn't easy or pleasant. I wrote him a letter, explaining my thoughts and feelings as best I could, and then we talked about it. He wasn't happy about getting a divorce, and as often happens when feelings are raw and unclear, we had a hard time for a while.

I took Brent and Laci and moved in with a friend in Escalon, then we rented a house in Modesto. Around Christmastime, Dennis and I got back together. The holidays were hard on both of us. But the reconciliation lasted only a few weeks, and this time when we split, it was permanent (though today we have a good relationship).

In early 1977, I moved to San Jose, thinking that was the change I needed, and got a job at an insurance company dealing with workmen's comp. But San Jose turned out to be too big a city for me. The nightly news was filled with reports of crime and violence, and I thought, Who needs this when I can have the quiet, comfort, and relative safety of a small town?

Within six months, I moved back to Modesto and rented a small two-bedroom duplex. The woman next door, Susan, had a son the same age as Laci, and we became friends. I also met her sister, Roxie, who had kids the same ages as mine. I appreciated being back home and woke up mornings feeling as if the sun was shining on me again.

I got an office job in the shipping-receiving warehouse for Standard Brands, which, after mergers and acquisitions, became Nabisco and then RJR. A few months later, my cousin Gwen called me at work and said she wanted me to meet a guy.

Even though it was a Friday night in November and I didn't have plans I said no. I wasn't in the mood for any kind of romantic stuff.

"Sharon, his name is Ron Grantski, and he's a nice guy," she said.

"No, thanks," I said and hung up the phone.

She called back three or four times and persisted until she wore me down.

Still, I didn't want to go by myself, so I brought a girlfriend from work. We met Gwen and her husband, Harvey Kemple, at a local hangout. At the time, Ron worked for Harvey in construction. Initially, Ron mistook my girlfriend for me. Wishful thinking, I imagine; she was very pretty. Nevertheless, he and I hit it off that first night. We talked and laughed for hours. I told my friends that he had made me feel comfortable, which wasn't easy given my thick reserve.

But I hadn't met anyone with Ron's qualities. I liked that he was at ease with himself and very confident. Born in St. Louis, Missouri, he lived in Nebraska and Oregon before his family settled in Sacramento, California. At nineteen, he joined the Navy. After boot camp, he married his high school sweetheart and they moved to Hawaii and had a son. At the time we met, he was divorced and in Modesto working construction. He was ambitious, solid, funny, and he made me feel good about myself.

A year and a half after Gwen introduced us, Ron and I moved into a three-bedroom home with Brent, then eight, and Laci, four. Why didn't we ever marry? Well, we planned to. In 1981, we were actually in the midst of making arrangements when my father was killed in an automobile accident. It was an awful ordeal and obviously everything was canceled. Then the next time we talked about getting married, Ron's father passed away. We got the message. Since both of us wanted to keep our mothers around, we agreed the only aisle we would walk down together would be one at the grocery store.

No one objected, including our children. Their thoughts were our top priority, and they were fine with our arrangement. Our family life was typical of two parents raising two little children. It was never dull or quiet. One Christmas, when Laci was around four years old, we were driving the kids around to look at the lights. As we passed a house with an elaborate display, Laci said, "Ooooh, pretty," and Brent took exception to the way she said that. It annoyed him, he said. So what happened? For the next few years, every time we passed that house, Laci would say, "Ooooh, pretty."

Laci liked teasing her big brother. I once took them to get ice cream sundaes and Brent asked Laci for her cherry. Even though she didn't like cherries, she said no. No matter how much he pleaded, she refused. I was almost as frustrated by her as Brent was, and so I made her eat it. And the next time Brent asked for the cherry, he got it.

Then there was the party at their grandparents' house when Brent dared Laci to take off her bathing suit. There were twenty-five to thirty people around the backyard pool. Laci, who was probably four years old, didn't hesitate. All of a sudden she was scampering around completely naked and laughing. She wasn't laughing nearly as hard as Brent, though. He was even more entertained when their grandma went over to Laci and said, "Honey, you're not supposed to be taking off your bathing suit."

It was around that same time that Laci made her debut in the kitchen. I was baking for the family and she wanted to help. She stood at the counter with all the confidence of Julia Child. I wrapped her in an apron, put a bowl in front of her, and let her cook. She put together a concoction that included milk, banana, a raw egg, and a few other things I can't recall. But I remember it was pretty gross, and when she asked me to try it, I said, "Why don't we let Ron taste it."

She took it to where Ron was watching TV in the living room. Grinning, she offered the glass to him. He took it from her appreciatively and made a nice show of being excited to try her first culinary invention; then he actually drank the whole thing down, pronouncing it delicious. I can still hear him say, "That was really good, Laci." She came back into the kitchen beaming with pride. Later the day I told Ron what had actually been in the glass and he gagged. "You let me drink that?"

Brent loved spending time with his father on his ranch, and at age nine he went to live there full-time (Dennis had remarried and had another daughter, Amy). My mom and dad also lived on a ranch, and Brent and Laci adored visiting them, too. We had big family gatherings there, and they were just like when I was a kid. Brent and Laci followed their cousins, Jeanette, Karen, Rene, and Rachel, out on the dirt road behind the house and listened to them tell stories about wolves and monsters coming out of the orchards, until finally the younger ones ran screaming to their grandma.

When Laci was in kindergarten, she drew a picture of all of her siblings and all of her parents, and beneath her colorful rendering, she wrote, "I love my family." She did, too. She felt that way her whole life.

Chapter Two

Every mother has a sixth sense about her child's well-being. You don't have to be told when something is wrong. You feel it in your gut, you see it, you just know. And I knew something was wrong with Laci. She was seven years old, and she didn't look or act like herself. She slept later than normal and didn't get up with her usual smile or bounce. She didn't eat normally and had dark rings under her eyes. She didn't complain, but she wasn't Laci-like.

I called the pediatrician to make an appointment, but the nurse couldn't get her in for a week or two because it was Christmas vacation. From the description I gave, the nurse made it seem as if it was probably the flu. It was flu season, after all, and everyone was under the weather. So I sent Laci to her dad's for the second week of her vacation as planned. But midway through, Dennis's wife, Nancy, called and said Laci's glands were swollen and she didn't look right to her. Nancy felt the same way I had—she wasn't acting like Laci.

I called the pediatrician again, and this time the nurse said to bring her in immediately. Nancy met me with Laci at the office, and I knew just from looking at Laci that something was terribly wrong. The doctor confirmed it. After examining her, he pushed on her stomach and said, "Look at this."

"What am I looking at?" I asked.

He pushed again; there wasn't any depression. Her stomach didn't go in.

"Nothing is moving," he said.

Indeed, her little tummy was rock hard, solid.

After undergoing a series of tests at Doctors Medical Center, including a CAT scan, Laci was sent to a surgeon. That threw me over the edge. How had we gone from the flu to a surgeon? The surgeon showed me her CAT scan and explained that Laci had a grapefruit-sized tumor in her stomach that was likely also causing an infection. He wanted to take it out as soon as possible. Before he operated, though, he wanted to try to get her temperature down, so he told me to take her home and make her rest, give her cold baths, and feed her lots of liquids. When I got her home, Laci wanted, of all things, Chinese food. Figuring it could only help her spirits, I picked up some egg flower soup.

She spent most of the night sitting in Ron's lap, resting her head on his chest as he rocked in a chair. In the morning, her temperature was 104, up from before. I called the doctor, who said to bring her in. He decided that her infection was getting worse, not better, and they operated a few hours later. I prayed it wasn't cancer, but I was told the surgeon wouldn't know exactly what was going on until he opened her up. I was told seven doctors were involved in the surgery. I was scared out of my wits.

After I don't know how many hours passed, the surgeon found me in the waiting room and said Laci was going to be fine. I was so relieved. I felt like I took my first breath in hours. Then the floodgates opened and I was awash in tears. According to the doctor, the tumor was a rare and unusually large dermoid tumor, and, thank God, it was benign. Laci had been so sick and run such a high temperature because the tumor pressed against her bladder, causing a kidney infection. He also said the tumor had attached itself to one of her ovaries, requiring its removal. I asked how that would affect her future.

"When we first saw the extent of the tumor, we feared we might have to perform a complete hysterectomy," he said. "Fortunately, we didn't. She'll be able to have as many children as she wants."

Relief. Joy. More tears.

Laci spent the next four days recuperating in the hospital. On the fifth day, I received a call at work saying I should pick her up. Laci had bounced back quickly. She had walked up and down the halls with her IV, which she nicknamed Charlie, and pressed the nurse's call button all the time, even when she didn't need anything, because she just wanted to talk. They thought she was adorable, but they were ready for her to go home.

"She's a good kid," the doctor said as I left the hospital. "She will be back to normal quickly."

Within days, Laci was back to her old self—bubbly, energetic, and happy. It was as if she'd never been sick.

She couldn't wait to get back to school. In class, she was always the center of attention. I can still picture her as a kindergartner, walking out the door with her Hello Kitty T-shirts, lunchbox, and notebook. All the parent-teacher conferences were the same. *Laci is a good student, but she's a little chatty.*

I think she was simply enthusiastic. For instance, Laci loved to dance. Actually, she didn't know how to dance, since she didn't have the patience for dance class, so she just kind of jiggled. I will never forget visiting her classroom for Show and Tell one day and seeing her shaking her head from side to side, with her little arms out in front, snapping her fingers, feet about shoulder width apart, and the biggest smile on her face.

After a minute, the teacher stopped the music and said, "Very nice, Laci."

"But I'm not done," Laci said.

I don't think she ever felt done.

Laci loved animals and all of God's little creatures.

One day, she had been outside playing when she burst through the door and came running into the kitchen where I was preparing dinner.

"Mom, look what I found," she said, holding out her hand.

I saw that she was holding several little bugs, rollie-pollies. It had rained the night before and she found them in the gutter near the sidewalk.

"Moooom. Do we have something to put them in? I want to keep them."

I took a lid from an empty jar and punched holes in it. Then I showed her how to put her rollie-pollies into the jar and close the lid so they wouldn't get out. Of course, she insisted on doing it all by herself and took off walking down the hallway toward her bedroom with jar in one hand and bugs in the other.

After dinner I went into her room and saw the jar sitting on the window seat. When I realized that the lid wasn't on the jar I took a closer look inside; there were no rollie-pollies in it. Instead, as Laci pointed out to me, they were rolling around on the carpet. She didn't put the lid on the jar because she was afraid the bugs would die. She didn't quite get the concept of the holes in the lid.

I had to laugh as I watched her crawling around on the floor trying to retrieve all the bugs. She picked them up and put them in the jar and, this time, I put the lid on it.

For her tenth birthday, we got Laci a ten-speed bike, which she'd wanted for months. She was overjoyed and grateful. Personally, I thought the bike was too big. It was nearly as tall as she was. But she climbed on anyway and sped down the block, as if to say, "See, I told you I was ready." Nothing intimidated her.

Around the same time, she talked on a car phone for the first time. Our friend Rob had one of the earliest car phones I recall seeing, and Laci adored him. One day Laci asked if he'd take her for a ride so she could use his phone. They hadn't even rounded the block when the phone rang. It was Laci.

"Mom, guess where I am and guess what I'm doing?" she said, laughing.

"I don't know," I said, playing along.

"I'm in Rob's car!" she squealed. "Can you believe it?!"

We always referred to that first conversation on a cell phone as a life-changing experience. She talked about it for the rest of her life, and every time she smiled.

Laci's zest for life and her sense of humor come out clearly in her old school papers, which I saved to show her children one day. Take the questionnaire titled *My Story*, which she filled out on the first day of fourth grade in September 1984.

"My name is Laci Denise Rocha," she wrote in a big, loopy, little girl's hand, clearly practicing her cursive. "I weighed 7 pounds. I now weigh 70 pounds and I am 4 feet-five inches tall. I have brown hair and brown eyes. I do not wear glasses.

"I do not have freckles," Laci continued. "I am right-handed. There are five people in my family counting me. They are my dad, mom, brother, me and my sister."

The second page is called "My Likes And Dislikes." Reading it, reliving her innocence and warmth, makes me smile:

EIGHT THINGS I LIKE ARE: *music, chocolate, roller skating, my cat, my best friend Amy S., Great America, sweats, and playing*

EIGHT THINGS I REALLY DISLIKE ARE: *shots, liver, waking up early, ciggerat smoke, cleaning my room, homework, mosiqetoo bits, and spinech*

On page three, she lists her "All Time Favorites":

NUMBER:	*Three*
COLOR:	*Blue*
SCHOOL SUBJECT:	*Socil studies*
ANIMAL:	*Unicorn*
FLOWER:	*Rose*
SONG:	*Mother's Girl*
TV SHOW:	*The Billy Cosby Show*
TIME OF DAY:	*3:00 pm*
DAY OF THE WEEK:	*Friday*
MONTH OF THE YEAR:	*May*
GAME TO PLAY:	*Scat*
PLACE TO VISIT:	*Great America*
SPORT:	*Softball*

FRIENDS:	*Amy S., and Mika L.*
HOLIDAY:	*Christmas*
NEWSPAPER SECTION:	*Movies*
MOVIES:	*Police Academy 2*
CAR:	*Lambregene*
RESTAURANT:	*Taco Bell*
RECORDING GROUP:	*Prince and the Revolution*
ACTOR:	*John Ritter*
ATHLETE:	*Joe Motana*
COMIC CHARACTER:	*Garfield*
TEACHER:	*Mrs. Fisher*
CLOTHING:	*Bathing Suit*
FOODS:	*Clam chadder, salad, shrip*
FOOD COURSE:	*Spare ribs*
VEGETABLES:	*Artichokes, sweet potatoe*
DESSERT:	*Hot Fuge Sunda*
SOUP:	*Chicken duddle soup*
CANDY:	*Worms*
ICE CREAM:	*Rocky Road*

These old papers have sat in a box for nearly twenty years. Looking at them now takes me back to much happier times. I'm so glad that I saved them. She was such a precious little girl, happy, outgoing, confident, and full of love—exactly the kind of adult she'd become.

"I see myself as a short person with brown eyes and brown hair," she wrote. "Also I see myself with criked [I think she intended to write *crooked*] teeth. And I feel terrific when someone kisses me because it gives me a tingle in my stomach.

"I try to help others feel good by giving them good comments and helping others out."

On another page, she drew pictures of the people in her family.

"My dad is Dennis Rocha, and some of the different jobs he had was being in the Marines. He now works at a dairy. His hobbies are collecting antiques and working with mules and cows.

"My mom was born in California. She works at Nabisco Brands.

Her favorite color is blue. The kind of music she likes is soft rock. And three things I enjoy doing most with my mom are cooking, going to Great America, and going shopping.

"My brother is Brent and my sister is Amy. They have brown hair and brown eyes. My sister is from a different mom than my brother. My favorite things to do with my brother and my sister is swimming, going to a parade, going to the ranch.

"My best friend," she wrote, "can be counted on to be trusted, kind when something bad happens, and funny.

"My friend counts on me to be nice, to be trusted, and to stock [she meant *stick*] up for her on certain things."

Here's another questionnaire she filled out later in 1984:

I DON'T LIKE: *A lot of things. Like the color dark green. I don't like to eat liver. I don't like to drink tea. I don't like to play Monopoly. I don't like to wear socks.*

IF YOU HAD THREE WISHES . . . *If I had three wishes, I would wish for money, health, scholarship.*

THESE ARE THE WAYS I SHOW MY FEELINGS: *When I feel happy I laugh so hard my face turns red and my sides hurt. When I feel sad I cry and my eyes turn red. When I feel angry I throw stuff around and yell. When I feel proud I brag a little and smile.*

WHAT ELSE DO YOU WANT TO WRITE? *Let's see, I can tell you something that makes me frightened. It's when I see a scary movie. I can tell you something that makes me shy is when I have to tell or sing in front of a lot of people. I can tell you something that makes me cry. It's when someone hurts me.*

In second grade, she received a certificate for "neatness," though her bedroom told a different story. On her fourth-grade progress report, her teacher wrote, "Another fantastic quarter for Laci. She has great potential." In fifth grade, she brought home straight A's. "Laci's grades speak for themselves," her teacher said in the remarks section. "She is an outstanding student and a cooperative member of the class. I enjoy being her teacher."

She had flair and personality, and I think it was evident in the adorable cards and notes she drew for every occasion—and often for no reason at all. For instance, I found a pretty drawing of wind chimes she made that had this acrostic verse:

Mom, you are to me . . .

Caring
Helpful
Intelligent
Marvelous
Excellent
Special

She stamped her loving spirit on everything. Here's another note I found. "Mom, I want to thank you for doing things for me," she wrote. "You're my favorite mom." On my birthday, she drew a large birthday cake with lots of sparkling candles, beneath which she wrote in colorful, flowing crayon, "To a special person. I love that person. She is a really pretty mom. Love, Laci."

Sometimes my mind will flash on something that happened to her at school or with her friends, but I won't be able to remember exactly, and I think, Oh, I'll just call Laci and ask. Sadly, I can't do that anymore. So I'm thankful I can refer to her old school papers and the cards and letters I saved. She wasn't perfect, but she was a good and loving kid, and that shines on almost everything she wrote. Occasionally I will read one of her old papers, close my eyes, and I can see her as if she is still talking to me.

"My mom is a special person," she wrote two days after her tenth birthday. "She works hard to take care of my brother and me. One thing about my mom—her and I have a lot of fun together. Well, that's all. Love, Laci."

A month later, she was already looking excitedly to the future. Let her tell you herself: "Well, I'm 10 going on 11, so you know I've been at this school [Sonoma Elementary] for six years. I can't wait until sixth grade. Everyone is glad to get out of fifth. Junior High will be fun. Until I start that, I guess I will have to wait.

"Bye for now. Laci."

Chapter Three

While looking through Laci's things, I found a paper she wrote at thirteen years old for a creative writing class at La Loma Junior High. I almost wish that I hadn't found it. The topic was scary movie villains and she surveyed a few of them. She wrote that *A Nightmare on Elm Street*'s Freddy Krueger "has a strange way to kill his victims," she said that *Psycho*'s Norman Bates "can fool you by looking and acting like a normal person," and after a sentence on *Friday the 13th*'s Jason Voorhees, she concluded, "Watch out who you meet in your dreams, the woods or motels!"

She wrote that paper fourteen years before she was murdered, but she could have easily been talking about the seemingly nice, clean-cut guy who surprised all of us by turning out to be a murderer. *Watch out who you meet in your dreams.*

As prophetic as these words strike me now, Laci was not haunted by any premonitions of a violent end. She was always cheerfully optimistic. I'm sure she thought life would keep getting better and better. She had no reason to believe otherwise.

On the subject of movies, her all-time favorite was *Superman*. How much more positive can you get than that story? She saw *Superman* at least twenty times. And she was a sap. She cried at the end of almost every movie I saw with her. She even cried while watching sentimental commercials. She had a big old heart and a lot of empathy and feeling.

As she reached her teens, Laci lost the baby fat that had made her look chubby and blossomed into an attractive, happy, upbeat young woman. I remember that period well. All of a sudden her precious Hello Kitty things went into the closet. Up went posters of her favorite rock stars. She permed her hair and developed a stylish flair when she dressed. She wanted to look perfect. Her clothes didn't have to be expensive or designer brands or even part of the latest trend. They just had to fit her vision.

In that vision she was about seven inches taller, with longer legs. But there was nothing she could do about her actual height.

"Mom, you lied to me," she once said.

"No, I didn't," I said. "When?"

"When I was in fifth grade, you said I would get taller," she said. "But I haven't."

Laci said she was five feet one inch, but that was probably an inch generous. One day she looked in the mirror and said, "Oh my gosh, I'm built just like Nana!" Maybe she did resemble Dennis's mother. Regardless, I can still hear her gripe: "It's not fair. Brent's tall and thin, and I'm short."

Still, she didn't let that bother her. In eighth grade, inspired by a pretty girl from down the street, Laci became a cheerleader for a football team in the local Pop Warner league. The yelling, the noise, the outfits, the attention—all of it was right up her alley. She loved it.

About that time she also discovered boys, and soon my little social darling got in trouble for the first time. I had dropped Laci and her friend Amber at Roller King, the local skating rink. Amber's mother would be picking them up. In between, the girls were supposed to skate. Before leaving, I reminded them to behave, to not make fools of themselves over boys and to not leave Roller King.

When Amber's mother arrived to collect them, the girls weren't there. She checked to see if I'd come by early. I hadn't. Finally, she saw Laci and Amber stroll la-di-da through the parking lot and go back inside Roller King. They'd left with two boys—boys who were already in high school, including one who had dropped out.

Laci knew that she was in trouble. She almost volunteered to be punished.

"I'm going to be grounded, aren't I?" she asked.

"Yes, you are," I said. "For two weeks."

"Okay. No problem," she said.

The punishment was minor, but she learned a lesson. Laci was really a good kid. She excelled in class. She played the flute in the school band. She liked sports. By the day of her junior high school graduation, her braces were gone. Talk about a big, bright smile!

In 1989, Laci started Thomas Downey High School. She walked to school until an older neighbor boy gave her a ride in his car, thus beginning her life as an independent young adult. Her personality ensured her popularity. She made the cheerleading squad freshman year, played on the basketball and softball teams, and earned good grades by studying hard.

I had my doubts about her making cheerleader. As we walked to our car after attending the initial meeting, Laci attempted to jump over a rope barrier in the parking lot. Everybody from the meeting was also in the parking lot. Needless to say, her foot caught on the rope and she fell flat on her face. But she sprang right up laughing at herself. It was typical Laci.

One Friday night Ron and I came home from dinner and a movie. It was about 10 p.m., and I checked on Laci as I always did before going to bed. She'd visited her friend Stacey Boyers earlier in the evening and was already in her bedroom. I thought she'd be sleeping, but when I opened her door she was sitting on the window seat, with the window wide open.

"Why are you sitting there?" I asked.

"I'm just thinking," she said wearily. "And getting some fresh air."

I asked if everything was okay. She said yes. We chatted for several minutes and then I said good night.

At that time, I worked with Stacey's mother, Terri Western, at Ambeck Mortgage (I'd left Nabisco after thirteen years to become a real estate loan officer), and on Monday afternoon Stacey was there visiting her mom when she came into my office to say hello.

"So Laci wasn't feeling very good on Friday night, was she?" Stacey said.

I shook my head no. I told her about Laci sitting in the window. Stacey laughed.

"I bet she'll *never* drink tequila again," she said. "She only had a couple of shots, but she was soooooo sick."

That night, as I set dinner on the table, I asked Laci what she wanted to drink. But before she could answer, I said, "How about a shot of tequila?"

The look on her face was priceless. Her mouth dropped open. For once, she was speechless. She just stared at me. I knew she was thinking, How could she know?

"By the way, I saw Stacey today," I said nonchalantly. "She came by the office to see her mom and she said hello to me."

Laci shook her head. "That Stacey!" she smiled. "She tells you everything."

I think it was a long time before she drank tequila again.

In tenth grade, Laci fell in love for the first time. She was at a party when a friend introduced her to a boy named Chad. Chad attended Davis High School on the other side of town. He was nice, polite, and handsome, and I approved. They spent time at each other's homes and hung out. Their relationship was innocent but their feelings were serious.

It was sweet; he was opening her heart for the first time. As I drove her home from his house or sat in her room after we got home, she filled me in on the details and let me in on her feelings. I treasured those conversations then, and now they're precious jewels in my memory. Her emotions were so pure, as they are when you're fifteen and in love for the first time. As such, I braced for the inevitable—the breakup.

It happened just before Valentine's Day, and she was absolutely crushed when Chad told her he wanted to end their relationship. I was at the dining room table and she came in sobbing like you do when your heart has been broken. She curled up in my lap the way she did when she was a baby, laid her head on my shoulder, and she just bawled until her eyes were dry. I felt as if I could see her aching heart;

she was raw and emotionally bruised and she didn't hold anything back.

I was so touched that my fifteen-year-old daughter had turned to me when she was in so much pain. Rather than cry to her friends, smoke cigarettes, drink, or do drugs, Laci wanted to sit in my lap and have me hold her. I squeezed her so tight that night. I was so grateful that she was just the kind of daughter I had hoped to raise.

I felt so bad for her on Valentine's Day. Her spirit was so low. I did something I shouldn't have—I sent her flowers. I thought they'd cheer her up but when they were delivered, she thought they were from Chad, and I instantly realized I'd made a mistake. She tried to be up-beat and appreciative after she opened the card and saw that it said "Love, Mom," but I saw she was disappointed and it was understand-able. The flowers weren't from the boy. It wasn't the best Valentine's Day for any of us.

By spring, Laci was dating a new guy, Kent Gain. He was two or three years older than she was, very handsome, and tall, with thick dark hair cut short. He was polite and made me feel Laci was in good hands. He was there for Laci's sixteenth birthday when I surprised her with a limousine that took them and another couple to dinner.

Laci adored that night. The expression on her face as she opened the door and saw the driver standing on the porch was priceless. She looked back at me and then beyond the driver to the limo parked at the curb. She laughed so hard that she doubled over, as was her way. That picture of her laughing—with one knee in toward her chest and bent at the waist—will stay with me forever. It was pure joy, and she was like that at the end of the night, too.

"It was so cool," she said. "I had so much fun."

Intent on getting her own car, Laci worked at a doctor's office and bagged groceries until her senior year when she finally could afford (with a little help from us) to buy a white Jetta. Soon, it seemed as if Ron and I frequently butted heads with her over things like curfew and chores and the amount of time she spent with her boyfriend.

Despite good first impressions of Kent, Ron and I began to have doubts as time passed. We couldn't put our finger on what it was, but we didn't like what we sensed beneath the surface. It wasn't apparent early in their relationship, but by Laci's senior year we were concerned because Kent appeared to have a very short fuse. Sometimes he left angry messages full of curse words on the phone machine in her bedroom. She kept it on the highest volume, which made it impossible for us not to hear it.

Both Ron and I took exception and discussed this with Laci. We thought Kent had real issues and feared he could turn on her physically. We tried discussing it with Laci, but she refused to hear anything negative about him.

"You don't know him like I do," she said.

That's what frightened us. Blind to his faults, she defended him and said she felt he would change. I could tell that she thought she was more adult than she really was.

In December, another issue came up. Despite knowing we were against her getting a dog, Laci came home with an Australian shepherd puppy that Kent had given her. Kent's dog was the puppy's mother. The puppy was adorable—a puffy white furball with crystal clear blue eyes. She snuggled right into Laci, who named her Samantha.

We couldn't make Laci give the dog back; that would've been cruel. So we laid down a strict rule—she *had to* take care of Samantha. And that is mostly what she did. She was very responsible, as was her inclination, and we excused the few times she wasn't around to feed her or was out when Samantha escaped for a visit with the neighbor's frisky boy dog. Those things happen.

But one night in mid-December when Laci was at Kent's house, Samantha got out and I called Laci and told her to come home and take care of it. I was angry. I'm sure she heard it in my voice.

In reality, I was angrier with Laci for spending so much time with Kent—and at his house—than I was about Samantha getting out of the yard. I wanted Laci to come home. She'd spent enough time with her boyfriend.

But Laci didn't want to leave Kent's, and unfortunately we had a scene on the phone. After a brief but heated discussion, she stalked into the house, fetched Samantha from the neighbor's, and then started back out the door.

"Where are you going?" I asked.

"I'm going back to Kent's," she said.

The two of us were standing near the front door. "No, you're not," I said.

With that, the long-brewing tension over Kent exploded. Neither Ron nor I knew it, but Kent was outside, waiting in the driveway for Laci. When Kent heard me tell her that she couldn't leave, he butted in and said that Laci could do whatever she wanted.

Ron said that this was between us and it was time for him to go home. Kent refused to leave and he and Ron exchanged words. Laci said she was going to leave with Kent.

"No, you're not," I said. "You're not going with Kent."

Suddenly, Kent pushed his way through the front door. I was standing behind the door and was shoved against the wall. Kent reached in and grabbed Laci's arm. She let him yank her outside and went with him to his car, and then they drove off.

Ron and I were in shock. We couldn't believe what just happened. Laci didn't behave like that. I was angry and disappointed in her, and I was even more upset when Laci called that night and told me that she was going to stay at her father's house in Escalon. I cried all night.

For the next few days we didn't speak. A few days before Christmas, I called her and asked if she'd help decorate the Christmas tree, something the two of us did together every year. She said no. She was being stubborn, and that hurt me. Laci and I had never had such a serious falling out.

A week later, she called, asking if she could come home. She wanted to make up. She said she was sorry and knew that she was wrong to have stormed out of the house. She missed her bedroom, her belongings, her dog, and me. From the sound of her voice and everything she said, I knew she was miserable. But as much as I missed her I didn't let her come back. There was a lesson to be learned.

She called again a few days later and this time I told her to come home. I couldn't wait to see her and vice versa. We had an emotional reunion and talked for hours. Laci apologized to me and Ron individually and both of us together. She realized that she'd been wrong and her behavior had been way out of line. She knew it wasn't the way you treated the people you loved.

Laci must have spoken to Kent because I also got an apology from him. I suspect she said something like, "If you want to continue seeing me, you need to say you're sorry." But he never said he was sorry to Ron.

Things returned to normal. That spring Laci spent a week as a science camp counselor, an annual off-campus activity for sixth-graders. On Monday morning, she was excited about being with the kids. When I picked her up that Friday, she was exhausted.

"Mom, you'll never have to worry about birth control with me," she said.

"Why's that?" I asked, suddenly more curious about that camp.

"All you have to do is send someone to science camp with a bunch of sixth-graders and they'll never have kids!" she said.

Then came graduation. She and her friends took a trip to Mazatlán, Mexico, and had a fabulous time. She sent us a postcard, calling the trip "the most fun I have had in my entire life." She came back sunburned to a crisp, exhausted, and yet still going strong. I marveled at how she'd grown up and was turning into a young woman.

Laci planned on continuing school the next year at California Polytechnic State University in San Luis Obispo, about 150 miles southwest of Modesto.

"Well, we have finally made it!" her close friend Stacey Boyers wrote in her yearbook.

Can you believe it? You have always been a wonderful friend through the years. Always remember these high school years and the killer times we shared! And the not so good ones, we can forget about. Always remember I'm here for you no matter how far away you live. Remember the telephone. But don't expect me to pay for the phone bills. Good luck in everything you do, and do your best at it.

I worried that only one thing might keep Laci from doing her best in the future—Kent. When she came home in tears from the post-party following her senior prom, the result of Kent not wanting her to go and then making her miserable after she insisted, I thought they'd finally break up. I was wrong. From his inscription in her yearbook, they seemed as tight as ever.

I'm glad that you and I have been able to make it through these past two years, three months and 11 days. I hope to spend the rest of my life with you together (not apart). That's in parentheses, because you do know how much I love you. Let's smooth out our rough spots and roll on through . . .

Love, Kent

Laci could hardly wait for college. She was inspired by her brother, a 1993 Sacramento State graduate who went on to McGeorge School of Law in Sacramento. In early spring, she was accepted at her number one choice, Cal Poly. The school wasn't taking many freshmen then, so it was quite an achievement. We celebrated with one of her favorite dinners, spaghetti.

I was very disappointed when I found out that Kent planned to follow Laci to San Luis Obispo. She knew it would upset me. Calmly, I asked why he was going with her. Laci said he planned to sign up at Cuesta Junior College—ironically the same school that Scott Peterson attended. Then, according to Laci, Kent wanted to transfer to Cal Poly.

I worried that if he failed, he would drag Laci with him. I didn't want her dropping out of school and making the same mistake I had. Fortunately, she didn't have any of those same concerns, and she sounded pretty sure of herself.

At the end of the summer, we made several trips to San Luis Obispo and found her a place to live. It was a tiny, adorable house in Morro Bay, a beautiful coastal town just north of San Luis Obispo. It felt great. From Laci's backyard, you could look out and almost see the ocean. The air was cool and the fog would roll in thick and gray till it felt like you were in a cloud. She loved it.

I cosigned for everything, and we made two or three trips down there to get the utilities turned on and everything set up prior to the start of classes in August. Her last summer at home flew by. I frequently think about how fast time goes by in general. Every cliché is true! You blink, and twenty years have disappeared without you knowing where they went.

The weekend before school started I drove to Morro Bay in the morning with my car packed full of her things while Laci waited at home for her dad to come with a trailer for her bed and other large pieces she wanted to take. Instead of arriving that afternoon, however, Dennis didn't show up until the following morning. But by Sunday, she was back on schedule, settled in, and eager to start college.

I liked seeing her so excited, and it made me think Kent wouldn't be able to exert as much influence as I feared at first. Once Laci set her mind to something she really wanted, she didn't change it. I felt even better a few days later when I received this card from her:

Mom—

You are a very special woman in my life. I just wanted to take the time to say thank you for all your support and love. Although we have our differences, I will always love you. I am going to miss you, but that's what a telephone is made for. I hope you can support and stand by me, even though you do not agree with the decisions I make for my future. I love you, mom, and you supporting my decisions means a lot to me. You mean a lot to me, and I hope nothing will ever come between us.

I want to congratulate you on your job, and all the great success you have accomplished. I knew you could do it!

I love you, mom.

Your daughter,
Laci

*Remember to always smile.

Chapter Four

T hat weekend Laci and I set up the kitchen in her new home. I'll never forget her bringing out a large stack of paper plates and setting them on the counter with a sense of purpose. I gave her a look that asked what that was all about, and she very matter of factly said she didn't plan to spend her time at Cal Poly doing dishes. And she didn't. Laci majored in ornamental horticulture and dreamed of opening her own plant shop—actually more of a specialty shop, as she explained it, with herbs as well as plants and flowers. She joined several clubs, managed the campus plant shop, and became an honorary sorority member. I had the impression she worked her butt off while enjoying every minute of college life.

I visited fairly often and I remember this one time a few months into the school year in particular. Laci and I were enjoying a long walk and she was catching me up on her life. I realized she wasn't saying much about Kent. Though they were living together, she didn't tell many stories that involved him. It was all about her busy schedule of classes and clubs. When I asked how Kent felt about her being so involved in school, she said he didn't mind. Her tone of voice led me to believe that it wouldn't have mattered if he did mind, she wasn't going to allow him or anyone else to hold her back. That told me enough. I knew his days were numbered.

When I got home, I happily announced my hunch to Ron. His only question was when.

"I think it'll be soon," I said. "She's growing bored of him. I can tell. I don't think she's going to let anyone hold her back."

But then came a scare when I thought Kent might be in her life permanently. A couple of months before her nineteenth birthday, she called and I heard a tone in her voice that immediately made me nervous. I took a deep breath and then dared to ask the question I dreaded: "You aren't going to tell me that you're pregnant, are you?"

Laci laughed. "No. I just wanted to tell you that I have a tattoo. It's a little rose on my ankle. I know how you don't like tattoos, so I was afraid you'd be mad at me." (She later had it covered with a sunflower.)

She played me perfectly. I breathed a sigh of relief.

"Compared to what I thought, it's not a big deal," I said.

Laci finally broke up with Kent toward the end of her freshman year, and fortunately that wasn't a big deal either. She was fairly matter of fact in the way she broke the news, more sad than emotional. Her tone on the phone was almost like, "Oh, by the way, Kent and I decided to break up." The decision was mutual, and she handled it better than her first breakup, with Chad.

"We're just not suited for each other," she said of Kent.

I was glad she came to that conclusion herself. According to Laci, Kent was going to stay in the house with her until June and then move in with his sister in Santa Cruz. But he lasted only a few weeks before leaving.

I don't think Laci ever saw him again. I knew she wouldn't put up with that type of guy. I'm sure she would've left Scott, too, if she'd known the *real* Scott, the one we met on December 24, 2002. She wouldn't have put up with him for even one day.

As for Kent, sadly, his life didn't improve. After he and Laci broke up, he became involved with a woman named Grace Ho. In 1997, they moved to Washington State. On January 17, 1999, they got into an argument and Kent shot her in the back with a .44 caliber handgun. She was seriously wounded but lived. Eleven months later, Kent was convicted of first-degree assault with a gun and sentenced to fifteen years in a Washington state prison.

From what I read, he professed to still love Laci.

Laci wrapped the year by receiving the ornamental horticulture department's outstanding freshman award and stayed in Morro Bay over the summer taking more courses. She adored her cute home and life in the college town. I heard the buoyancy in her voice whenever we spoke, and I saw her zest for life and a new maturity when I visited. I frequently drove down and spent the night at her place.

Both of us appreciated our close relationship. It was easy for us and enviable. The fun we had is something I miss terribly. We'd come through the hard part and we were able to talk about anything and everything.

Confident, enthusiastic, talented, and capable, Laci knew what she wanted and her vision of the future included marriage, children, a beautiful home, and her own plant shop. Between the way she talked about her goals and her ability to go after whatever she wanted till she got it, I had no doubt that her life would turn out the way she envisioned.

But then you never know. . . .

During her time at Cal Poly, Laci was friendly with her next-door neighbors in Morro Bay. One day in late spring the woman from next door took Laci to a small restaurant on the embarcadero in Morro Bay, the Pacific Café, where her boyfriend worked, and it was there that Laci first laid eyes on Scott Peterson.

Scott waited tables there part-time. Laci spotted him and thought he was cute. I don't know if they spoke that day but the next time she and her neighbor went back, Laci wrote her telephone number on a slip of paper and asked her neighbor's boyfriend to pass it on to Scott.

At first, Scott thought it was a joke and tossed the paper in the trash. Even when the neighbor pointed to Laci out front, Scott still didn't believe him. But finally he was convinced it wasn't a prank and dug the paper out of the trash can. Eventually he called Laci.

I heard about Scott a day or two after they'd talked that first time. I asked if they'd gone out yet. Laci said no, but they had a date planned, and then a few days later they went out. Scott took her deep-sea fishing, and she got violently seasick. But Laci was laughing about it on the phone when she told me how she'd turned green, thrown up, and been extremely embarrassed, and yet still had a wonderful time with him.

For Laci, I think Scott was love at first sight. She described him to me as early twenties, handsome, smart, nice, ambitious, and well-rounded. She said Scott had told her that he'd traveled, enjoyed good wine, and had once thought about becoming a pro golfer. As for background details, she told me that Scott was the youngest in a large family from San Diego. His parents, Lee and Jackie, had a home in Morro Bay. Warily, Laci said that Scott had dropped out of college but planned on attending Cal Poly in the fall.

Laci knew how strongly I felt about getting a college degree, and she emphasized that Scott was bright and really did fully intend to go back to school. She said he'd gone to Arizona State University, in Tucson, on a partial golf scholarship, but withdrew after a semester. She didn't know why he'd left. In fact, I don't know if she ever found out the real reason.

Following her murder, though, we heard a couple of rumors as to why. In light of what he did to Laci, anything sounded possible. We also found out that he hadn't even stayed the entire semester, as he'd claimed to Laci. I'm pretty sure she didn't know that either.

After ASU, he moved into his parents' home in Morro Bay and worked a few jobs, including the Pacific Café. He seemed to be a hard worker, but she'd said something else that bothered me. While at ASU, he'd lived with an older woman.

"How much older?" I asked.

"She was twenty-three, I think," Laci said. "He was nineteen."

"Hmmm."

I couldn't think of anything else to say. I didn't want to be too critical. She was just getting to know him. But she fell for him hard and quickly. As we talked one night on the phone, she confided that after just one real date she had a feeling about him.

"I met the man I'm going to marry," she said.

"Really?" I said.

"Yes," she replied.

I was delighted that she was falling in love, but I had concerns. I used myself as an example. Since I'd married out of high school, divorced, and always felt like I'd gypped myself out of life experiences, I advised Laci to live away from home and learn about the world before settling down. I also thought Scott sounded a little too good to be true. Ron was skeptical, too.

"I hope he's not full of bull," I said to Ron.

My feelings, however, took a backseat to Laci's. Her heart was way out in front of her head, and that made me curious about Scott. "You've got to come down here and meet him," she said. "You'll see. When are you coming?"

A few weekends later in late August, I left Ron at home and made the four-hour drive to Morro Bay from Modesto. The older Laci got, the more we treasured those moments when we could be together and talk. We drove to the Pacific Café early that evening for dinner. We got there a little before our seven o'clock reservation and walked around the embarcadero, shopping, gazing at the ocean, talking, and catching up on Scott. By then, Scott and Laci had gone on a few more dates, and she liked him even more. I was even more eager to meet him.

We strolled up to the café at seven and Scott was standing in front, waiting for us. I saw his grin from far off. Laci was right; he radiated charm. And he was good-looking. As we approached, Laci introduced us and he said, "It's nice to meet you, Mrs. Rocha." (He called me Mrs. Rocha until the day they married. After that I was Mom.)

Scott then looked at Laci and with a huge grin on his face said, "I have your special table waiting for you."

He was trying to be very suave, and it was cute.

"Right through here, ladies," he said.

I glanced at Laci, who was waiting anxiously for my reaction. I nodded approvingly—so far so good. She was barely able to contain her delight as Scott led us to a table by the window. In her excitement, she looked like a little girl to me. It was a small restaurant, with only a half dozen or so tables in the entire place. He had roses waiting for us on the table—twelve white roses for me, and twelve red roses for Laci.

"I hope it's okay, but I went ahead and ordered for you," he said as he pulled out the chairs for each of us.

"That's so nice," Laci said.

"I also have a bottle of wine coming," Scott added.

"Very nice," I said. "Thank you."

Laci couldn't stop grinning. He put on quite a display, I must admit.

"Mom," Laci said as he walked away from the table and went behind the bar, "doesn't he have the cutest butt?"

"Frankly, Laci," I said, "I'm not really looking at his butt."

Scott was extremely attentive as we chatted over dinner and white wine. He came over to our table numerous times to ask if we were enjoying our meal. Laci smiled and flirted when he was close by, and each time he left she turned to me and asked, "What do you think?" I thought he was very gentlemanly and I told her so.

For me, the highlight of the meal had nothing to do with Scott. Midway through our meal, Laci leaned toward me and lowered her voice so Scott couldn't hear as he tended to a couple at a nearby table, and said, "You were right about Kent. We really weren't suited for each other."

I was pleased to hear her give me credit.

"Well, you had to discover that for yourself," I said.

"I knoooooow," she said, dragging out the *oooooow*—the way she always said it when she had a change of mind or in this case a change of heart.

"But I'm glad it didn't get any more serious or last any longer," she confessed.

I was impressed by her budding maturity.

"Okay," she said, smiling, "now you can say 'I told you so.'"

"I'm not going to say it," I said. "I don't have to say it. You already know it."

Laci knew I couldn't resist. She just grinned until I broke. It took about a minute.

"But I did tell you so," I said.

At the end of our meal together, Scott picked up the tab. As we headed for the door, he said that he enjoyed meeting me. Outside the restaurant, he gave Laci a kiss good-bye and wished us a good night. Back at her house, she wanted to talk about Scott, asking my opinion about every detail. I was willing just as long as she didn't ask what I thought about his butt.

Again, I treasured the intimacy and openness of our relationship, and overall I gave Scott a good review. I'd say three stars out of four. I'd just met him, and our contact had been minimal, consisting basically of the roses, white wine, and watching the two of them make gooey eyes at each other. What did I know? Let's just say from what I'd seen and heard, I saw no reason to spoil Laci's mood.

The next night Laci fixed us dinner, a salad, pasta, and a nice loaf of bread. Afterward, she asked if I felt like dessert. I said sure, expecting her to get something from the fridge. But no, instead she quickly changed clothes and raced over to the Pacific Café to pick up dessert. We'd talked about Scott all day and she'd expected to hear from him, but when he didn't call, she cooked up this dessert scheme in order to see him.

A few minutes later she returned. In addition to dessert, she brought me regards from Scott. She also explained that he hadn't called all day because he knew I was still visiting and he didn't want to interrupt our time together.

Laci gave me a look that asked, "Isn't he great?"

Yes, he seemed pretty great. But given what I know now, I wonder.

At the beginning of September 1994, I visited Laci again. Wildfires had burned the hills above Morro Bay, destroying many homes. I remember the hills were black and the highways were clogged with different-colored fire trucks from neighboring counties. I got to Laci's house and saw the flames had stopped several hundred yards up the hill from her backyard. She'd lost her power and was scared to be alone.

I asked if she could stay at Scott's place until her power was restored.

(Though they hadn't dated that long, I knew their relationship had progressed quickly. They'd gone to Mexico the previous weekend and she'd already met his parents.) After I left, Laci spent the next couple of days at Scott's. I remember she called one of her professors and got a test postponed after explaining she'd lost her power—as no doubt other students had, too—and hadn't been able to study.

That was so Laci. I wouldn't have thought to call the teacher. I would've taken the test.

Scott spent Thanksgiving at our house and it was clear that he and Laci were serious about each other. He was very polite. He insisted on sleeping in a different room from Laci; he cleared the dishes and helped out. He didn't volunteer conversation, but he readily answered questions, and he appeared to have a sense of humor. We thought he was nice and solid, and he left well liked.

I had one reservation, and I didn't hide it from Laci. I said I'd like him better when he made good on his promise to return to school.

During Christmas break, Laci bought Scott a golden retriever puppy, which she named McKenzie. He was the cutest pup in the litter, but he was kind of lethargic, low on energy. The lady who sold him to us said the mama dog had dropped him on the concrete floor, and she showed us a bump on his head. That endeared him even more to Laci, who cradled him all the way home.

But that bump took a toll on the pup. That evening when our Christmas tree fell over in the living room, shattering glass ornaments on the coffee table with a thunderous crash and scaring the bejesus out of Laci and me as we watched TV, McKenzie slept through the whole disaster. We figured the little guy had to be sicker than we thought, maybe on his last breaths.

It turned out he was merely tired. He got a little better and stronger each day, eating and playing more like a puppy, and when Laci returned to school she and Scott took him to the vet, who pronounced him healthy. According to Laci, Scott adored McKenzie, and they took care of him together. I remember Laci telling me that Scott was the disciplinarian; she babied the dog.

That was also the Christmas he and Laci took another big step in their relationship by moving in together. They rented a small one-bedroom home in San Luis Obispo and then moved to a ranch just north of the city on a large lot with two other homes. The front porch was built around a large tree, which inspired us to refer to the place as "the tree house," and a creek ran through the front yard. It was a charmer.

I can still hear Laci say, "Mom, I don't know if I have room for more than a TV, but I don't care. I love it here." Indeed, despite the cramped quarters, they were happy. McKenzie barked at the neighbor's chickens and loped through the tall grass, and Laci and Scott were both very busy with school and work. In retrospect, though, there was a potentially troublesome blip on the radar screen.

Laci mentioned on the phone that Scott had lost his job at the golf course. She said it casually, but that she brought it up at all indicated that it bothered her. Apparently Scott had been fired for stealing money, but Laci quickly added it was actually a mistake; she called it a *misunderstanding*. She said that Scott had straightened out everything.

After I pressed for more details, she said that the problem involved missing cash, but the club's owners didn't want to pursue it and Scott agreed to leave. He wasn't going to work there again (and he didn't).

I wish I knew more about what really happened. Excusing it as a *misunderstanding* doesn't sound credible now, and it didn't ring true when Laci told me then. I remember thinking that Scott was covering up the truth or not telling the whole truth. Laci didn't seem alarmed. She was more upset that Scott lost his job over something he didn't do. She felt it was unjust.

I remember thinking it sounded as if Scott had fed her a line, and I can still hear Laci on the phone as if she had just told me.

"He didn't do anything," she said. "Mom, they shouldn't have fired him if he didn't do anything. It's not right."

"You believe him?" I said.

"Yes, Mom," she said matter of factly. "Why would he lie?"

Chapter Five

After Laci was murdered, I realized that I really didn't know much about Scott Peterson.

How can you not know a member of your family? You can imagine how many times I've asked myself that question. I don't have an answer.

Laci brought Scott to the house as often as possible. But even during the best of times, he was a tough person to get to know. His guard was always up. Why was he so enigmatic? Good question. But from everything we saw, he treated Laci well, and she adored him.

I remember playing a lot of Yahtzee with Scott and Laci when they were at the house. I seemed to win most of the time, which brought out the competitiveness in all three of us. Scott was determined to beat me; he never did. But we laughed about it and had lots of fun. I miss those times so much.

I never suspected he might one day murder Laci. Nothing remotely like that ever entered my thoughts. It still sounds absurd.

Scott was the youngest in his family, the baby, "the golden child," as he was called—and was, as we learned later, praised and spoiled to the point where, at least in my opinion, he grew up without any accountability for his actions. Why should he have felt responsible when he was told everything he did was perfect? It makes sense to me. I can imagine him going through his entire life like that. How else could he so strenuously deny something that we saw so clearly?

Since one is arguably a product of their upbringing, I wish I'd known more about his parents, Jackie and Lee. Jackie, who'd been raised in an orphanage after her father died, had three children from previous relationships, two of whom she'd given up for adoption. Lee also had three children from a previous marriage.

Scott was a young man with a megawatt personality, and depending on how you felt about him, he either was charming, charismatic, and full of potential or, as Ron would later say, "a silver-tongued devil who knew what people wanted to hear and said it." Laci saw only the former. To her, Scott was the total package of looks, intelligence, and ambition. He was her Cary Grant, the handsome sophisticate who said all the right things and was going to take her small-town-girl's dreams of living happily ever after with the man she loved and turn them into reality.

Laci predicted they'd get engaged, we expected it, and then it happened in December 1996. Laci called with the news shortly before Christmas vacation. She didn't have a ring yet but she said that Scott planned to get one soon from a friend in San Francisco. She was excited.

"Sounds good," I said.

I might've said more, but I didn't, and Laci picked up on my restraint.

"Oh, I know what you're thinking," she said.

"You do?"

"You don't have to worry. We're not going to get married right away. I'm waiting until I graduate."

"Good. Get that out of the way," I said, relieved.

When they came home for Christmas, Scott formally asked us for permission to marry Laci. As Laci looked on, he explained in an earnest manner and softer-than-usual tone of voice how much he loved Laci and then he said something to the effect of hoping he could have our blessing. It was sweet, and we said yes.

Their plan was to get married after Laci graduated. Since she'd tacked on another semester in order to get a business-agriculture minor, she wasn't going to finish till the next December, a full year away, which was fine with me. But the next month Laci and Scott moved their wedding date to August. "I know what you're thinking—we won't have graduated," Laci said. "But it's okay. I'm going to finish school. I promise."

As long as she promised, I didn't see the point in going over that old ground. It wasn't worth fighting that battle. Laci knew my feelings about college, and I felt confident that she respected them and would keep her word. I asked the obvious—why had they moved up the wedding date?

According to Laci, they didn't have any particular reason. Like a lot of young engaged couples, they were eager to get married and simply didn't want to wait more than a year before becoming Mr. and Mrs. Scott Peterson.

She wanted an outdoor wedding in the garden at the Sycamore Mineral Springs Resort in Avila Beach, and she wanted it on her grandfather's birthday, but when that date wasn't available, she and Scott decided on August 9.

For the next seven and a half months, Laci planned the wedding. It was like a full-time occupation. Between her classes and work at a florist shop in San Luis Obispo, I don't know how she managed her schoolwork, but she did. She was a dynamo. She picked the menu, tasted all the food, figured out the bridesmaid dresses, piped in on the design of Scott's tux, and had a hand in creating all the flower arrangements, from her bouquet to the table centerpieces.

Though she knew what she wanted, Laci called all the time to discuss every detail. While I marveled at her vision and organizational skills, I appreciated that she still wanted my opinion or just wanted me to hear her latest thoughts. At some point, I figured out my actual role was as the voice of reason—keeping Laci from spending like she was royalty.

Picking out her bridal dress was a special experience I won't ever forget. Laci pored through bridal magazines, ripped out photographs, and then we laughed our way through Modesto's bridal stores. Her initial vision for a fancy, billowy gown with lots of tulle and lace was dropped after she tried on several such dresses and the fabric consumed her petite frame. All sixty inches of her, from her head to her toes, literally disappeared.

"Where's Laci?" I said, laughing.

"Don't worry, Mom," she replied. "I'm somewhere in this wedding dress."

In March, Laci settled on a beautiful, traditional white dress with stitched pearls and a long train. She ordered a size two and still needed it altered—that's how tiny she was. During the fittings, I couldn't take my eyes off Laci. She looked beautiful, like one of the girls in the bridal magazines. Her eyes lit up every time she looked at herself in the dress.

"Mom, I'm so excited," she said. "I can't believe it."

I couldn't believe it, either. When had my little girl grown up?

Lee Peterson owned crating businesses in Morro Bay and San Diego, and Jackie had an antiques shop in town. Jackie's interest in collectibles and her strict adherence to etiquette appealed to Laci's budding aspirations for a quality life. In the beginning she was impressed by both Jackie and Lee.

I've read that in private Jackie didn't think anyone was good enough for Scott, including Laci. I first met Jackie at lunch in San Luis Obispo, and I got the impression that she and Laci were close. Laci wanted me to like her and forewarned me that Jackie had a bronchial condition that required her to use an oxygen tank. I thought Jackie was fine—attractive, pleasant. We talked a lot and I got the impression that she enjoyed the way Laci looked up to her.

Over time, I felt as if I saw past her public smile and I wondered if that attitude wasn't in reality a way of distancing herself from a past that I think might have caused her pain. I don't think she talked about her background with anyone, even with her family. Scott hadn't known, for example, that she'd given up her first two children for adoption until the children had separately sought her out.

Several weeks before the wedding I had gotten a call from Laci, who was stunned by this surprising revelation.

"Mom, you're not going to believe what I just found out," she said.

"What?" I asked.

"Jackie had a son—has a son—that she gave up for adoption when he was little," she said.

"How do you know?" I asked.

"Because he contacted her!" Laci said. "He got in touch with her a while ago, and we just met him."

Laci liked Don, who was then in his mid-thirties and lived in Pennsylvania with his wife and three small children. Laci had real difficulty reconciling Jackie's secret past with the woman who had passed herself off as a model of propriety. I don't know how much Laci ever found out. I remember she told me that Jackie's father had passed away when she was young and then her mother got sick and she was put in an orphanage. But Laci never mentioned that Jackie's father had been murdered. I don't think she knew. We learned about it during the trial. We had heard that he was murdered on December 21, 1945. I often wonder if it was coincidental or intentional that Scott murdered Laci so close to the date that his grandfather had been murdered.

When I asked her what Scott thought about his new brother, Laci said he handled it well.

"At first, he was surprised," she said. "He didn't know about him. But Scott was great when we got together. I think he liked Don."

"What did you think?" I asked.

"I thought he was really nice," she said. "We invited him to the wedding, and he can come."

"That's great," I said.

"Why not?" she said. "It's a family occasion."

Shortly before the wedding, Laci called with the additional jarring news that Don wasn't the only child Jackie had given up for adoption. It turned out that she'd also had a baby girl, and that girl was now a thirty-two-year-old woman named Anne Bird. They arranged a meeting, which Laci didn't attend but heard it went well. It was all a lot for her to digest. According to Anne, Jackie told her that Scott was about to get married and while she wanted to invite her to the ceremony, she apparently said that "Laci didn't seem all that comfortable with the idea." But that's not what I was told. I remember Laci saying that they invited Anne to the wedding, but then explained that Anne declined because she didn't want to have anything to do with Jackie or Jackie's family. It isn't what Anne wrote in her book, but it's what Laci said— and Laci didn't lie. (That doesn't matter. I liked Anne's book.)

Laci was really disappointed with Jackie. She'd always been in awe of Scott's mother, but her opinion changed slightly after she found out about Don. Then, after learning about Anne, she felt betrayed. She thought her soon-to-be mother-in-law had portrayed herself as something she wasn't. She didn't believe in the image and she lost her trust in Jackie.

"Laci, you have to understand that this is not something people talk about openly or easily, especially if it's something they're ashamed of," I said.

"That's not it," she said. "It's not the fact that she had two children that she gave up for adoption. I understand that. They probably ended up with better lives. I'm sure it was also very hard for Jackie."

"Exactly," I said. "So what's the problem?"

"Jackie made herself out to be someone she's not," Laci said. "It's a lie. It's like she's lied to me. I'm hurt."

Laci was too practical to hold a grudge against her soon-to-be mother-in-law. She accepted what was and moved on. Her girlfriends threw her a fun bridal shower and Scott took a couple guys, including Brent, to Lake Tahoe, where they golfed and gambled (I heard the guys were tamer than the girls). I ran into a little glitch at the bridal store picking up her wedding dress when they couldn't find the receipt, but I got it to Laci in time for a final fitting on the Monday before the wedding and that's all that mattered.

On Friday night, there was a rehearsal dinner at an Italian restaurant in Pismo Beach. Both families mixed and mingled with one noticeable exception—Dennis. He didn't show up. After a time Laci shrugged and figured Dennis would show if he showed. Otherwise everyone enjoyed the celebration, especially Scott and Laci, who were laughing, talking, and partying every time I glanced at them.

Around midnight, though, the phone in my hotel room rang. Ron picked it up and the tone of his voice alarmed me. When he hung up, he turned to me and said that had been our friend Richard.

"He said you need to call Laci. She's crying and she needs to talk to you. She called the hotel and asked for you but the operator put her through to Richard's room."

I immediately picked up the phone and dialed her home number. She answered on the first ring. I could tell she had been crying. I asked frantically, "What's wrong?" She started sobbing and I could barely understand what she was saying. I told her to take a couple of deep breaths and try to calm herself.

Despite continuing to cry, I could understand most of what she was saying. She had doubts.

"Mom, I don't know if I should get married," she said. "If I get married, I'll lose my ethnic name."

Okay, I thought, she's having prewedding jitters. This didn't seem like an insurmountable problem. She could always keep her name, I said, and hyphenate it. Rocha-Peterson. But Laci had thought of that and didn't want to do it.

I got another idea.

"Look at it this way," I said. "Your name is Rocha and it'll change to Peterson. My maiden name was Anderson and it changed to Rocha. So in a sense your new name will be very similar to my old name."

It sounds pretty weak now, but it made sense to her then. Laci chuckled, which told me that she felt a little calmer.

"Laci, are you having second thoughts about getting married?" I asked.

"No," she said.

"Are you sure?" I pressed. "It's okay if you want to change your mind. You don't have to do this if you really don't want to."

As I spoke, I realized I was slightly panicked. What if she wanted to call it off? How were we going to reach everyone before three the next day? Oh well, I told myself, we'd manage.

But Laci didn't want to change her mind.

"Are you absolutely sure you want to get married tomorrow?"

"Yes, I'm sure."

I knew she had had a few glasses of wine earlier; maybe that had contributed to her state of mind.

"Where's Scott?" I asked.

"He's here—in bed."

"Is he sleeping?"

"No. He's awake."

"Can he hear what you are saying?"

"Yes."

"Well, honey, how does he feel about this?"

"He thinks I shouldn't be worrying about changing my name. But, Mom, it's important to me."

We talked for a long time, and eventually Laci calmed down. I kept her on the phone until I felt sure that she was really, truly confident about the next day's big event. She ended up laughing at herself for getting upset over her name change. After we hung up, I told myself that she'd become emotional after having a little too much to drink at the party. It happened, it was normal, it explained everything, and yet I don't think I convinced myself 100 percent. Call it intuition, I don't know. But I couldn't help but wonder if something else was bothering her, something that she couldn't bring herself to tell anyone, including me.

I still wonder, and I always will.

Early in the morning, Laci met her bridesmaids at the beauty salon where they had breakfast and got their hair and makeup done. That afternoon at the Sycamore Mineral Springs Resort, Laci handed out flowers to her bridesmaids from a big Styrofoam ice chest she'd brought to keep them fresh. When I arrived to help Laci get dressed, they were sipping champagne, taking photos, and having a good time. I had a glass of champagne myself, took pictures of the chaos, and enjoyed seeing Laci happy.

Of course, amid the tension, there were some laughs. One of the bridesmaids, despite several earlier fittings, couldn't zip up her dress in back. After a brief moment of panic, the wedding coordinator and I removed the large bow that streamed down the back of the dress over the zipper, safety-pinned the zipper together, and replaced the bow.

It was an exquisite afternoon for an outdoor garden wedding. The sky was blue and the temperature was mild, with flowers perfuming the air. The wedding was scheduled to start at three. About an hour before guests started to arrive, I went outside to survey the grounds and ran in to Scott, who'd just finished taking pictures with his family. Laci was still up in the room getting ready. Scott spotted a swath of white fabric in the distance and thought it was her.

"Is that my future bride?" he asked, grinning and pointing.

I peered in the direction of his finger, looking for Laci.

"No, that's a tablecloth," I said, laughing.

Scott chuckled, too. It was a nice, light moment. I was glad to see him calm and happy. Laci was excited and collected, too. When I think about the hours prior to the ceremony, I might've been the only one with butterflies in my stomach.

Laci did a great job handling the situation with her dad. With less than an hour to go, Dennis still hadn't shown up. He hadn't phoned, and he hadn't returned Laci's calls. Somehow Laci kept it together without losing her temper. Finally, a few moments before three, Dennis showed up. I felt bad for Laci. She didn't need that on her wedding day.

She'd already planned to have Dennis's father—her much-adored Papa—walk her down the aisle along with Dennis, so that alleviated one concern. But now Dennis needed a tuxedo. Amy's half-brother, Nathan (Dennis's wife, Nancy, had been married previously, and he was from that marriage), who was one of the ushers, gave his to Dennis. Unfortunately, it was too small and when Laci saw her dad come out in it, she said, "You are not walking me down the aisle like that."

Seeing that Laci was on the verge of losing her grip, the wedding planner stepped in, and thank goodness she did. Trading on her connections, she persuaded the local tuxedo shop to open up and sent someone into town to get Dennis a tux that fit. She also persuaded Laci that although we were starting about an hour late, it didn't matter, this was her special day, and she shouldn't pay attention to anything other than the feelings that led her to this moment. And she was right.

Once the string quartet began to play the opening notes to Pachelbel's Canon in D, the drama was instantly forgotten. The setting was like a page from one of Laci's bridal magazines. Chairs faced a gazebo where the ceremony took place. Rose petals were strewn on the grass to create a pinkish white aisle. And on the wedding video, which I occasionally watch, you can see the caterers putting the finishing touches on the three-tiered wedding cake moments before Laci appears. When I saw Laci walk down the aisle on the arms of her father and grandfather, I choked up. Little things got me. For instance, before Dennis gave her hand to Scott, he pulled a tiny strand of hair off her forehead. It was a small gesture, but it emphasized that the wedding was a celebration of our love for Laci as well as hers and Scott's.

Laci smiled throughout the twenty-minute ceremony and stared at Scott. He looked into her eyes with an equal amount of affection and promise. They handed Jackie and me each a long-stemmed rose, read each other a poem, kissed, put on their rings, and kissed a few more times. Then everyone partied and danced. I can still picture Laci toward the end dancing and laughing to the B-52s' "Love Shack." I'd never seen her having a better time. I sometimes watch the wedding video just to see her in that moment.

"My dad always told me something when I was growing up," said Lee Peterson, raising a glass of champagne to the newlyweds. "He said, 'Son,' and I pass this on to Scott, 'son,' he said, 'when you marry a girl, make sure she's beautiful. You're going to have to look at her the rest of your life.' Scott did that." He paused. "Um, that's about all. God bless you kids, and be happy."

Then the microphone was handed to Scott. He stood up and smiled. I'd never seen him as happy as he looked at that moment, and he was handsome in his tux. Still, he apeared to be slightly nervous, as he thanked his friends, instructors, and others he hadn't seen in a long time for helping him to celebrate this special occasion. Then he turned his attention to Ron and me:

"The toast is to Laci's parents and grandparents," he said, "because they've given me the one thing in life that will keep me happy forever."

Chapter Six

Laci came back from her honeymoon in Tahiti and told me that she'd taken off her bikini top on the beach, which surprised me.

"Everybody was topless, so I thought I might as well," she said. "But I only did it once; I got sunburned."

Good for her, I thought, and I said something along those lines, too. I was proud of her spirit and passion for experiencing the pleasures of life, even when it meant taking tiny risks like going topless on the beach. In December 1997, she graduated from Cal Poly. There was a small celebration back at their house at which Scott praised Laci for her accomplishment.

Eager to start a career, Laci got a job as a marketing rep for a wine distributor in Richmond. That meant moving to the Bay Area from San Luis Obispo and leaving Scott on his own. She wasn't thrilled by the choice, but she knew it was short-term, only until he was out of school, and Scott was supportive of her decision. Laci took McKenzie and rented a three-bedroom mobile home in Prunedale, a small town off Highway 101. She and Scott talked several times each day and saw each other every weekend. He sometimes spent the night during the week, too.

Scott lived in a house with three other guys. By all appearances, he and Laci were 100 percent committed to each other. I knew she trusted him. Which led me to believe that Laci had no idea that Scott had begun having an affair with Cal Poly sophomore Janet Ilse almost as soon as she had moved away.

It would turn out she did know something about an affair, though I'm not sure about the extent to which she knew the details. Laci never directly told me about the affair. But there would come a point when the detectives told us about Amber Frey and Janet Ilse, and afterward, I spent every waking minute thinking back on my conversations with Laci and I remembered a time when I was visiting her in Prunedale and she may have hinted at trouble. The two of us were out and she tried calling Scott numerous times without getting him. She left numerous messages, but never heard back.

That really bothered her. She got angry with him, something I rarely saw. I asked if everything was okay.

"I'm going to have to have a talk with him," she said. "He's living with three single guys and acting like he's single again. And he's not. I have to straighten him out," she added. "He's not acting like a married man with responsibilities."

Generally, though, Laci liked her job and living in Prunedale. Whatever was going on with Scott, she was thrilled to be on her way in her career. She told me that she didn't want to go back to San Luis Obispo and life in a college town. She enjoyed living close to San Francisco and wanted to take advantage of the opportunities of a big city. Boy, did I remember those feelings from when I was her age.

After Scott graduated in June, he was supposed to join Laci in the Bay Area and look for work. I know he applied for a couple of jobs there but ruled them out for one reason or another right after the interviews. Despite their agreement, he wanted to stay in San Luis Obispo, where he was comfortable. Laci was disappointed, but she put her marriage first, quit her job, and came back. She spent two months as the banquet coordinator at the Sycamore Mineral Springs Resort, but after getting her degree and working she wanted more challenges.

Around that time is when Scott sold the Morro Bay packing business his parents had given them and together he and Laci opened the

Shack, a tiny restaurant that became a popular hangout for students. The two of them spent months readying the Shack, and Laci's touches were apparent when it opened in spring 1999. They poured themselves into the place. Scott cooked and ran the business side, and Laci hostessed, waited tables, and oversaw the Shack's trademark chalkboard menu, which featured a daily special along with a trivia question. The place had spirit, lots of it Laci's, and it took off immediately.

Behind the scenes, though, it was a grind. Running a restaurant was very hard, and by the next year both of them were tired of it. They sold it in early 2000 and decided to move to Modesto as Laci wanted to be closer to family following the death of Dennis's mother the previous year from lung cancer. If she couldn't be in San Francisco, I was glad Laci was moving back home where I could see her more often and she could be with friends.

In May, I went to San Luis Obispo for one last visit. In a sense, it was my good-bye to that town where Laci had gone to college and we shared good memories. I also wanted to visit Hearst Castle, the landmark estate of newspaper baron William Randolph Hearst. I'd wanted to see it since Laci had been accepted to college and had never gone there. I knew if I didn't make one last attempt before she left, I'd never do it.

I met the two of them in San Luis Obispo and then Scott drove Laci's black Jetta to San Simeon. We had lunch at an Italian restaurant in Cambria. But throughout the meal, Scott was on his cell phone with the Shack. He'd finish one call and the phone would ring again with another problem. He wasn't pleased. He kept saying that this was supposed to be his day off. Laci nodded in agreement.

"This is why we sold it," she said. "Even when we're away, we're not away."

Laci was, I realized, developing other interests. As we drove, she started asking about pregnancy and childbirth. It was a conversation we hadn't had in such grown-up detail, and she asked questions rapid-fire: What does it feel like to have something growing inside you? ("Strange," I said.) How long does morning sickness last? ("Not long.") What does it feel like when the baby moves and kicks? ("You can imagine its little arms and legs scrunched up inside and how it's trying to stretch.") How much does it hurt to give birth? ("A lot. But then it's all over and done. The pain doesn't linger.")

Finally I asked her a question of my own: "Are you thinking of getting pregnant?"

"Not right now," she said. "But one day. Maybe not that far in the future."

Scott was quiet throughout the conversation. He didn't ask any questions or offer comments, unlike Laci, who was full of questions. Her clock was ticking. She wanted a baby. Later, I snapped a photo of Laci on the dock. It's a favorite of mine. Her arms were folded, she looked relaxed, and she had that big, beautiful smile of hers. I only wish we'd taken off our sunglasses.

On the way back to San Luis Obispo, we stopped at a restaurant where Scott knew the owner. We only had a drink because it was so busy. On the way out, someone spilled a beer on Scott, but he simply wiped it off. We ended up eating a late lunch at the Pacific Café, which had an obvious sentimental attraction as the place where Laci and Scott met and where I first met Scott. We ordered a bottle of champagne to celebrate Laci's birthday and upcoming Mother's Day. After Scott filled our glasses, Laci accidentally knocked the champagne bottle over and with it went our glasses. Laci was animated when she spoke, gesturing with her hands, just like me. But we laughed and had a good time. Not only was Scott covered in beer, he also wore the champagne home.

In June 2000, Laci and Scott moved to Modesto. They stayed with us while they looked for jobs and a place of their own. I remember Ron commenting about Scott's morning trips to Starbucks for coffee. He wondered what was so great about a nearly two-dollar cup of plain coffee. I chalked it up to a lifestyle habit, not an insult to Ron's daily brew. But before Ron could try making a latte—ha! fat chance—Laci and Scott rented a three-bedroom house several blocks away from ours and were on their own.

They also found jobs. Through a Cal Poly connection, Scott

landed a position with a company owned by Spain-based Technocrop selling large sprinkler systems to farmers and ranchers. (The following year he left that division and went to work selling fertilizer.) Laci got a job marketing wine and stocking grocery store shelves. But she had trouble lifting the heavy cases. "I'm just not big enough," she told me. But I give her credit. As much as she disliked the job, she stuck with it because she and Scott were looking to buy a place of their own and would have to apply for a home loan. With help from their real estate agent, Terri Western, who just happens to be Stacey Boyers's mother and had known Laci most of her life, at the end of the summer they purchased a green ranch-style three-bedroom home. It had two fireplaces and large backyard and was located on a tree-lined street between Laci's old junior high and East La Loma Park. They were thrilled when their offer was accepted and their loan went through. They took possession in October and set about turning it into their home. One of the things I'll always remember is how Laci looked at that house before they moved in and envisioned its potential, testimony to both her talent and positive outlook. I didn't see what she saw when I first toured the house, but Laci shut her eyes and saw the whole picture: cozy, beautiful rooms, a kitchen she could work in, and a place where they could raise a family. Then she made that picture come true. She and Scott painted and added French doors leading to the back. Laci also put in a vegetable garden, planted herbs, removed and added trees, and replanted the courtyard with roses and jasmine.

When the garden was in full bloom, the walk leading to the front door was like a perfumery, with all those roses and flowers. You entered the house and were in the dining room, where they had a large pine table, a pretty chandelier, and candles on every flat surface. This was also the room where they put their Christmas tree and presents.

Laci's favorite room was the kitchen. It had pine cabinets, pots that hung from the ceiling, and a wine rack above the counter that they kept stocked with good vintages. Both of them shared a passion for good wine and food. One of the highlights of Laci's life was an eleven-day trip she took to Italy to attend cooking school. It was everything she'd hoped and more. She came back filled with new skills, knowledge, and enthusiasm. After that trip, she kept a variety of olive oils and cooking utensils on the counter next to the stove that let you know she was serious about food.

The family room, past the kitchen, was furnished with a sofa, an oversized chair, and a TV. The washer and dryer were behind accordion doors. The three bedrooms were in the back of the house. Scott and Laci painted their room light yellow, and the windows were covered by brown roman shades. Laci's clothes filled the master bedroom closet, and Scott's filled the closet in the guest bedroom.

Laci was, I thought, delighted to be back home. She renewed her friendships with Stacey, Rene, Lori, and other longtime girlfriends, some of whom were married and starting families, and she hosted gourmet dinner parties that impressed her friends for their Martha Stewart–like taste and sophistication. But the truth is, Laci did all that to entertain herself as much as her friends. From decorating her house to attending cooking school in Italy, she was all about making her home and her life comfortable and inviting. She saw what her life could be, she saw the potential, and she went after it.

Soon after moving into their home, Laci and Scott hosted a house-warming party. Everyone had a wonderful time, and from what I observed Laci was pleased with the way things turned out. But later that night, after we'd gone home, she called in tears. At the party, my friend Linda had pressed Brent and his wife, Rose, on when they were going to start a family, and they somewhat reluctantly said Rose was already pregnant. Laci, sniffling, admitted that while overjoyed for her brother and his wife, she was disappointed she wasn't pregnant, too.

"You've got plenty of time," I said. "Your time will come."

After a brief pause, Laci began to sob again.

"What's wrong?" I asked.

Laci said she didn't know if her time would ever come. That sort of negativity wasn't like her. For a moment, I thought she might've been concerned about a Pap smear she had before getting married. It came back positive, and her doctor explained that she had some precancerous cells on the walls of her uterus, a fairly common condition called dysplasia. But the cells were removed and she was given a clean bill of health.

That wasn't the problem. Laci let me in on a bigger issue that was troubling her.

"Scott said that he's not ready," she said. "He doesn't even know if he wants any kids."

"He said this?" I asked. "Recently?"

"Yes. He said he didn't want to have children," she explained. "First he said that he wasn't ready, and then he said he doesn't think he wants to have children."

Hearing that made me mad. Scott knew that Laci wanted a family. She'd made that clear in numerous discussions, in my presence, before they married. I had never heard him say anything to the contrary. But then, as we've come to understand, he was a master at telling people what he thought they wanted to hear. I've since heard about instances when he told others, too, that he didn't want children.

So who knows what he really wanted? Actually, in fact sadly, tragically, we do know what he wanted. He told Laci as much after everyone left their housewarming party.

He didn't want children.

Laci—who left her marketing job in early November and began substitute teaching at local schools, including her old junior high, where some of her former teachers said she still looked young enough to be a student—didn't give up. Over Thanksgiving, the two of us were in my kitchen when she said she was quitting birth control pills in December. I stopped whatever I was preparing and looked at her with raised eyebrows.

"Really?" I said.

"We're going to try to get pregnant," she said excitedly.

I still had to ask about the conversation that we'd had a few weeks earlier. I thought Scott didn't want to have children. What accounted for his apparently sudden change of mind on such a large issue?

"We talked about it and he said he wants kids," she explained. "He said he's ready."

"Are you sure?" I asked, hoping I didn't seem badgering. "Laci, I know you want to be a mom. But you have to make sure . . . he has to, too. . . . You both have to make sure he's ready to have children. Because you can't give the baby back after it's here."

After that last sentence, I added a nervous laugh. I wanted to lighten the mood without losing any of the seriousness.

Laci nodded.

"No, no, we've talked about it, and he swears he's ready," she said.

In retrospect, though, I wonder if that conversation she had with Scott was what set him down the path of doing such an unimaginably horrific thing. I wonder if that was when the time bomb in his mind began to tick. I don't know what to believe anymore. Was everything a ruse or did he ever really care about her? Did he care about anyone, for that matter?

So many lies have been told that I don't believe anything Scott has said. I go only by what I know to be true, what I saw, and what my gut felt. I could be wrong, but I think that at some point Scott Peterson really did love Laci.

Intent on getting pregnant, and now open about feeling that special stirring inside her, Laci stopped taking her birth control pills after Christmas. Everyone knew. She even announced it at our friend Richard Taylor's annual holiday party. With a drink in her hand, she told people she was saying good-bye to alcohol. If they didn't pick up the hint, she explained that she and Scott were trying to have a baby.

Every picture I have of her from that party has her holding a drink, looking downright gleeful, and talking to someone. She was so funny. I had to rescue some guests from her. I imagined them waiting for her to take a breath so they could excuse themselves, but she never stopped talking. As for Scott, he smiled as Laci spoke about their baby plans, and at the time we took that to be a smile of approval.

Laci couldn't wait to become pregnant. She was so excited about being a mother.

Chapter Seven

Whenever Ron needed to clear his head or just relax, he went fishing, so it's no surprise that he thought it would be an excellent way to get to know Scott better. In November 2001, after Ron had bugged him for months, Scott finally agreed.

They met at the house one morning at six thirty and drove to Lake Amador, where they spent a few hours sitting on the bank and talking about things guys talk about when they fish. Ron remembers it being the one time they ever spent time alone together.

And the fishing? According to Ron, Scott had a nice rod and reel but he didn't pack much in his small tackle box for that type of fishing. He tried a couple of lures, walking up and down the bank, but Ron had their only catch of the day—and he lost it at the bank! Ron didn't think much of Scott's ability as a fisherman, not from the way he tied his knots or cast his pole.

On the personal side, Scott said things with him were going fine. He didn't go into great detail, but Ron didn't remember Scott having any complaints. When they returned home, Ron asked Scott if he wanted his fishing pole. Scott said he'd get it later. At the time, Scott was traveling a couple days a week for work, and it would've been easy for him to forget about a fishing pole. For whatever reason, he never came for the pole. It's still sitting in our garage.

Laci was working as a substitute teacher, which she liked. She also flirted with ideas for her own businesses. She briefly thought about opening a restaurant and even printed sample menus. She also talked about making her own mustards and selling them at gourmet shops. Another idea was an etiquette school for children. That amused her friends. I can still hear Lori Ellsworth saying, "Laci, you know that we aren't in Beverly Hills or New York, don't you?"

I wish she would've gotten the chance to open the little plant and herb shop she dreamed about. Laci was so knowledgeable and she loved growing her own backyard herb garden of oregano, catnip, and basil. She would've enjoyed having the shop and helping other people grow their own gardens.

Laci was meticulous, but at the same time had a good sense of humor. After their swimming pool was completed in March 2002, she planted groundcover in the border along one side, but the extremely compact soil made it difficult for plants to survive. One day in late spring she was replacing dead or dying plants. At the same time, their heating and air-conditioning unit was being replaced on the rooftop. The installer was on the roof, and as Laci got up to retrieve a gardening tool, she lost her balance. She told me that she'd hoped the man on the roof didn't see her fall in the pool. But when she surfaced, he was looking right at her. In typical Laci style, she giggled and waved and announced, "I'm fine! I'm fine!" Then she crawled out of the pool and dragged her wet and fully clothed body into the house, where she proceeded to laugh hysterically. One thing about Laci: she could always poke fun at herself.

One day Laci and her friend Stacey were in the backyard, and Stacey pointed to a large bush near the pool that had a dead limb jutting out.

"Why don't you clip that dead part?" Stacey asked.

"No way," she explained. "Scott's tried. But that's where my dragonfly sits and watches me work in the yard."

As Stacey recalled, her eyes widened. Her dragonfly? Sure enough, as they spoke a dragonfly landed and stared at Laci, who shrugged.

"It's good luck," she said, laughing.

Laci hoped for some, too, as she wanted to get pregnant. Unfortunately, Laci had trouble getting pregnant as quickly as she wanted. For someone who did everything by a schedule, it frustrated her. I felt bad for her. She was so determined, and there was not much she could do unless she and Scott saw fertility specialists, which they weren't ready to do. I knew when she was ovulating and when the pregnancy books said was the optimum time for her and Scott to try. Perhaps it was more information than I needed, but that was Laci.

By spring 2002, Laci had done a lot of research on fertility treatments, looked into doctors, and spoken about her concerns with Scott. As far as I knew, Scott had never expressed any concerns about Laci's ability to get pregnant, but she told me that he'd agreed to get tested to see if one of them had a problem. From what I knew, she believed he was willing to do whatever it took for them to have a baby.

That apparently wasn't true. After Laci's disappearance, Brent's wife, Rose, told detectives that on Christmas Eve 2001, Scott had said he was "kind of hoping for infertility." I want to think that if Laci heard anything remotely close to that I would've heard about it from her. She would've been very hurt and we would've talked about it.

As it turned out, she got pregnant naturally. She was on the verge of scheduling fertility tests when she got the good news. It was June 9, a Sunday. The phone rang at seven a.m. Ron and I were still in bed. He picked it up and Laci blurted out the news. I was still half asleep when Ron handed the phone to me without having given anything away. He simply said, "It's Laci."

I sat up in bed and took the receiver.

"I'm pregnant!" she said. "Mom, I'm pregnant! I can't believe it. I just took the test. I'm pregnant!"

"It finally came back positive?" I said.

"Ah-ha," she said, thrilled. "I'm pregnant!"

"That's great news, Laci," I said. "Congratulations!"

That evening Laci and Scott came over. As expected, Laci was beside herself and wanted to talk about everything from when she took the home pregnancy test and how she watched it change color to how she envisioned decorating the baby's room depending on its sex. Scott didn't contribute to the conversation or share Laci's excitement. He didn't show any of the joy that you'd expect on such a momentous day.

It was noticeably weird. Laci and I were standing at one end of the dining room table and Scott sat at the other end, looking glum and moody.

"Scott's having a midlife crisis," Laci said.

I looked at Scott and asked, "A midlife crisis? Why?"

He didn't say anything, but Laci did. "It's because he's turning thirty and becoming a father all in the same year."

"Oh, get over it," I said lightheartedly. "Thirty is not midlife and becoming a father is supposed to be a happy time."

He said nothing. His expression remained the same.

I turned to Laci. She looked pained, as if she'd already dealt with his mood. I raised my eyebrows, asking if she wanted to say anything more. She didn't go in to further detail, but I saw she was troubled.

His crappy mood bothered me then, and it still does. Could that have been the moment he turned into the other Scott, the Scott we didn't know? It was clear to me that something was going on in his head. Most people would've been overjoyed at the prospect of their first child. But he showed no signs of joy. In fact, his attitude seemed so inappropriate to me. Knowing what I do now, I think that Laci's good news was the beginning of her end.

The next day I shared the good news with friends and family, including my cousin Gwen. The two of us have always been extremely close. We've had a relationship that goes beyond enjoying each other's company. It's deep, in the place where intuition and emotion intertwine and you know each other's thoughts without even having to speak.

As I told her about Laci, she must have heard a note of apprehension in my voice. It wasn't anything I was aware of, but after listening to me describe my original conversation with Laci and then dinner later on, including Scott's cranky reaction, she asked, "What's wrong?"

"Nothing," I said. "I couldn't be happier for Laci. Why?"

"Well, you don't sound like you're *really* excited," she said.

"I'm thrilled for Laci," I said. "She's wanted this for a long time."

"Yes. But something's bothering *you*," she said. "I can hear it in your voice. Tell me."

I was amazed by the power of her perception, but she was on the money. I hadn't even told Ron. Until that point, in fact, I hadn't even fully confessed it to myself. Yet beneath the surface, I was dealing with an irritating, totally irrational fear that I couldn't erase no matter how strongly I told myself to forget it.

I debated whether to admit as much to Gwen, but I thought, If I say what's on my mind, if I actually speak the words, it won't happen. I took a deep breath.

"I just feel like there's a dark cloud hanging over me," I said. "Why shouldn't the sun be shining through right now? I should be so excited and happy for Laci. She's so excited and happy. But I have a terrible feeling—and I hate saying it but I'm going to put it out there anyway. I have a terrible feeling she's not going to survive this pregnancy." I didn't elaborate. Nor did I feel any better for having said it.

Gwen asked why I felt that way. I wasn't sure: maybe it was because Laci was so small; or maybe it was because of her past medical history.

"I'm probably just being a mother," I said. "I'm worrying when I shouldn't."

"It's normal to worry," she said. "Laci is young and healthy. She'll be fine."

"You're right," I said, relieved . . . somewhat.

Later, as I thought about it, I attributed my worries to Scott's bad mood the previous night. I didn't understand why he couldn't smile, and I felt bad for Laci, whose grin, fortunately, only grew brighter.

On July 4 Laci and Scott hosted a barbecue and invited some friends and family. Laci had done all the prep work and Scott barbecued the chicken on their recently installed gas barbecue. Scott became frustrated when, no matter what adjustments he made, the flames continued to flare up and burn the chicken. It was obvious to everyone that he was very upset, so we tried to reassure him that it was no big deal. I tried to lighten his mood and told him not to worry about it, it's difficult to barbecue chicken without burning the skin. I joked that we could call it jerk chicken, as in jerk the skin off before eating it. I don't think he found much humor in what I said, but eventually his mood changed and we had a great dinner.

I'm glad I had my video camera with me that day. I videotaped Laci as she was lying on the lounge near the pool. She was only a few weeks pregnant at the time, and I teased her about how big her tummy was, which of course it wasn't

I watch that video often. I look at her, listen to her voice . . . and I remember.

I'll never forget how much fun Laci had lighting the fireworks. There were only a couple of young children at her house, and then there was Laci. She was bouncing around like a little kid, waving sparklers in the air, and running into the street to light more fireworks as soon as the last went out. I remember thinking that night how much enjoyment I got out of just watching her. She was so excited, so happy, so full of life.

Laci relished every minute of being pregnant. From almost the first week, she talked about how she was getting *sooooo* big. In reality, she hadn't gained an ounce. We kidded her all the time about that. But she was just so excited about everything, even morning sickness. For her, pregnancy was the ultimate in fun adventures. She couldn't wait for each new change or development. She treated her first ob-gyn appointment as if it were a holiday. She called me after she left and said her doctor had officially confirmed her pregnancy to her and Scott. (He'd gone to the appointment with her.) She sounded so happy, and relieved. It was a good time for them, I thought.

Unbeknownst to me, she started to keep a diary of her pregnancy. The pages were cataloged as evidence and weren't brought to my attention until after Scott was convicted. I've read and reread each page umpteen times. It's like hearing Laci all over again. Her voice is so clear and clearly excited, starting with the very first entry on July 16, 2002.

Well, it's official. I am with child. Today Scott & I had our first sonogram. The baby looked like a peanut. So small, with a strong heart beat & active. She/He rolled over, kicked its arms & legs. I didn't realize a baby at 10 weeks would be so developed. My true feelings would be excitement & relief. I can't wait for the changes to come.

Laci came to our house for dinner that night. Scott was out of town. As she walked in the door, she was practically in tears. I asked what was wrong. She said she lost the sonogram, which she'd wanted to show me. As far as she knew, she'd left it on the front seat of her car, but she'd run an errand before getting to our house, so I thought maybe it fell out.

We searched her car and when we didn't find it, we drove in my car to Long's Drugs, the only place she'd stopped. We searched the parking lot and didn't find anything. Laci was distraught. I suggested she get a copy from the doctor, which she did a few days later and which she gave to me. It's the only photo I have of my grandson.

I don't know how she could've lost it. Unfortunately, Scott's betrayal leads me to question everything about him and sometimes I wonder if he grabbed it from her car and threw it out.

In her first trimester, Laci suffered morning sickness, and to counter it ate toast or cereal as soon as she got up. Like so many moms-to-be she read the classic book *What to Expect When You're Expecting*. She also couldn't wait to start wearing maternity clothes and was obsessed with getting bigger. One day she stopped by her friend Stacey's house and, according to Stacey, wouldn't stop patting her tummy until Stacey commented on her "bump."

"You had to acknowledge how thick she was before she'd stop," Stacey told me. "And Laci rarely stopped talking."

July 25, 2002
> *Today I realized I can no longer fit into a pair of pants that I love. My tummy is getting bigger and I have a hard time sucking it in. I'm still real sleepy, but my headaches aren't as bad. I had to buy a new bra this week, and I know a new wardrobe is on its way sooner than I thought!*

For Laci, this was that special time in her life, a time only a woman appreciates and knows. It also drew her closer to me. We discussed the changes she was experiencing as well as her hopes and dreams. I think generally there's something about being pregnant, about creating a new life and feeling it grow inside you, that releases not merely a torrent of hormones but an even-more-powerful sensation of optimism about life, and that was true with Laci.

In July, her friend Rene Tomlinson gave birth to a girl, Emma. Laci visited them in the hospital and called me right after, as if she'd witnessed a miracle. She went on and on about the baby's size and looks. She couldn't get over how cute she was, so small and lovable, all swaddled and sleepy. She was so happy for Rene, she told me.

"I can't believe I have a baby inside me," she gushed. "This is so amazing."

August 15, 2002

    On my way to the mall I had a big sneeze, and a few seconds later I felt something that I had been waiting for. I felt the baby move. It was a small flutter on the right side of my stomach. I had been reading about what the first movements would feel like, but I didn't expect it so soon. I am only 14 weeks pregnant but my body is starting to show signs that I am pregnant to everyone else.

A week later, Laci had another appointment with her ob-gyn. Scott again accompanied her. Afterward, she wrote:

August 20, 2002

    We heard the baby's heart beat today. The doctor had to chase the baby around with the machine, but she finally cornered her/him. The heart beat was strong and loud. It's amazing to have a living human inside of me. I can't wait to meet her/him.

I'm inclined to think that Laci's body wasn't the only change occurring at their home. Thinking back, Scott's behavior seemed to change in the months before Laci's murder. We didn't know about the big things occurring in secret, but there were little incidents that did happen in front of us, but since they weren't huge red flags I didn't give them a lot of thought. Take, for instance, when my sister's granddaughter stayed with me one weekend. Her name is Lacey, pronounced the same as my Laci but spelled differently. I promised to take Lacey to the county fair and then swimming at "big Laci's" house.

As it got to be time to leave for the fair, though, Lacey thought that maybe it was too hot for the fair and we should just go swimming. Fine with me. We went over there and Laci sat on the lounge and watched Lacey play in the water. She said Scott was inside taking a nap. He came out a while later and wasn't friendly at all. That wasn't the Scott I thought I knew. I'd never seen that side of him. I asked Laci if he was okay.

"He's been working hard," she shrugged. "He's just tired."

By Labor Day, Laci was starting to show. She and Scott were at our house for lunch and I took a picture of her pressing her shirt down so I could see the little bump in her tummy. Brent and Rose and their baby were there, too. We sat out on the patio and enjoyed the late summer afternoon. Laci was talking about baby names. All of us chimed in and gave our own suggestions. Scott suggested Ripley.

I looked at him and said, "You can't do that to your son. 'Ripley' will always be followed by 'believe it or not.'"

He laughed and said he hadn't thought about that.

Laci was so proud of the progress she was making and couldn't wait to get fatter. Up till then, she'd mostly borrowed clothes from Stacey. I can still hear Stacey say, "That little shit is telling people that she's wearing my shorts. Why not just say, Isn't Stacey fat?" But Laci was thrilled the time had come when she could buy her own maternity clothes. It added to the excitement. Most important, she felt terrific.

September 5, 2002

The second trimester is great! I have so much energy & I feel like my old self again, except for the extra 10 pounds. I am wearing my maternity clothes now. My tummy is growing a little each day, and my bathroom trips are less frequent. I'm 17½ weeks and the count down has begun until my next doctor's visit. At that appt. we will find out the sex of our child.

I was convinced she was having a girl. I worked with a woman, Kathy, known for being able to predict the sex of babies. I had Laci come to the office and I introduced her to Kathy. The three of us went back to my office. Kathy had Laci lie on the floor and then did her little thing. A girl, for sure, Kathy said.

September 24, 2002

I am 20 weeks pregnant and my tummy is finally bulging out. Today we had another sonogram and we were able to find out the sex of our child. It's a boy. We were excited to know the sex of our child. It makes our pregnancy even more realistic. Now we need to focus on names and decorating the nursery.

Laci called to tell me the news. Then she stopped by my office to tell me again in person. Each time, I asked if she was sure—that's how steadfastly I believed the baby was a girl. We had a good laugh over that when she showed me the sonogram photo.

"You can't argue with that," she said.

Laci was thinking of everything. Shortly after she learned her baby's sex, Rene, Laci, and I went to Babies "R" Us so Laci could register for her baby shower in January. Because Rene had a gorgeous three-month-old girl, Laci decided she was the Babies "R" Us expert, and it turned out she was. We spent three hours in the store, and Rene knew every item's location.

At one point, as Rene walked up and down the aisles saying, "You need this and this, oh, and you won't survive without this," I said, "How much time have you spent in this store?" She didn't have to answer. Another customer walked up to her and asked for help. Rene said she didn't work there. "I heard you telling her [she pointed at Laci] where everything was, so I thought you worked here," she said, surprised. "Sorry."

If only Scott had caught the same spirit. To help him through his depression, Laci wanted to throw him a thirtieth-birthday party. I know she envisioned a big blowout, something over the top, but Scott was out of town before his birthday and she had trouble getting him to commit to a date when he'd be home. Still, she lovingly put together an elegant dinner party for seven couples that included a multi-course gourmet dinner and gifts.

Why wouldn't he commit to a date? That was always curious, not the norm. Then during the trial, we learned that the night before his thirtieth birthday, Scott was partying at a convention in Anaheim, where he asked Amber Frey's friend Shawn Sibley if she knew any single women that she could introduce to him. He told her that he was single and ready to meet someone and settle down.

So was he excited about fatherhood? Scott's behavior provides the best and most honest answers. And I think deep down Laci must have had concerns.

October 29, 2002

The baby has been moving a lot lately. It feels like little punches. Some times they're big enough to move my hand if it's placed on my tummy. Today we had an appointment or check up for a better word. Scott and I heard the baby's heartbeat and the doctor said it sounded normal. The doctor asked if Scott had felt the baby move yet and he excitedly replied yes. October 27 Scott felt the baby move for the first time. We were at the Tomlinson's watching Game 7 of the World Series, between the Angels and the Giants. I felt releaved [sic] because I didn't want to be the only one experiencing such a beautiful moment. Now Scott, in my mind, can enjoy my (our) pregnancy even more now. Scott didn't show a whole lot of excitement, but I know he really was.

Chapter Eight

Laci felt healthy and energetic through most of her pregnancy, and that was due in no small part to eating properly and exercising regularly. To keep in shape, she walked McKenzie through East La Loma Park. Getting there was simple. She walked out the front door, turned left, and walked about a block to the end of the cul-de-sac, where she scooted down a fairly steep dirt path to the park.

In the best of conditions, the path was slippery and rutted by mountain bikers and weather, and therefore it required sure-footed steps. Laci was very careful. Upon reaching the bottom, the park opened up into a huge expanse with trees, a creek, and acres of well-lit paths that were used by bikers, joggers, Rollerbladers, and moms pushing strollers.

Laci always walked the same path, past the swings and jungle gym and the tennis courts, where she turned around and came back via the restrooms. The circuit took her about forty minutes. I went with her enough times to know. She was in good shape and walked at a brisk pace. She always carried a bottle of water. Sometime in late October, though, Laci started to have problems. While walking in the park, near the restrooms, Laci became dizzy. She also got sick to her stomach suddenly and threw up. As she told me later, it was different from morning sickness, and so she picked up the pace, hoping to get home before she got any sicker. She also told me that she was embarrassed about vomiting in front of two maintenance workers as well as worried about the dizziness. I advised her to tell her doctor. She thought I was overreacting and tried to blame it on something she'd eaten or simply that she was tired.

"It's nothing," she scoffed. "I was dizzy for a minute. I threw up a few times. Then it went away."

"Please do me a favor," I said. "If you continue to walk, please take a cell phone. You can call if anything happens again."

A few days later, sure enough, the same thing happened. Laci was walking in the park again when she had another dizzy spell. This time, rather than hurry home, she sat down on the ground and waited until the dizziness and nausea passed. She didn't throw up, but I know it scared her. She called her doctor as soon as she got home. The doctor thought she was probably dehydrated and said that since her February due date was so close, she should probably stop walking. If she really wanted to walk, the doctor suggested going later in the day so her body had time to rehydrate. But in general, Laci was told to take it easy.

And she did. As far as I know. Laci gave up her regular walks in the park and instead started prenatal yoga classes at the Village Yoga Center. She and Scott also attended two private Lamaze classes that were held at the home of their friends Kristen and Greg Reed. Kristen was also pregnant—about three months ahead of Laci, I believe—and they compared notes. When Laci and Scott dropped off my birthday gift on November 1, she was pouty—not blatantly but enough for me to detect. I got her to admit she was a little annoyed that Kristen had named her baby Conner. "Mom, she knew I wanted to name my baby Conner," Laci said. "She had five names on her list and Conner was the last choice."

I knew how she felt, but I still pointed out the foolishness of thinking you could own a name. I told her no matter which name she chose there would always be someone with the same name, so she should call him Conner if that's the name she liked. She laughed at herself and realized there was no reason to be upset.

November 14
> *My little baby boy is growing every day. It seems like every morning I wake up and my belly seems bigger. I love feeling him move*

*inside of me. We've decided to name him Conner Latham Peterson. I
enjoy talking to him and rubbing my tummy to let him know I'm
thinking about him. Pregnancy is such a wonderful experience.*

Six days after that journal entry, Scott met Fresno massage therapist Amber Frey, a young, single, seemingly earnest mother whose
girlfriend, Shawn Sibley, led her to believe—as Scott had told her—
that he was single and looking for a committed relationship. They met
at a bar, had dinner at a Japanese restaurant, and then went back to his
hotel where they continued to drink and spend the night together.

Scott never mentioned that he was married and a couple of months
away from becoming a father. None of that was in his script. It seems
to me that it was pure ad-lib, whatever he needed to say to get what he
wanted. When Amber asked Scott about his plans for the upcoming
holidays, he said that he was off to fish in Alaska over Thanksgiving,
then at the annual family get-together in Kennebunkport over Christmas and with friends in Paris for New Year's.

What a guy!

What a liar!

Amber didn't know it.

We certainly didn't.

As for how Laci and Scott really spent the holidays, they alternated
each year between our house and his family's in San Diego. This year
they were scheduled to have Thanksgiving in San Diego and Christmas with us. As pregnant as Laci was in November, she didn't mind
the long drive to San Diego, but the Petersons planned a family trip to
Disneyland in Anaheim, and Laci didn't feel up to that. Her feet were
swollen and she was tired.

"Why are you going?" I asked.

"Because Scott's never been to Disneyland and Jackie wants to
take him," she said.

Given Laci's condition, I thought it was inconsiderate to insist on
the trip to Disneyland. Why couldn't it wait until after Laci had the
baby? And the central premise—that Scott hadn't been there—turned
out to be untrue. As I learned later, he'd gone as a child. The Petersons
were also throwing Laci a baby shower for their side of the family. I felt

bad for my daughter. On November twenty-fourth, they came for dinner, and Laci, though in good spirits, seemed a little tired. Maybe she wasn't enthused about the trip.

During dinner, Laci informed us that Scott had joined Modesto's exclusive Del Rio Country Club. As she told us, Laci looked at Scott and shook her head. He grinned and rubbed his hands together. He didn't have to say anything. I thought he looked as though he was envisioning long days on the golf course.

"Great," she said. "Now I'll see you less than I already do."

"You'll still see me," he said, adding, "or you can come with me."

On November 26, they drove to Disneyland and met up with Scott's parents, his brother John and his family, and his relatively new half-sister Anne Bird and her family. Later, when I asked her about the trip, Laci said Scott pushed her around the amusement park in a wheelchair. She didn't offer many details but I knew she was relieved to get through it.

From what I later read about it, she had good reason to feel that way. Supposedly, Scott was aloof and antisocial at dinner. He consumed an expensive bottle of wine by himself and talked constantly on his cell phone—to guess who? He left Laci with the rest of the family. According to Laci, Jackie always criticized something about her, whether it was her clothes, the way she decorated her house, or her cooking. This time it was the new name Laci and Scott were considering for the baby. Laci told her mother-in-law that they were thinking of Logan, not Conner, at least for the moment, but for whatever reason Jackie didn't like it.

I was gratified by Anne Bird's account in her book of Laci on that trip. She said Laci's smile was unfailing no matter the circumstance, and she described her as resilient, strong, and always maintaining a good, positive mood. That was my Laci—the silver lining in a dark cloud. As for the rest of that Thanksgiving, Scott's family gave her a baby shower and I know she appreciated the gifts and had a good time, but she didn't say anything else about the Petersons. Knowing Laci, that spoke volumes.

In a moment of weariness, Laci had once told me that Jackie made her feel like she was never quite good enough. I never knew the extent of what she put up with until I read that Jackie had even found fault in the thank-you note Laci wrote her for the shower. Jackie called it "too by the book." Why not just be grateful?

Laci was looking forward to the future: Christmas, her baby shower in January, her growing tummy, and the excitement she felt as she got closer to her due date in February.

Dec. 1

On our trip down to San Diego for Thanksgiving, Scott and I came up with another name for the baby, Logan. We will have to start using that name when speaking to the baby to see if we like the sound of it. Connor is still on our minds, but we are not certain. If we do go with Connor, we need to decide on how we are going to spell it, er/or.

That was the last entry Laci made in her pregnancy diary. I wish she'd written more. I wish she were still here to write. I can't begin to describe the deep pain I feel when I think of her heading into the future with such excitement, and all of us helping her and cheering her on, while at the same time Scott was at the dinner table or in bed next to her, plotting her murder, and none of us had any awareness that we were nearing the last day of Laci's life.

I've heard that a sociopath can live a fairly normal life without any obvious signs of trouble for years. As long as their lies are minor, they can maneuver through their complicated situations. But if they feel backed into a corner, they can become dangerous. I've often wondered if that's what happened to Scott.

On December 6, three days after he'd helped Amber pick out a Christmas tree, Scott was confronted by Amber's friend, Shawn Sibley, who'd heard that he was married and wanted to know the truth.

At first Scott denied it, but then he called her back and said that he had been married but he lost his wife. Was that the first tick of the time bomb? It might not have been the first time Scott had imagined his life without Laci, but it may have been the moment when he decided to act on it. I don't know, but it doesn't seem coincidental that he told Amber's friend he lost his wife. Then on the very next day, December 7, he searched the classified ads for a small boat. On December 8, he used the Internet to check the currents in San Francisco Bay. On December 9, he purchased a boat for $1,400. On the fourteenth, he and Amber went to a Christmas party where she introduced him as her boyfriend and he didn't bother saying anything to the contrary. Earlier that morning, he told Laci that he had to meet a business associate in San Francisco and couldn't attend a party her friend Stacey Boyers was having that night. I talked to Laci later that morning and I remember asking her if Scott couldn't reschedule his trip for another day because the weather was stormy and the drive would be treacherous.

"Can't he go on Monday?" I asked Laci. "The winds are terrible. It's going to be a really bad drive."

"I told him the same thing," Laci said. "He said the guy has a stopover in San Francisco, before heading to Mexico. This is the only time he's going to be here, so Scott has to go today."

Before he left, Laci and Scott went to a local pawnshop together and sold several pieces of jewelry that Laci had inherited from her grandmother. I didn't know all this until it came out during the trial. Apparently Laci had been there a few days earlier and had done the first round of paperwork in her name. According to testimony at the trial, she wasn't in a good mood when they went back. At one point, Scott jokingly put his arms around her stomach, in a ha-ha kind of way, and she brushed them off. Laci may have been annoyed about being there in the first place, and additionally, she forgot her driver's license, which was necessary to complete the transaction. That wasn't like Laci. But instead of running back home to get it, Scott did all the paperwork himself and used his ID. I don't know what significance to ascribe to all of this, if any, because Laci never told me they were selling the jewelry. That may be significant itself. I'll never know. But it all strikes me as odd, especially in light of Scott telling her that he was going to San Francisco when in reality he was going with Amber to a Christmas party.

The same night, Laci drove herself in the howling wind and cold to

Stacey's party. She arrived carrying freshly made crab cakes and an ivy plant, but what people noticed was the way she looked in her burgundy pantsuit and high heels. As Stacey told me later, Laci was "radiant" and "glowing." Still, Stacey couldn't help but make fun of her for being so dressed up on such a wet, dreary evening.

"The streets are flooded," Stacey recalled saying. "And you're pregnant and in high heels!"

"Hey, I had to make use of this outfit somewhere," Laci cracked.

Ron and I got up early the next morning and went fishing near Oakdale. We went to one of his favorite spots along the river. The weather was still cold and icky. For my taste, it wasn't a great morning to be outside, but Ron thought the conditions were heavenly. Since I didn't have a license, I bundled up, sat in a fold-up chair, and read the Sunday newspaper.

We were home by early afternoon. Laci called and invited us for dinner and to watch the season finale of *The Sopranos*, one of Ron's favorite programs. They had a satellite dish and received the early feed from the East Coast, allowing Ron to watch *The Sopranos* at six o'clock rather than nine. In those days he went to sleep pretty early, so her invitation was appreciated.

"I can't go over there unless we're going to have dinner," Ron joked. I relayed his message to Laci, who was amused.

"Let me call you back," she said. "I want to check with Scott."

She called back a short time later. Now I know that she must have reached him either at Amber's or on his way back to Modesto.

"Come for dinner," she said. "Scott's going to make lasagna."

Since the show began at six, we got to their house early. The dining room table was set. But Laci was already apologetic. She was serving a frozen lasagna because Scott had arrived home too late to make his. Usually she made everything from scratch. I told her that we didn't care. In fact, I sheepishly admitted that I liked the frozen kind better and laughed.

At dinner, I said that Ron and I had gone fishing earlier in the morning. Laci's eyes widened. I rarely went fishing with him, so it was news. And it prompted a funny description of me bundled up in a chair beside the river. It was also a perfect opportunity for Scott—or Laci—to mention that he'd bought a fishing boat the week before. But the subject never came up because (a) Laci didn't know and (b) because Scott didn't want us to know.

For some reason, Laci mentioned that Scott had told her that the warehouse he rented for work in an industrial part of town was so full he had to step over things to get to his office. I'd never seen the warehouse myself. I didn't even know what it looked like until I saw photos at the preliminary hearing. By that time I couldn't remember why she had brought it up, but I knew it didn't have anything to do with a boat.

I asked Scott what his mother and father were doing for Christmas. He said that his entire family was getting together at one of his brother's or sister's homes. When I asked if he was going to miss being there, he grimaced, as if to say no, and made a comment about how his family was so dysfunctional. Although I'd heard him make comments before, I'd never heard him dismiss his whole family like that. Scott was clearly going through something. Now we know; then, we didn't have a clue and he wasn't about to let on. When I asked about the drive to San Francisco the previous day, curious whether the strong winds had made the roads more treacherous than normal, he cocked his head to the side, thought for a moment, and then simply said it was okay. Then he changed the subject and raised his wineglass.

"I want to make a toast to Mom for having such a wonderful daughter," he said.

That was Scott's trick, something I didn't notice then. If he didn't want to talk about something, he quickly and smoothly changed the subject. Once dinner was finished, he didn't have to worry as *The Sopranos* took over. He and Ron moved into the family room—Ron sunk into a sofa, Scott sprawled on the floor—while Laci eagerly guided me into the baby's room and showed me the colorful mobile she'd put over the crib and the red-and-white life preserver on the wall. Scott had also hung some shelves over the dresser that he was supposed to convert into a changing table. The room had really come together and was adorable. We also looked at her baby shower gifts.

"We're just waiting for the baby," she said, putting some tiny T-shirts into a drawer.

And it seemed the baby was also waiting for them. Shortly after Laci and I joined Ron and Scott for the second half of *The Sopranos,* Laci said the baby was kicking and asked if I wanted to feel him. I'd never felt him. Every time I'd tried, he stopped moving. It was like a game of hide and seek. I was so determined to feel him kick. Laci just beamed with each movement.

She said he was moving all over the place, but when I moved next to her and put my hand on her tummy, the same thing happened— nothing. I didn't feel a thing; the little guy quit moving. Determined to feel him, I kept my hand on her for the rest of the show. It would've been kind of funny if not for a comment that Laci made that bothered me. As I complained about not being able to feel the baby, she said Scott didn't like to leave his hand on her stomach.

"He takes his hand away if he doesn't feel it immediately," she said.

I don't know if Scott heard what Laci said, but he didn't acknowledge it.

Laci offered a half smile, as if to suggest, What are you going to do? but I saw the hurt in her eyes. I felt so sad for Laci. I didn't understand why he wasn't more involved.

Even after *The Sopranos* ended, I still had my hand on Laci's belly. I couldn't take it off. Even if he wasn't going to move, I wanted him to know I was there. So before Ron and I left, I laid my head on Laci's stomach.

"Hello, little Conner," I said. "This is your nana talking to you. I love you. I can't wait to meet you."

I didn't get to meet my grandson. I never even got to feel him move.

The next day, December 16, was Ron's birthday. He wasn't at home when Laci called to wish him happy birthday, but the two of us spoke. She and Scott were going to Carmel for three days with Scott's parents, and she asked me to take care of McKenzie and their cats. I said sure and assumed that McKenzie would come to our house while the cats would fend for themselves. That's how it always was when they left town.

But this time there was a change in plans. Laci told me that Scott wanted to leave McKenzie at home, too. I was shocked. That dog was treated like a baby. It was mid-December and cold outside. McKenzie was going to sleep outside for three days? I didn't understand. It didn't make sense. As I said, they always brought him to our house. Once Brent offered to take care of him and Laci quickly said no thanks, explaining that McKenzie enjoyed being spoiled at our house, it was like a vacation at the Ritz.

"Why aren't you bringing him to us?" I asked.

"Scott seems to think that he'll be okay here," she said.

I could tell from her voice that it wasn't her choice to leave him. As far as I knew, McKenzie had never slept outside in the cold; he slept in their bedroom.

"Laci, it's freezing cold," I said. "You know it's fine with us. It's not a problem."

She hesitated.

"Scott said he'll be okay," she said.

Again, I heard a note of concern in her voice, the same way I'd heard sadness in her voice the previous night when she said that Scott didn't leave his hand on her stomach. It didn't sound right to me.

The next day, a Tuesday, Scott and Laci met up with his parents in Carmel. Laci wasn't as enthusiastic about the trip as she'd been in previous years. At almost seven and a half months pregnant, she was uncomfortable during her best moments. It was hard enough at home; why would she want to go on another long drive and stay in a hotel?

I didn't speak to Laci while they were in Carmel, but I called her on Thursday evening after they returned home. Though she sounded like she'd tried to make the best of the trip, I heard the fatigue and strain in her voice as she told me that Scott and his father spent the entire day on the golf course, leaving her with Jackie, whose breathing problems made it difficult or impossible to walk to the shopping area. Later, Scott's phone records would show that he called Amber every day. So how much attention did Laci get? I'm sure it was harder than she let on.

But I could hear that she was already more comfortable being back in her own environment, around her own things. She sounded even better the next day. She mentioned having a routine doctor's appointment the following Monday, December 23, and then she and Scott were going to preregister at the hospital.

When we spoke on both Friday and Saturday, we talked about the baby shower Heather Richardson and Rene Tomlinson were giving her on January 11. As she went over some of the details, she sounded like herself again, which made me feel better. Rene joked that Laci had pretty much planned her own shower, including the menu. And she was still planning it. As we spoke, Laci changed her mind about having a cake—first she didn't want one, then she decided I should bring one.

"Make up your mind," I teased.

"Right now I feel like having my cake," she said.

On Monday, December 16, I'd spoken to Laci and invited her and Scott to come for dinner on Christmas Eve. Laci wanted to but said she needed to ask Scott and then would get back to me. Hearing nothing, on Thursday, I asked again if they wanted to come for dinner, and, again, she said that she had to talk to Scott.

She was the one who kept track of their social calendar and normally she would've gotten right back to me. This sort of indecision was unusual. I didn't say anything, but I now wish I had asked if everything was all right.

Why after eight years of babying McKenzie did they suddenly leave him outside for three days? (Actually, as Laci said, it was Scott's decision, not hers.) I think it's because he wasn't concerned about the dog anymore. Why couldn't she get him to commit to dinner at our house on Christmas Eve? I think it's because he knew what was going to happen. He killed Laci long before he murdered her.

Still, he let all of us go on making plans as if everything was normal, as if Laci had a future beyond Christmas Eve. Laci invited us for brunch on Christmas morning. She also asked Brent and his family, Amy, Dennis, and their grandfather, Bob. I asked Laci if she was up to cooking for such a large group and offered to host everyone at our house, but she insisted she was, and in typical Laci form she changed the menu several times.

I've read that she planned to make French toast. She may have, but I don't recall her mentioning that to me. At one point, she discussed making quiche and another time she talked about a favorite egg dish she'd enjoyed at Easter.

On Saturday, the twenty-first, I made a bunch of Christmas cookies for family and friends; I wanted to drop some off at Laci's that afternoon.

"Oh, Mom, please don't bring any to me," she said when I called. "My doctor told me to watch my weight, and I won't be able to resist them."

I listened to her. I wish I hadn't. I could've seen her one last time.

But only one person knew the end was drawing near. For the rest of us, and especially Laci, everything was normal. On Sunday, December 22, I delivered my Christmas cookies to family and friends. Afterward, Ron and I were out for a while and returned a little after 9 p.m. When we got home, I had a message from Laci.

"Hi, guys," she said, upbeat in tone. "I guess you aren't there. Call me when you get home. I have Ron's birthday gift and want to bring it to him."

I checked the time on the kitchen clock. It was past nine—too late to call Laci back, I thought. I didn't want to wake her in case she'd already gone to bed. I knew she'd been tired lately. I figured we'd talk in the morning.

As it turned out, we kept missing each other and played phone tag throughout the next day, December 23. Later, I learned that late that afternoon, Laci's sister Amy cut Scott's hair at Salon Salon, the shop where she worked, and she gave Laci some tips on using her curling iron. They also chatted about Laci's Christmas brunch. Amy said she'd ordered a gift basket of fruit for her and Laci's grandfather, which needed to be picked up at Vella Farms early afternoon on Christmas Eve, and Scott offered to do it for her. He must've been in a generous mood. Before leaving—at about 6 p.m.—Scott invited Amy to the house for dinner. They were picking up a pizza, he said.

She declined, explaining she was meeting a friend from out of town. Wasn't that convenient for Scott?

I've always wondered if she had mentioned meeting her friend before he invited her. Amy couldn't recall.

About eight thirty that night, I was on the phone with my friend Sandy and we were talking about each other's holiday plans. I said that I was still waiting to hear whether Laci and Scott were coming for dinner on Christmas Eve. I mentioned that it was unlike Laci to keep me waiting until the last minute, but I said, laughing, that I expected them to say yes and had already bought the groceries.

At that moment I heard the call-waiting beep and clicked over to the other line. It was Laci.

"Finally!" I said.

She told me that she and Scott were going to come for dinner on Christmas Eve. I wanted to ask why she'd taken so long to get back to me about dinner, just in case something was wrong or perhaps they'd had other plans, but I decided to make that inquiry the next day. It wasn't crucial.

Nor was it as interesting as what we did talk about—her visit to the doctor earlier in the day. Laci went through the whole exam, as she always did, so excited about the approaching due date, and she said everything was fine with her and the baby. I knew she and Scott were also supposed to have preregistered at the hospital, but I didn't ask how that went. I thought I'd save that, too.

"Who's going to be at dinner?" she asked.

I ran down the guest list. It was just family: Ron, his mother, his sister and her son, and me.

"I feel kind of funny because I didn't buy gifts for everybody," Laci said.

"That's okay," I assured her. "As a matter of fact, Ron and I talked about it and, you know, our families are getting too big to buy presents for everyone. We're going to do things differently next year. So don't worry about it. I just want the two of you to be here. That'll be the best gift."

"Okay," she said. "I'll see you tomorrow."

"I love you," I said.

"I love you, too," she said. "Good night."

"Good night."

It was a short conversation. I wish we had talked much longer.

It turned out to be the last time that Laci and I spoke.

Part Two

Her Daughter's Mother

We get to a point that I want Laci home,

and I get tired of waiting for her to come home.

We keep hope that she'll come home alive . . .

Each day it gets a lot harder.

Every single day is harder.

SHARON ROCHA TO LARRY KING,
FEBRUARY 25, 2003

Chapter Nine

December 24, 2002. Christmas Eve.

At first, Scott would tell a couple of people that he went golfing, but he told others, including me, that he left the house at nine thirty and went to the Berkeley Marina, where he went fishing. Both versions turned out to be untrue. He didn't leave for probably another half hour, and, as we now know, he didn't go fishing.

That morning I was on the phone with Sandy, picking up where we had left off the previous night. We arranged to meet at the movie theater and see a matinee of *Two Weeks Notice*. I thought about asking Laci to join us, but figured she would probably be too uncomfortable to sit still for the duration of the film. Since I was seeing her later, I didn't call her.

After the movie, I went home and got ready to make dinner. As I worked in the kitchen, Ron was reading the paper in the living room. I remember checking the ingredients in the fridge and realizing I'd forgotten to pick up whipping cream earlier at the grocery store for the chocolate pie I'd made. I asked Ron to call Laci to see if they could bring a pint. He left a message at their home. I never heard back, but I didn't expect her to call. I thought she and Scott would just show up with the whipping cream.

At five o'clock, I was actually preparing the dinner—ham and scalloped potatoes. I put the casserole dish of potatoes into the oven, but they never got cooked. (Two weeks later, I opened the oven and found the casserole dish still sitting on the top rack.) I remember standing by the stove and looking at the clock. It said 5:15. I'd told everyone to come at six. With forty-five minutes to pull myself together, I took another minute or so to finish in the kitchen and then I went into the bedroom to change my clothes and freshen up.

That's when the phone rang. It was the moment when time stopped, when normal life was replaced by a nightmare that shattered everything I knew to be true and right, when the calm and familiarity of daily routine was blown out of the water, when the shadow of death draped itself over our lives.

"Hi, Mom, is Laci there?" Scott Peterson asked.

"No," I said with my voice rising as if asking a question myself. I wondered why he was asking.

Scott paused and went *hmmmmm.* I wish I could've seen his face as he thought of what to say next. He had a way of cocking his head to the side and squinting his eyes when he was working out a scenario.

Then he said those words I'll never forget. "When I got home Laci's car was in the driveway and McKenzie was in the backyard with his leash on and Laci's missing."

I thought about what he'd just said. He got home. The dog was in the backyard. Laci was missing.

What did he mean, "missing"?

That word annoyed me. It was such a strange choice. Both of us knew that Laci wasn't the type to go missing. She was too practical, reliable, organized. They were coming for dinner. She wouldn't have gone anywhere without leaving word. It struck a nerve, more so than I initially realized.

"What time did you get home?" I asked.

"A quarter to five," he said.

And what time was it now? I wish I'd asked what he'd been doing for the past half hour. I didn't think to do that, I didn't grasp the situation that quickly. According to what Scott told the police—details that I didn't know until months later—he claimed that he came home from his fishing trip, fixed himself a snack, threw his dirty clothes into the washing machine, showered, changed clothes, and moved the bucket and mop he said Laci used to clean the floor. At that point he called me and asked if Laci was at my house.

If I'd known he did all that, I would've asked why he waited so long to call. I'd have asked a ton of questions. How concerned could he have been if he waited that long?

"Call her friends and ask if anyone knows where she is," I said. "See if anyone talked to her today. Then call me right back."

I hung up, took a deep breath, and tried to stay calm. *She's not missing*, I told myself as I turned to go tell Ron about Scott's call. I got as far as the bedroom door, about two or three steps, when I heard Scott's voice in my head: *Laci's missing*.

Suddenly I couldn't hear anything else but the word *missing*.

When I thought back on that call a few weeks later, I realized it was that word that had sent me into a panic. I said it to Ron, I said it to Sandy, I said it to Gwen and my sister, Susie, later that night. He'd said she was *missing*. That wasn't a word I would've used. I would've said I didn't know where she was. I think most people would have said it that way. But Scott didn't—and it set me off. I remember the feeling: a combination of sickness, panic, and fear sweeping through me like a virus. Everything got tight. I threw open the bedroom door and ran down the hall yelling to Ron: "Ron! Laci's missing! Scott just called and said that Laci's missing!"

Ron, in the living room, tried to calm me down by assuring me that she wasn't missing.

"She has to be around somewhere . . . with her friends, or out shopping . . . she's somewhere."

Then the phone rang again. It was Scott, and he sounded more concerned this time.

"Nobody has seen or talked to her today," he said.

"Check with the neighbors," I said. "Maybe she's at someone's house delivering cookies or something, since her car's in the driveway. And call me right back again."

He called back a few minutes later.

"I checked with the neighbors," he said. "Nobody's seen her."

"I'm going to the park to look for her," I said.

Since Scott had said McKenzie had been found wearing his leash, I assumed Laci had taken the dog for a walk. If I'd been thinking clearer, I would've realized that that didn't make sense. It was freezing cold outside and the steep trail leading into the park would've been muddy, wet, and difficult to navigate—in other words, a risk—even if Laci weren't nearly eight months pregnant. That, and she hadn't walked in the park for two months. Furthermore, she hadn't told anyone that she was going for a walk.

Anxious and on the verge of panic, I sprang into action. I told Ron to call the hospitals and 911 while I changed into warmer clothes and got set to go to the park. When I came back into the living room, I wanted him to tell me that he'd located Laci at a hospital. But he didn't. None of the hospitals had her registered as a patient. Nor did they have any Jane Does. Ron said the 911 dispatcher had told him to wait at home for an officer. I couldn't wait. It was dark and cold outside. *I had to find Laci.*

I called Sandy and in a panicked voice I told her what Scott had told me. I asked if she'd pick me up and take me to the park. Later my phone records showed that I called her at 5:32—about fifteen minutes after Scott's original call. I wondered how many friends Scott could have called and how many neighbors he checked with in that brief timespan.

I called Scott on his cell from Sandy's car. We were driving over the bridge leading to the park. It was 5:49.

Scott said he was already in the park.

"Meet me at the tennis courts," I said.

Sandy drove down the sloping road leading into the park and parked in the lot. I don't think I waited for the car to stop before I jumped out and started to run all through the area near the tennis courts. I started in the well-lit areas along the paths and worked my way into the darker fringes, screaming Laci's name: *"Laci! Laci! Laci!"*

The park was empty on Christmas Eve. There was no sign of Laci or anyone else.

Laci! Laci! Laci!

I was frantic. The thought of one of my children being missing had never entered my mind. They were adults. They weren't supposed to go missing. I needed to find Laci. That was the only thought in my head. I didn't know how to do it, I just knew I needed to find her, so I reacted to instincts and impulses. I moved, ran, searched, yelled. I caromed across the grounds in the park. I looked inside the first trash can I came upon and I continued to check every other one. I was afraid that someone might have hurt her and tried to hide her in a trash can. I wasn't even thinking what I'd do if I found her in one of them.

At some point, I turned around and ran back toward the parking lot, where I saw that Amy Krigbaum, who lived across the street from Laci and Scott, and her father had pulled up in her car. They'd come to look for Laci. Scott had knocked on her door and asked if she'd seen her.

(Almost a year later, during the preliminary hearing, I learned that Amy had asked where he'd been that day. Scott told her that he'd been golfing.)

I still hadn't seen Scott. Even if we'd started out in different sections of the park I should've seen him by now.

Where the hell was he?

I scanned the grounds for Scott and spotted a jogger running up a nearby hill. I chased after him, yelling for him to stop. At the sound of my frantic voice he turned, then stopped. Despite the freezing temperature, he wore running shorts and no shirt. (It's strange what the mind remembers.) I asked if he'd seen a young, pregnant woman. I blurted out her name as if he'd know it.

I remember he took a wary step backward. I don't blame him. It was nighttime, on Christmas Eve, the park was empty, and I'd darted at him from out of nowhere. I'm sure he thought I was a crazy person.

I quickly explained the situation as best I could and gave the jogger another description of Laci—pregnant, brown hair, large eyes . . .

He shook his head and said he hadn't seen her. He asked if I'd called the hospitals. I said yes. The jogger said he was a cardiologist and could check all the local hospitals with a single phone call if I wanted him to. I said yes, grateful for any help, and then I stood by as he dialed and gave Laci's name to the person on the other end. A minute later, he shook his head no, explaining that none of the hospitals had admitted her.

I thanked him and hurried back in the direction of the parking lot, my heart sinking . . .

I didn't know what to do, which way to turn, or where to look. From the park, I called my sister Susie. Crying, I told her the story. At first she didn't understand, thinking of her granddaughter Lacey, and she thought that I meant Lacey, not my Laci, was missing. That frustrated me.

"Not her!" I screamed. "My Laci. Big Laci! She's missing. We can't find her. She's gone. Something's happened to her!"

Suddenly I saw Ron's nephew, Zachary, in the parking lot. His mom, Carol, Ron's sister, had gotten a call from Ron. I ran a few steps toward Zach and then for some unknown reason turned around and ran back into the park, still calling Laci's name. I guess I was torn on which way to go. Anyway, at that moment, I had my back to the parking lot and was facing into the park when I saw Scott walking along the side of the creek that ran the length of the park. He had McKenzie with him, the leash in his right hand, and he looked toward the creek. (Only later did I realize that I never heard Scott call out Laci's name. And if he had a flashlight, I didn't see him use it.) I called out his name, but he didn't acknowledge me. I kept calling his name. I recall thinking, *What is wrong with him? I know he can hear me. Why doesn't he answer me?*

Suddenly, out of the corner of my eye, I saw Zach run past me. He went straight to Scott, who, forced to acknowledge he wasn't alone, stopped. I quickly joined them. They were only a few yards away. I wanted Scott to say something to reassure me that things would be okay. But he never even looked at me; he just gazed into the distance.

"Do you have any idea where Laci is?" I asked.

"No," he said softly, still not looking at me.

"Was her purse at the house?" I asked.

"I don't know," he said.

"Is the house unlocked?" I asked.

He said yes.

"I'm going to the house to see if I can find her purse," I said. "Where does she keep it?"

"On the hook by the front door," he said, not looking at me.

I turned to look for Sandy so she could take me to Scott and Laci's house. On my way, I saw a group of police officers arriving in the parking lot. I introduced myself and said that I wanted to go back to Laci's house to see if her purse was there. An officer stepped forward and said that he should go inside first.

I guess it was around six thirty when we pulled back in front of Laci's and I got out. The police were there ahead of us and they were waiting for other officers, including detectives, as I later learned, and they never did let me or anyone else, except Scott, go in the house that night. Scott arrived several minutes later. He didn't look very upset, and certainly not panicked—and why should he have, since *he knew* what had happened to Laci—but her disappearance was already a big deal, and of course the attention was going to magnify every day, so I wonder if he had even an inkling of concern that the situation was going to boomerang beyond his ability to control it.

I saw the officers disappear into the backyard and waited for what seemed like an eternity before one of them emerged. I walked over to him, and asked if they had found her. He said no.

"Did you look in the pool?" I asked.

"Yes. She's not there."

"Did you lift the lid and look in the hot tub?"

"Yes."

"And in the ivy?"

"Yes. Nothing."

I'm sure they'd looked everywhere, but I had to ask.

Then he disappeared again and other officers arrived. I waited in the driveway for a while, periodically asking one of the officers if it was okay for me to take a look around. The answer was always no.

Scott was there, too. But I didn't speak to him until later.

I kept waiting and waiting. Finally, the officers came out from the backyard and approached Scott. They conferred briefly and then all of them disappeared through the gate. Several minutes had elapsed when Scott reappeared, with an officer, through the gate and returned to the driveway, where by then quite a crowd had gathered. This scenario re-peated itself throughout the entire evening.

When Susie and her husband, Gil, arrived, I was across the street and crying so hard I couldn't stand up. Susie, gripping my arms as tightly as possible, helped me sit down on a step next to the curb. Eventually, I saw Scott standing in the driveway by himself. He was staring into the distance, looking toward the park entrance. I'll never forget the strangely blank look on his face. Much later, I realized that except for the time he was with the police, he spent most of the evening by himself, speaking very little to anyone.

Scott didn't look at me when I approached him. But I still felt awful for him. He had to be scared to death, I thought, confused, and in shock just like us. I thought, Poor Scott, he needs a hug. I stepped forward to put my arms around him and he turned slightly toward his left, away from me. That was odd. I tried a second time and he did the same thing. What was going on? I never did hug him.

"Have you called your parents?" I asked.

"No," he said.

"Tell me, what were Laci's plans for the day?" I asked.

"She was going to the store," he said. "Then she was going to bake gingerbread and take the dog for a walk."

"What time did you get home today?" I asked.

"A quarter to five," he said.

"Why'd you wait so long to call me?" I asked.

"I thought she was at your house, and I was running late so I took a shower," he said. "Then I called you."

Though we were speaking, Scott still wasn't looking at me. I didn't understand why. I was too concerned with Laci to give it much thought.

I asked how he'd spent the day. He said he left the house around nine thirty and went fishing.

"Fishing? Where?" I asked, surprised.

"The Berkeley Marina," he said.

Silence. I didn't know what to say. I stood there, next to him in the driveway, not looking at him. Fishing? In Berkeley? Ninety miles away? Several weeks earlier, Ron had gone deep-sea fishing. The boat had departed from the Berkeley Marina and he'd left home at 3:30 a.m. to be there in time to make the boat launch. Scott said he left home at

9:30. Since I didn't know he owned a boat, I assumed he went deep-sea fishing and I wondered if those boats left that late. Weren't all departures early in the morning? But I didn't ask. I also remembered that he and Laci were supposed to have preregistered at Memorial Hospital. For whatever reason, I asked if they'd done that. He said no and didn't offer further explanation. Again, I didn't ask why. I just wanted to know where Laci was.

But Scott wasn't offering much information. Every bit was like pulling teeth. I figured he was beside himself and didn't want to talk. He kept his distance from everyone, and while it was bizarre, especially the way the rest of us found support among one another, I didn't dwell on it at that time.

More and more people showed up. Like my cousin Gwen Kemple. She had thirty people for Christmas Eve dinner. As soon as they received the call from Ron—we don't know where Laci is—they got up from the table, all thirty of them, and came over to help look for her. Laci's neighbors pitched in, too. Besides offering coffee and sandwiches, they opened up their homes and their hearts. I sat inside someone's car or on a neighbor's front step, waiting, praying for news. Cold and tired, I knew something horrible had happened. I was so afraid for her. I wanted her back. Immediately.

After Ron had called several friends and family members, asking for their help to find Laci, he left our house and went to hers. I don't know when exactly he arrived. I didn't see him right away. He started talking to a couple of cops at the end of the driveway and at some point in that conversation Scott saw him and came over. Ron was glad to see him.

"How was your golf game today?" Ron asked.

Scott said he didn't play golf, he went fishing.

"Fishing?" Ron said, puzzled. "What time did you go fishing?" He didn't know Scott to go fishing that much; and he'd gone himself that morning. They could've gone together.

Scott told Ron that he had left around nine thirty.

Surprised by his answer, Ron jokingly said, "Nine thirty? That's when I come home from fishing, not when I go."

From what Ron told me, Scott didn't say anything, he just walked away. The two officers listening to the conversation traded glances that caused Ron to feel like he'd screwed up by putting Scott on the spot and possibly making him look like a suspect to police. But we didn't talk about it until much later that night. There wasn't time, and in those early hours we weren't focused on who was responsible for Laci's disappearance; we wanted to find her.

The night had turned bitterly cold, and I was frozen to the bone. As the temperature dropped, so did my hopes for a quick and happy resolution. I couldn't stop shaking—a mix of the cold and anxiety. I had Sandy take me home, where I gathered an armload of jackets, sweaters, sweatshirts, gloves, and blankets and gave them to those waiting outside Laci's house. Amy got the red fleece sweatshirt I'd worn when I went fishing with Ron on the fifteenth. I loaned out every item I brought except a thick patchwork quilt that my mother had given me years earlier. I was saving that to wrap around Laci.

"She's going to be really cold when we find her," I told Sandy. "I need her to be warm."

We were told that a helicopter with infrared search equipment had been called in to help, and it couldn't come quickly enough for me. For the first time since Scott called, I felt hopeful. *Yes, that's what we need. As soon as possible. The helicopter with its infrared light will be able to find Laci.*

About eight thirty, the helicopter arrived with the loud *whoop-whoop-whoop* of its giant blades chopping the quiet sky.

Thank God. Now we can find Laci.

The police cleared the park. They didn't want any interference with the infrared light as it sought her out.

I stood in the street with my eyes riveted on the helicopter as it began to fly above the park, its bright light shining down and sweeping the dark ground like a beacon of hope. I'll never ever forget that sight and those sounds. It flew from one end of the park to the other, several miles in length. I held my breath through the first long pass. I just knew they were going to find Laci, they had to. But then I heard it coming back for another pass over the park.

Okay, they missed her the first time, but now they're going to find her.

At the opposite end of the park, the helicopter turned around again.

What's wrong? Why can't they see her?

With each pass, I felt fear replace the hope I'd had when I first saw the helicopter. I don't know how many passes it made. I didn't count. But then the rumbling became fainter and fainter, and suddenly I realized I couldn't hear it at all.

"Where's the helicopter?"

I rushed over to one of the officers who seemed to be in radio contact with the searchers and asked about the helicopter.

Reluctantly, he told me the pilots had finished their search; they didn't find her.

No, no, no. They can't leave. She's there, in the park. She needs to be found. Tell them to turn around and come back. Please, please don't let them leave. She's there. I know it. She's there.

For about the next couple of hours we did our best to remain hopeful. No one said much. Around 11 p.m., Modesto Police Det. Al Brocchini approached me and Ron. He was a stocky, tough-looking man in his forties. He'd been among the first of several investigators on the scene. I noticed that he spoke to Scott a couple times but mostly went about his business inside the house where we couldn't see him. At some point, he approached us in the driveway. I couldn't believe I was talking to a detective in front of Laci's house late at night. It was surreal. As I've said so many times, I kept waiting to wake up from this terrible nightmare.

But it was clearly real. I saw that Detective Brocchini was concerned.

"You may as well go home," he said. "There's nothing else you can do here tonight."

I felt what little strength I had left draining out of me. It was impossible to believe that only hours earlier everything had seemed normal. I'd gone to the movies. I'd forgotten to buy whipping cream. Why couldn't we go back to that? How could everything have changed so quickly?

Ron put his arm around me as we listened to Brocchini explain the next steps. He said he was going to take Scott to his warehouse, then to the station for additional questioning—all routine, he assured us—and then he'd be able to come home. We had no idea, but Brocchini already suspected that Scott was the key to Laci's whereabouts, and perhaps a lot more.

"When you're finished with Scott, please bring him back to our house," I told the detective. "There's no need for him to stay here all alone."

Then I found Scott and told him to come to the house when he was finished.

"Don't worry if it's late," I said. "We'll be up."

Back at my house, a large group of us—Ron, Brent and Amy, Amy's half-brother Nathan, my cousin Gwen and her husband, Harvey, my sister and her husband, and several others sat in the living room, looking bewildered and feeling helpless.

None of us knew what to think. I didn't have a good feeling. I kept praying that Laci would walk through the door. Gwen put her arm around me, literally holding me up as she offered comfort. She'd known Laci since I gave birth. When Laci had been little, Gwen enjoyed asking when her birthday was and hearing Laci say, "It's May foth."

I was frightened beyond my wits.

"It's going to be okay," Gwen said.

"I need to find her," I said. "I need to have her home."

"Everyone's looking," she said. "We're going to find her. She's coming back."

As I've said, I didn't have a good feeling. Earlier, when we'd first walked into the house and nobody else could hear, Ron had told me about a conversation he'd had with Detective Brocchini, wherein Scott claimed to have left home at nine thirty that morning, gone to his warehouse, then left there and launched his boat around one.

"What boat?" I asked.

"His boat, I guess," Ron said.

"Scott doesn't have a boat," I said. "Did he borrow someone's boat? Can you rent a boat at the Berkeley Marina?"

"I don't know," Ron said. "The detective said Scott launched *his* boat, so I thought he bought one and I just didn't know about it."

I tried to comprehend what Ron had said, but it didn't make sense. It was like putting a square peg in a round hole. As far as we knew, Scott didn't have a boat. Scott didn't go fishing regularly, either. I didn't know what was going on, but I knew something didn't add up.

"I don't think he has anything to do with Laci's disappearance, but I know he's lying about what he did today," I said to Ron. "Something just isn't right. He's hiding something. Either he has a girlfriend, and that's where he spent the day, or he's selling drugs or something like that. I don't know what it is, but he's hiding something."

By 2 a.m., everyone had gone except for Brent, but we still hadn't heard from Scott. I wondered how he was faring with Brocchini. Brent called Scott's cell. Scott picked up and said he was still at the police department. (In reality, as we'd learn months later, Scott was already at home, having been dropped off by detectives at 1 a.m. I wonder how things might have been different if we'd checked with the police and asked if Detective Brocchini was finished with Scott. But we didn't.) Scott told Brent that he'd call him back later.

At 4 a.m., we still hadn't heard back from Scott. Brent called his cell again. When Scott didn't answer, we became concerned. Brent drove to Laci and Scott's house to see what was going on there. He came back without any news. He'd seen a light on inside the house, but he hadn't knocked on the door.

"Why don't you try calling him again?" I suggested.

This time Scott answered. Groggy, he said he'd just gotten home and fallen asleep in his bed.

"He's not coming over," Brent said. "He was asleep."

How could he possibly sleep when he didn't know where Laci was? None of us could imagine going to sleep. I was too frantic to lie down, too worried to shut my eyes, too scared for my daughter and her baby. What if Laci screamed and I didn't hear because I was asleep? I thought of so many *what if*s. I vowed I wasn't going to shut my eyes until I saw her again.

Chapter Ten

What I didn't know then was that even though it was postmidnight on Christmas Eve, many different people had sprung into action to help find my daughter.

One of Laci's girlfriends knew the owner of a local copy shop and asked if they could open up and make missing person posters. Though it was already very early on Christmas morning, the owner didn't hesitate, and she and the girls spent the next few hours making hundreds of posters, and then began putting them up all over town before sunrise.

They weren't the only ones at work. Around midnight, Rene Tomlinson, after searching the Internet, called Kim Petersen, executive director of the Carole Sund/Carrington Foundation, a Modesto-based organization dedicated to raising awareness about missing persons and providing support and resources to families. Brent put in a call about an hour later.

Kim, visiting family in Los Angeles, listened to what they'd done—working with police, making posters—and said that's exactly what she would've advised. She promised to get involved the next day when she returned to Modesto. Like Laci's friends and Kim, hundreds of others canceled their plans and made finding Laci their priority. Total strangers joined in, including so much unconditional generosity from merchants and volunteers from the community. I was up all night trying to figure out where she was, wondering if she was cold or uncomfortable, imagining her calling for me, hoping she wasn't in pain, or worse. I felt that I could hear her, and it drove me crazy.

I kept wondering what else I could do, what else we could do. Since there weren't any blueprints to follow, I wanted to do everything.

Just before dawn, I jumped off the sofa, layered myself in warm clothes, slipped on a pair of heavy boots, and was prepared to go back to the park to resume my search for Laci. I tried to hold back the tears and ignore the fear and exhaustion. I had one thought: I *needed* to find Laci before one more night had gone.

Brent drove his car and Ron and I drove together in ours to Laci's house. When Ron and I arrived, I saw police cars lining both sides of the street for more than a block—all the way to the park entrance. We found out later that they'd searched the park and the neighborhood throughout the night. As we got out of the car, Ron and I shared a similar apprehension about the situation. Even with all those people looking for Laci, there were no results. It wasn't a good sign.

I don't remember whether or not Scott was there, but I spent several minutes inside the house, checking the rooms for signs of Laci or any clues that might have been overlooked by police the night before. I opened her jewelry box, thinking that she might have gone to the park wearing a lot of jewelry and been mugged. But Laci didn't wear a lot of jewelry, and from what I saw in her jewelry box, nothing was gone.

I sat down for a minute in the room outside the kitchen, trying to think of what to do next, and I sensed that I should go to the park. A second later, I was hurrying down the street. Halfway there, I was stopped by a police officer who asked if I wanted to speak to a chaplain. I'd been asked the same question the night before but said no. It seemed so defeatist then. We were going to find Laci, and she would be fine.

But the situation now seemed bleaker and more complicated, and I sensed the need for more support, and so I said yes.

Even so, I wasn't planning to concede anything in terms of Laci. In fact, as the officer radioed for the chaplain, I continued toward the park and got all the way to the entrance. There, confronted by the street sign that warned of a dead end, I stopped.

The steep path that led down the embankment and into the park was covered in wet, slippery mud, and I realized I couldn't go in there. If something had happened to Laci, I didn't want to be the one to find her. It was more than that, though. Several days later, I remembered the muddy, slippery slope and realized that Laci wouldn't have gone down that path and risked slipping or falling and injuring her baby. She wasn't in the park.

When I turned around to go back, I saw Scott, holding McKenzie on the leash, walking toward me, just a few feet away. He seemed to materialize from out of nowhere. I assumed he'd been out looking for Laci, like everyone else. I said that I was going to my friend Jane's, who lived on the street behind their house. Exactly one week earlier, after feeding McKenzie and Laci's cats at Laci's house, I'd attended a Christmas party at Jane's. It seemed like a lifetime ago, not just one week.

"I'll walk with you," Scott said.

We walked almost to the corner without saying anything to each other. I'd never known Scott to be very talkative, so I attributed his silence to the trauma and confusion all of us felt. I figured he didn't know what to say. As we passed the police officer who'd asked me about the chaplain, I told him where I was going to be. At that point, Scott could've asked why I wanted to speak to a chaplain, but he didn't.

When we got to Jane's, I knocked on the front door while Scott leaned up against the side of her house near the door. Jane didn't see him, but I didn't give her any time to look around. As soon as she opened the door, I stepped in and started to cry. She hugged me tight and sat me down on the sofa, where I cried even harder.

I asked Jane if she heard or saw anything going on at Laci's the day before or noticed anything unusual in the neighborhood. She said she hadn't. We talked for several minutes and when I couldn't sit still a moment longer we walked back to the park entrance, Jane wearing only her nightgown and slippers. We got to the entrance, where we stood for a few minutes before I realized, as I had before, that I didn't want to be there, and then we went back to her house where Sandy arrived soon after.

Jane and Sandy were literally holding me in their arms while I cried and trembled in a state of shock when Modesto's police chaplain Donna Arno showed up. Donna and I moved to the kitchen table where she said a prayer and we talked. We stayed there for a while and then Sandy and Donna walked me back to Laci's.

Gwen had arrived a moment ahead of us. I walked through the house again, giving each room another look. I didn't see anything out of the ordinary. It was tidy, as always.

Actually, one thing did stand out—a lampshade. When I first arrived at the house earlier that morning, I noticed a Tiffany style lampshade on the floor next to the dining table. I knew Laci would have been upset if it got broken, so I moved it into the guest bedroom. But now it was back—in the exact same place. Strange.

I also remember feeling Laci's absence. I can't pinpoint what it was, but the house felt different, empty. I hated that sensation. I didn't want it to be true. I needed to feel her.

A short while later, I was resting on one of the two white chairs in the sitting room, facing into the kitchen. Gwen was standing near me, and Scott was in the kitchen with his back to us. Casually, he turned toward me and said, "The police want me to take a polygraph."

"Good," I said. "When will you be taking it?"

"I don't know," he said. "They said they had to set it up and then they'll let me know."

I thought for a moment.

"Well, at least it will clear you, and that'll be out of the way," I said.

"Yeah, that'll be a good thing," he said.

I went into Conner's room, sat in Laci's rocking chair, and felt my entire body disintegrate into what seemed like one giant teardrop. Donna and Gwen knelt beside me, letting me have my space and time without saying anything. They didn't have to say anything. I was comforted by their presence. Sometime later, after Gwen left the room, Donna asked if she could say a prayer. I nodded, feeling like faith was very much needed right then.

When I finally left Conner's room and walked back out into the kitchen area, Gwen was talking to Scott in the sitting room. I asked Scott if he'd talked to his parents yet.

"No, they aren't home," he said.

"I remember you told me that everyone was getting together at your brother or sister's, I can't remember which one," I said. "Have you called there?"

"They changed their number," he said. "I don't know the new one."

"Did you try information?" I asked. He said, "It's unlisted." His demeanor surprised me, and I wondered why he hadn't called another family member to get the number.

"Do your parents have a cell?" I asked. "I'm sure they do. Did you try it?"

I never got a response to that question, and then Scott left the house.

Less than ten minutes later, the phone rang. I asked my friend Linda to answer it. It was Jackie, looking for Scott. As soon as I heard it was Scott's mother, I took the phone from Linda and asked her to go outside and find Scott. He hadn't been gone long, so I figured he was in the courtyard or the front yard. I took the phone into Scott and Laci's bedroom and sat on the bed. Scott's side of the bed was unmade, while Laci's was neat.

Jackie asked how I was holding up.

"I'm not doing good," I told Jackie.

I can't recall much of the conversation, but I do remember Jackie saying she was concerned the police were going to frame Scott. She said that had recently happened to a boy in San Diego. I recall she repeated her concern about Scott being framed three different times in that one conversation. In retrospect, I find that unnerving. We didn't yet know that a crime had been committed. We didn't know anything.

Jackie also said she and her husband, Lee, were on their way to Modesto. I thought Scott must have reached them as soon as he walked out the door and they were at home, getting ready to pack. But then Jackie told me what time they expected to arrive. I looked at my watch and calculated the number of hours it took to drive to Modesto from their location and realized they'd been on the road for a while.

Something wasn't right. Why did Scott tell me he hadn't talked to his parents, when obviously he had?

I couldn't process that information at the time. I was too concerned with finding Laci and getting her back home. I couldn't think about anything else. I curled up on the living room sofa. I could've easily drifted off, but I willed myself to stay awake. I didn't want to miss a thing.

I remember hearing people talk in the kitchen. Two women I'd never met before, Lucene and her sister Brucene, were on their way to see a movie when they stopped at the Walgreens and recognized Laci on a "missing" poster. Lucene was a teacher at the school where Laci had worked. Instead of going to the movie, they came to the house to see if they could help. They ended up spending almost every day at the volunteer center, epitomizing the generosity of spirit of so many people. I also remember a student of Laci's, a seven-year-old boy who heard what happened and was so upset he didn't want to sleep alone. He wanted to find her. His mother brought him into the volunteer center several times to pick up flyers. When I met him I saw that he was fighting back tears. I hugged him and he began to cry.

My sister Susie and her husband, Gil, arrived later that morning. I also remember Gil had a bad headache, and I called Ron at home and asked him to bring some aspirin when he came back to the house. Again, it's strange how those little things stay with you. All I could do was wait.

Eventually, I joined Nathan by the dining room windows that looked out onto the courtyard. I put my arms around him and rested my chin on his shoulder. We stood like that for a moment without saying anything.

"Nathan, do you feel her?" I asked. "Do you feel that she is still here?"

He nodded.

I desperately needed to have someone assure me she was still here.

"I didn't *feel* her leave, Nathan," I said. "She has to still be here; otherwise I would've felt her leave me."

Months later I concluded the reason I didn't *feel* Laci leave me was because she didn't. She's never left.

She'll always be with me.

I don't know when it happened, but at some point late that morning everyone left the house, leaving me and the chaplain, Donna Arno, by ourselves. I sat in a chair, in that daze, and I didn't notice the surrounding quiet until it was broken by a loud moan from outside. To me, it sounded like, "Oh, nooooooo . . ."

I flew from my chair and started toward the French doors that led to the pool area when Donna grabbed me.

"Sharon, it's not Laci!" she said. "It's not Laci."

I tried to pull away. I didn't want to hear what she said. I had another image in mind. But Donna kept hold of me.

"It's not Laci," she repeated.

I sank to the floor and sobbed uncontrollably. She sat on the floor with me and held me in her arms while I cried.

I wanted it to be Laci. I wanted her found.

We also got word of a press conference at the police station scheduled for that afternoon. We didn't have to attend, but Ron, Brent, and I wanted to be there. Ron took me home so I could change clothes, which I barely managed to do. I showered and tried to put on makeup but I was crying so hard I couldn't do it and simply gave up.

As we pulled in front of the station, I had a moment where I shuddered with disbelief at what was happening to us. Laci was missing. Scott had a boat. I'd met with a detective in the middle of the night. Now we were doing a press conference. It was too unimaginable to seem real. Honestly, I kept waiting for Laci to show up and end this nightmare.

But there was no mistaking the painful reality of walking into the police station. I'd never been inside it before. Ron and Sandy walked on either side of me. A bunch of us went, but only a few were able to attend the actual press conference. Sandy told a photographer not to take any photos of the family or me, but he ignored her and snapped away.

"I told you not to take pictures," she said angrily.

This time he stopped.

We stayed in the background and let the police speak to the press. Modesto P.D.'s public information officer Doug Ridenour provided the basics about Laci's disappearance, physical appearance, and background. Lt. Bruce Able explained that thirty officers and six firefighters had combed the park and the creek on foot, horseback, bicycle, and raft, through the night and all Christmas Day up until that afternoon, without any results.

The point of the press conference was to let people know that Laci was missing, get her picture out to the public, and spread the word about the reward offered for her return. The reward had started out at $100,000, but in the event money could motivate someone to step forward, it had already been increased to $125,000. I left there trying to feel hopeful. I had to be hopeful; there was no other choice.

Afterward, we went into another conference room where everyone who'd come with us had waited. This room had stadium seating and most of us took chairs in the top three rows. I remember Scott was standing about three rows below us when he asked everyone from the police department to leave. I wondered what was going on. Once the police officers and detectives had left, Scott turned to us and announced that his dad had told him not to take a polygraph, not to do anything in fact, before they got there and helped him retain an attorney.

I was a little surprised but didn't dwell on it. After a few moments Rene Tomlinson stood up and told Scott that she wanted him to know that we stood behind him. She said that Laci loved him very much and that of all her girlfriends, Laci was the only one who never had a single complaint about her husband.

I didn't hear Scott's response, but I was later told that he'd said, "You're making me feel bad." *Feel bad? Your friend just told you how much your wife loves you and you feel bad?*

Before we left, Ron had a brief conversation with Detective Brocchini. I wasn't there, but according to Ron, Brocchini had told him that he wanted to clear Scott and that he could help by getting him to answer three questions:

- Why wasn't there any salt water on his fishing line?
- Why had he used lures? (And one of them was still in the package, unopened.)
- Why was he fishing for sturgeon?

"We want to clear him," Brocchini had told Ron. "But if he can't help us, it makes the job harder."

We didn't know what to do or make of things. We talked about what might have happened and places we should look. We tried to keep from falling apart or falling further apart. They were doing a better job than I. Someone in the house offered me a sedative, and I refused.

I didn't want to shut my eyes. I felt if I did, I'd lose the chance of seeing her. *What if she called out and I didn't hear?*

Where is she?

Is she hurt?

Is she cold?

Is she hungry?

Is she being cared for?

Who has her?

Who would want to take her away from us?

Is she crying out for help?

Is she dea . . .

I sat up the entire second night, Christmas night at that, on the sofa surrounded by family and friends, including Gwen, Susie, Patty Amador, Lisa Ribiero, Lin Pereira, and Dina McCall—all of whom should've been at home celebrating Christmas with their families. But as one of them said so convincingly, they couldn't celebrate when I was in such dire pain. It was a time to be together.

That night my friend Lissa McElroy called. She was driving back to Modesto from Southern California, after having had a premonition that something was wrong and she needed to return home right away.

She canceled her holiday plans and got in the car. Soon after arriving at home, she'd received a call from Patty, who told her about Laci. Then she got a hold of me and we talked.

"Where was Scott the whole time?" she asked.

"He was launching the boat?" I said weakly.

"What boat?" she asked.

According to Lissa, my voice changed from a whisper to almost a yell:

"They don't even have a boat!"

Where was Scott Christmas night? We hadn't seen him since the afternoon press conference. Nor had we heard from him. As it turned out, his parents had arrived and, unbeknownst to us, they had a sit-down Christmas dinner. Karen Servas, the neighbor who'd found McKenzie wandering on his leash the day before, testified that she had received an invitation after she stopped by to see if there was any news about Laci.

She excused herself, telling the Petersons she was a vegetarian and went home. Several minutes later, though, Scott called and said he'd found tortellini in the freezer and insisted she come back over for dinner. At that point she agreed to join them. I was told that Scott even made a point of serving the correct wine to go with tortellini.

And what did they talk about at dinner? Among other things, I learned that Scott told his parents that he'd offered to take a polygraph, but the police had told him it probably wouldn't be a good idea because he was too upset.

Why had he told us something different?

Chapter Eleven

On December 26, I woke up and counted. It was the second morning since Laci had disappeared.

The *Modesto Bee*'s first story came out that morning and was headlined "Woman Vanishes on Walk." So much of what was reported as fact in that first account later was proved untrue, including that Scott had returned from a day of fishing; that Laci had been on a walk when she disappeared; and that she was last seen in the park at 10 a.m.

One of the only facts that held up was the description Rene Tomlinson's husband, Jeff, gave of Laci as "a fun-loving girl." He added, "She's always smiling and joking with you." And that was so true.

At some point, my friends Lissa and Shelly came to the house and found me on the sofa where I'd been stationed since the middle of the night. I didn't even look at them as they entered.

"Is that Lissa?" I asked.

"It's me," she said.

As soon as I heard her voice, I started to cry. I was always on the verge of tears, and the littlest things set me off.

Shelly sat on the end of the sofa by my feet. For some reason it seemed important to me to point out to her that I had on two different socks. Nothing matched, I thought, just as nothing made sense anymore.

I'd planned for the girls to take me to Laci's house that morning, but I couldn't seem to move, and I didn't get to Laci's until after noon. When I arrived, Jackie was already in the kitchen. We hugged and then she did something that still boggles my mind. She took off her shoe and showed me her foot.

"I had a pedicure," she said, smiling as if she wanted approval. "I knew Laci would give me a bad time if I didn't get one."

I didn't know what to say. Later, though, I wondered when she'd had that pedicure and when she'd decided it was *for Laci*? She hadn't planned to see Laci over the holiday as they were spending Christmas in San Diego.

I didn't see Lee and asked where he was. Jackie said he'd taken a couple of his sons to look for Laci in the Sierra foothills.

I didn't stay at the house long since I had to be at the police station for an interview with the media and then another press conference. Brent and Jackie drove to the station and on the way there she talked about her Jaguar. Once there, Jackie, Scott, Brent, and I did an interview for national TV, and Scott, for some reason, insisted that the interview air unedited. He made a big issue out of it, even down to insisting that it run at the agreed time.

More reporters and photographers than previously attended this press conference, and more of us showed up, too. Ron, Brent, Rose, Amy, Nathan, Dennis, Susie, Gil, Gwen, Harvey, Sandy, and Laci's friends took seats at a long table. We were joined by Jackie and Lee. For some reason known only to him, instead of sitting at the table Scott knelt at the very end.

The police answered the majority of questions, but I think the most revealing answer of the whole press conference didn't even involve an actual response. It happened when a journalist asked if the police were looking at the husband, and with that Scott immediately walked out of the room and left the station and, in fact, he never appeared at another press conference again.

After the press conference, Ron, Brent, Rose, and I met with Modesto Chief of Police Roy Wasden, as would be our routine following each press conference for the duration of the case. Along with some of the detectives working on the case, we discussed the latest information and asked questions, not all of which were able to be answered.

Later, Ron got ahold of Scott and let him know the cops thought his "fishing story was fishy."

"They think you have a girlfriend," Ron said. "Do you?"

Scott said no, then he walked away and they didn't speak again.

That afternoon Sandy, Lissa, and I went to the park. I felt like I needed to look around again. Others were there looking around, too. Sgt. Ron Cloward, the officer in charge of the Modesto P.D.'s mobile command center, showed us maps of the places they had already searched and the places they would be searching. I learned that a bloodhound was on its way from a neighboring county to track what would ultimately be Laci's last movements. Ron explained to me that they were hoping the dog would give them the lead they needed to be able to find Laci.

Late that same day, an official volunteer center opened at the Red Lion Hotel. Realizing the search effort had outgrown Laci and Scott's home, Stacey Boyers's mom, Terri Western, contacted the Red Lion's management. They donated two rooms and a space in the courtyard that became the headquarters for the hundreds of people who had dropped everything on their holiday to help look for Laci. Tables, computers, message boards, maps, and stacks of posters and flyers seemed to appear from nowhere. One entire wall was covered with photos of Laci.

I was amazed the first time I walked into the volunteer center. Everyone shared the same single-minded purpose—finding Laci. Their spirit, concern, and generosity overwhelmed me. I wanted to thank every single person, friends and strangers alike, but I was unable to find the words, and so I simply hugged people. The media also gathered there, using it as their base for picking up the latest tips on stories.

Shortly after my first walk-through of the volunteer center, I met Kim Petersen, the executive director of the Sund/Carrington Foundation. The foundation was developed after Carole and Juli Sund, a mother and daughter, and Silvina Pelosso, a family friend visiting from Argentina, were abducted while visiting Yosemite National Park in 1999 and eventually found murdered. Carole's parents, Francis and Carole Carrington, had offered a sizable reward for information, which ultimately led to the arrest of Cary Stayner, who was convicted of the murders.

The Carringtons believed the reward money and the media attention it drew was a factor in receiving the tips that led to the discovery of the bodies and Stayner's arrest. That led them to start the foundation to provide similar resources and support for other families of missing and murdered loved ones and to help convict the monsters who commit such crimes.

Starting with our first meeting, Kim took charge of the situation, which made me like her immediately. She cleared one room of everyone but family and spoke to us about the necessity of using the media to get information out to as many people as possible. She impressed me as organized, efficient, knowledgeable, and direct. And she didn't waste time. She said the reporters at the center wanted to speak to someone from the family, and she asked who was going to be the spokesperson.

Nobody stirred.

I was leaning against a wall. Almost everyone else, including Scott and his parents, sat on the hotel room beds.

Kim wanted an answer.

Scott's sister, Susan, had taken the lead at that afternoon's press conference, but Ron and I thought she'd sounded flat, as if she'd been talking about a stranger, not our Laci, and she didn't reflect our urgency. We didn't want a repeat performance. But no one, including Susan, stepped forward. Kim asked two more times and then laid out the facts.

"If the family doesn't talk," she said, "those reporters are going to start talking to anybody out there they can get their hands on."

At that point, someone suggested Susan speak again.

"I guess I can do it," she said hesitantly, glancing around the room. But in the next breath, she said, "No, I'm not going to."

The room was silent again. With Susan out, who was going to be the spokesperson?

I felt frustrated. Laci needed someone to speak for her. Then I was struck by the obvious choice.

"Fine, I'll do it," I said.

I didn't like speaking in front of a group of people, and the few press conferences we'd had confirmed that feeling. However, as I looked at Ron, then at Brent, and then at the Petersons, I knew in my gut that I was the one for the task. Who better than I to speak for Laci? I was the natural, obvious choice. She'd come from my blood and womb. I'd raised her for twenty-seven years. She was my daughter, my baby, my best friend. She needed me, and I needed to be there for her. I had to speak for Laci and about Laci. I was, and remain, Laci's voice.

I love her, and that love gave me strength and courage to do the right thing, to do anything necessary. When I walked out and back into the main room, with Ron and Kim on either side, and stood in front of several television cameras and many reporters, I began the gradual, painful, necessary transformation into a fighter.

I didn't prepare any remarks. As Kim advised, I talked from my heart and the right words came out.

We need to find Laci, I said. She needs to be home. If anybody knows where she is, call the police, call the hotline. Then, specifically addressing the person who had her, I asked them to please take her to the police station or a hospital or fire department. Take my daughter anyplace. Just please let her go. Let us have her back. We love her.

That evening the police, armed with a warrant, searched Laci and Scott's home and his warehouse. The house was closed off with yellow crime scene tape, officers were posted outside, and Scott, his parents, and the rest of his family stayed at the Red Lion for the next two days.

The next morning, December 27, Modesto Police Chief Roy Wasden appeared on *Good Morning America,* and our family tragedy mushroomed from a local story into a national one. A photograph of Laci was broadcast. Her charismatic smile had always won new friends, and it didn't fail this time either. From then on, millions of people knew about Laci's disappearance on Christmas Eve.

That afternoon, I stopped by the mobile command center in the park and asked Sergeant Cloward about the story in the morning paper

Fall 1975.

With a
chocolate
smile.

Laci dancing,
age 2.

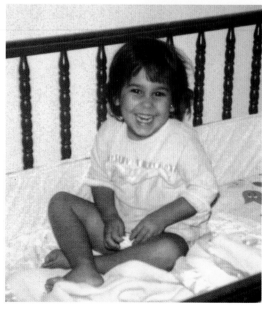

The way I was
greeted every
morning.

Kindergarten Halloween party, with an oatmeal witch's nose.

Laci, 5, and Brent, 9.

Age 9—playing one of
her favorite sports.

Talking talking talking—
Laci on the phone, age 12.

Laci, 17, and Samantha.

Laci with her grandparents Bob and Helen Rocha at her high school graduation in 1993.

Graduating Cal Poly, December 1997, with her mom and dad.

Laci doing what she loved best—working in the yard.

Amy Rocha and Nathan Hazard, Laci's half sister and her stepbrother.

Three generations: Me, my mother, and her granddaughter,
Christmas 1999.

Enjoying the beach, May 2000.

Wedding day,
August 9, 1997.
*(Courtesy of
Stacey Boyers)*

that reported the bloodhound brought in the previous night had turned away from the park where Laci was believed to have been walking when she was abducted. It had reportedly followed another route out of the neighborhood. That was the first clue I knew of suggesting she hadn't gone for a walk, which refuted Scott's story, and I wanted to know if it was true and if there was more.

Sergeant Cloward didn't give me much more than a recap of what was in the newspaper.

He was tight-lipped about the investigation, as was everyone involved. As it turned out, they were already checking on Scott's receipts at the Berkeley Marina (during the trial we learned he was one of only three people who'd entered the marina that day) and looking for witnesses there; they also confiscated his computers (we later heard that among the Web site addresses found on his computer was one on how to beat lie detector tests).

We gave a press conference that day. Scott didn't attend and his absence seemed to fuel reporters' curiosity as to why the authorities were paying so much attention to him.

Modesto P.D. public information officer Doug Ridenour would only say that Scott wasn't a suspect. We were emphatic in expressing our belief that he wasn't responsible. Brent told reporters that Scott loved Laci and that he was suffering more than anyone. All of us agreed that we thought Scott had nothing to do with Laci's disappearance.

We may have had questions, but we honestly believed, at that time, that Scott was not involved in Laci's disappearance. Scott's inconsistencies hadn't yet begun to sink in. As I've said, it was so much easier for me to excuse his strange behavior and conflicting statements. If I thought he was responsible, I then had to realize that we weren't going to ever get Laci back. I think that Brent and Amy felt the same way.

I didn't know it then, but the police were on to him. Others also saw him more objectively than we did. I remember a friend of Kim Petersen's saw Scott that day at the volunteer center standing over a table of food and watched as he carefully considered each item before putting it on his plate. Kim's friend later remarked that Scott seemed to be making decisions most people in his situation couldn't make for months.

Kim called that night to tell me that someone I knew but who wished to remain anonymous had added $375,000 to the reward, bringing the total for Laci's safe return to a half million dollars. It was an overwhelming example of the kindness, generosity, and concern people showed us. I choked up as I told Ron and Brent.

The next day, December 28, a new lead surfaced. Susan and Rudy Medina, who lived across the street from Laci and Scott, came back from Christmas vacation on the twenty-sixth and found that their house had been burglarized during their absence. I had hope, again. Find the burglars and we might find Laci.

As soon as I heard about this, I called the detective in charge of the case and asked for details. He said they were still investigating. He also said a woman claimed to have seen an off-white van parked in front of the Medinas' home.

I tracked down the woman and called her up. She seemed sure that it was about 11:45 a.m. when she noticed the van. It was off-white or cream-colored—she wasn't positive, but she knew it wasn't a dark color—and she thought she recalled seeing one person on the lawn and two people standing at the rear of the van. Grateful for the tip, I arranged for a dozen or so people to meet the next morning to look for the van. Almost thirty people showed up and we canvassed the city, writing down the license plates of every white or cream-colored van we saw. Then I turned the numbers over to the detectives to investigate.

As it turned out, there was no connection. But we didn't find that out for a while. I'm sure we created more work for the detectives, but I couldn't just sit still and wait. I wanted Laci found now!

In the meantime, Scott's sister Susan called a family meeting. She'd gone on the Polly Klaas Foundation Web site and downloaded information about a seven-day plan for organizing and searching for a missing person. We met at the volunteer center, in the room adjoining the center. I got there early and saw Scott talking to someone. It was my chance to ask him the questions that had been weighing on me. I took hold of his arm and said, "I need to talk to you," while simultaneously guiding him into the second room and shutting the door.

This was the first time we'd been alone since he walked me to Jane's house on Christmas morning. I didn't waste a moment of this opportunity and jumped right in to it:

"What were you doing when you last saw Laci?"

Scott said he left the house around nine thirty, stopped by his office, and then went fishing.

I asked what Laci was doing when he left, and he grinned and said, "She looked so cute. She was sitting on her little bench, styling her hair the way Amy had shown her the night before."

What *bench*? I'd never seen a bench in her bathroom.

I wasn't aware that Scott had told the police that Laci was mopping the floor when he left their house.

I hadn't known that Amy had done Laci's hair; I made a mental note to follow up with her.

I had so many questions for Scott, including the fact that he'd bought a boat without telling anyone, but a couple of minutes into our conversation Susan knocked on the door. I tried ignoring it and kept talking, but she banged again—and harder.

"We've got to start the meeting," she said firmly.

That was it, the door opened, and he walked away. I lost my chance and wondered if I'd ever get one again. Susan handed out pages of information she'd taken from the Web site and explained the seven-day program. Ron scanned the notes and I saw he was put off. Then I heard as much when he asked Susan why she thought Laci would be missing for seven days or more.

"What direction are you headed in?" he asked. "What about having a positive attitude?"

I agreed with him. I still felt we would find Laci alive or someone else would and they'd bring her back. We already had a media strategy, posters, a volunteer center, hundreds of people looking for Laci, national TV interviews, and a police investigation under way. We had to find Laci.

Thus far, the meeting struck me as a waste of time, but then it got downright absurd. Scott stepped to the center of the room and said he had taken steps on his own to find Laci by hiring a dog psychic to interview McKenzie. He was serious. He said he'd already spoken to the dog psychic and agreed that we'd pay her airfare, hotel bill, and fee. He added that she was arriving the next day.

Ron and I traded shocked looks that expressed our amazement at Scott's idea, otherwise the room was absolutely silent. Maybe everyone was as dumbstruck as we were. His plan was ridiculous, I was outraged, and I said so.

"You've got to be kidding," I said. "We don't want a dog psychic." Then I just let go with my anger. "You need to contact her and tell her, no, the family is not paying for her trip out here. Make sure she cancels everything. We don't want a dog psychic."

No one disagreed. I don't think they dared. Even Scott didn't argue. I never heard Scott or anyone else mention a dog psychic again. I wasn't against psychics. I didn't know how desperate I'd get, and I didn't want to rule out anything. But a dog psychic? I didn't bother to hide my disgust. I'd had Scott alone in a room and felt like I was about to get some real information from him, and now I didn't know if I'd ever get that chance again. I couldn't believe it was interrupted for such a mind-numbingly stupid idea. Laci had been gone four and a half days without any clues and McKenzie was supposed to tell us what happened to her?

That night I called Amy and followed up on the information I got that afternoon from my brief talk with Scott. I didn't tell her that I'd spoken to him.

"Did you cut Laci's hair on the twenty-third?" I asked.

"No," she said. "But I did show her how to style it."

She said they also talked about the brunch Laci planned for Christmas Day.

I told her what Scott had told me Laci was doing when he left that morning.

"What bench?" she responded.

Exactly as I had reacted, too. As far as either of us knew, Laci didn't have a bench in her bathroom.

Later that night, despite my effort to screen calls, I picked up one that left me shaken. The caller was a woman, and she sounded scared as she explained that she had to talk softly because her husband, who was in the next room, didn't want her to call. But, as she said, she had information about Scott Peterson. I could've answered calls all day long from people claiming to have information. More than 300 people had already called a special police hotline just for tips. I urged the woman to leave her name there. But she refused to hang up.

I'm not going to repeat her story because it was wrong and could hurt other innocent people if I gave any details. But a part of her story was that Scott was having an affair. She described a situation that caused my mind to picture the worst-case scenario. I hadn't thought about Scott in that way and I was doing everything possible to keep hope alive for Laci. I called Kim Petersen, described the call, and asked her what to do. She advised me to call one of the detectives.

At first, I was hesitant. It was Saturday night and I didn't want to disturb anyone. But I called anyway. Detective Brocchini picked up right away and told me that I could call at any hour. I relayed my information, and he recognized the story from the tip line. He recalled some additional details and knew it came from an older woman. Apparently she'd left a message there, something she didn't tell me, and Brocchini said they'd already checked it out.

"But let me ask you a question," he said.

"Okay," I said.

"Would you be surprised if Scott was seeing somebody else?" he asked.

"Yes, I would be surprised," I said.

I still don't know why Brocchini asked, though. He wouldn't hear from Amber Frey for two more days. Perhaps he sensed it from Scott.

"I'm sorry," he said. "I just wanted your opinion. Anyway, we checked out your caller. It was nothing."

Chapter Twelve

On December 29, the media reported that the police had widened their search the day before to the rivers and wetlands outside of Modesto, but had failed to turn up anything. They also admitted that, based on reports by the dog handler, Laci wasn't on a walk in the park when she disappeared. The bloodhound had, in fact, followed streets that first led to a Dumpster near Gallo Winery, and then toward the 132 Freeway that led out of town, and so they targeted those areas.

At eleven in the morning, Ron and I met with detectives Craig Grogan and John Buehler at their office. They were methodically interviewing everyone in the family, and our turn had finally arrived. We'd seen the two detectives at the house, but this was the first time we spoke at length, and I felt like I could trust them. They were extremely professional and didn't mince words. As we got to know them better, they turned out to be some of the most caring, devoted people we'd ever met.

It was jarring when they got down to business. I told them that I had a million questions and needed to know where Laci was, but they politely and firmly let me know they didn't have those answers, yet. It wasn't long before I realized, if they suspected anything at this point, I wasn't going to be told about it.

I didn't understand why they wouldn't tell me anything. I was Laci's mother. Didn't they know what I was going through? As I later discovered, they knew, and they couldn't have been more sensitive or sympathetic. But since I would be considered a potential witness if there was a trial, as would Ron and everyone else in the family, they weren't able to share information that might cloud my judgment or influence me in any way.

Was that frustrating? Absolutely. But thank goodness they didn't violate any procedures that might have given cause for a mistrial.

We didn't know the extent of the information they'd already collected, but we sensed an impressive thoroughness from the recently concluded search of Scott and Laci's house. Still, as they explained, they wanted more—the intimate sort of details about the ways they thought and behaved. They started with Laci, questioning us about her habits and friends, and I had the feeling we told her entire life story. Scott was different. We were less certain about our answers. We shifted in our chairs as we searched for answers. The more they asked, the more I realized I really didn't know as much about Scott as I thought I did.

"I only know what Laci told me and what little Scott said about himself," I admitted. "He never volunteered much."

I recounted what I knew about the basics of his childhood and family and how he and Laci met at the Pacific Café in Morro Bay. I also explained the concerns I had about them finishing college, and I said Laci graduated a semester ahead of Scott.

"Do you know if he has more than one diploma?" Grogan asked.

"No, I don't," I said. "I don't think he does. I don't see how he could. He left Arizona State during his freshman year. He didn't stay there very long. And then he graduated from Cal Poly."

Did he take any courses that I didn't know about? I tried to think. I glanced at Ron. He didn't think so.

"Does he have another diploma?" I asked.

"We're asking you," Buehler said.

During the trial, we'd find out that Scott had three diplomas— religious studies from Arizona State; finance from the University of San Diego; and psychology, also from the University of San Diego, all fakes that he bought online. He'd claimed to police that Laci had ordered them as a joke, but the order forms had his e-mail address, credit card, and cell phone number. On one form, in a box titled Verification, it read, "I'm hoping nobody checks."

In addition, I remembered Laci commenting during dinner at our house on November 24 that their finances were tight and instead of buying a new changing table for the baby's room, Scott was going to convert an old dresser, something he never did. Given that money was tight, Laci wasn't the type to spend $300 on "joke" diplomas. (My theory is Scott thought that Laci would be gone by the time those diplomas arrived.)

At two o'clock, the detectives let us take a break so we could attend the regular afternoon press conference. Afterward we resumed for a couple more hours. We talked more about their finances. They asked if we'd lent them money. We hadn't, I said. They also asked what we knew about Jackie and Lee and their background, and I said we didn't know them very well.

Finally, they showed us some clothing—women's underwear that had been ripped, a frayed jacket, and a colorful dress—and asked if we recognized any of them, but we couldn't. As we drove home, however, I continued to think about the dress and thought it might be similar to the dress Laci had worn to an Elvis-themed party she and Scott had attended at the end of October. I wasn't sure. I knew she'd rented her dress and turned it back in. But just the mere suggestion that they'd found something that might offer a clue to her whereabouts made me anxious for more information.

When I arrived home, I mentioned the Halloween dress to Kim Petersen, who relayed that new information to Detective Grogan. He looked at a picture I had taken of Laci in that dress and determined it had no connection.

On Monday the thirtieth, I started the day at Laci's house. Patty and Lissa were with me. We were doing an article with *People* magazine, and Scott went into the family room to look through photo albums for pictures of Laci. Lissa offered to help him, thinking Scott would have a hard time going through all those memories. She was stunned when he pulled out a photo of himself with some guys at a bachelor party, one of whom was mooning the camera.

"How about this one?" Scott cracked.

He quickly made a face that said, "Just kidding," but a moment later he held up a picture of Laci in a bikini.

"This will get some attention, don't you think?" he asked, grinning.

It was so inappropriate, Lissa didn't know how to respond. He pointed to another photo, one of Laci when she took cooking classes in Italy. According to Lissa, he said, "She made such great pasta. I wish I had some now."

Scott and I were standing at the kitchen counter that morning when he turned to me and with a big smile on his face, said, "I'd really like to have some of Laci's pasta right now." That comment came out of the blue. I didn't know until that afternoon that Scott had said something similar to Lissa.

She was repulsed as she recounted that scene to me and Patty. In my mind, I was running through Scott's behavior, all of it odd, and his demeanor, which hadn't been normal, and even though I didn't fully realize where my thoughts were headed, I wasn't able to excuse him, and I lost control.

"He missed Laci's pasta?" I shouted. "What about missing Laci?"

After the daily press conference, Patty asked me to meet the crew from Ambeck Mortgage at Mallard's, the restaurant where we held our monthly office meeting in a private banquet room. The decision was mine, she emphasized. There was no pressure to go.

My first inclination was *No, I can't go there. I have to look for Laci.* I couldn't think about socializing. But Patty and Lissa encouraged me to reconsider; Patty said it would help everyone to see me and know I was okay.

"I can go for a little while," I said.

From the police station, we weren't far from Mallard's. As we drove, I went through a sort of emotional spin cycle and finally admitted to myself I had all these horrible doubts about Scott that weren't going away. Each time I said Scott had nothing to do with Laci's disappearance, I believed it. Then he'd do or say something that would cause me to doubt him. I was in constant turmoil. *Could he have done something to Laci? How could he do something to Laci? Did he love Laci?*

Now there were too many doubts to ignore. I think it was the combination of being physically and emotionally drained, overwhelmed, angry, and confused; and also being in a kind of protective cocoon of a car with friends I trusted, but suddenly I had to speak the unspeakable. I needed for someone to tell me I was wrong to think Scott could have something to do with Laci's disappearance. I needed objectivity. I needed to look my friends in the eye and see their reaction.

"I don't want either of you to repeat any of this because I feel guilty thinking this, much less saying it," I said, struggling to come up with the right words to explain my feelings. "Something's not right about Scott." That was the first time I recall saying that to anyone, even Ron. "I've been struggling with this for a few days and I feel guilty even thinking it. Please don't let anyone know."

Patty and Lissa promised.

"I don't know what to think anymore," I said. "If Scott didn't have anything to do with this and Laci comes home, she'd be devastated that I thought her husband might have anything to do with her disappearance. I don't want to do anything that would harm our relationship."

"That's understandable," Patty said as she parked the car by the restaurant.

"You're just thinking both sides," Lissa added.

She was right, but truthfully I didn't know what to think about Laci being gone or whether Scott was involved. I hated feeling so overwrought and anguished. I hated being in this nightmare. I let all of that and more pour out of me.

"Nobody knows how torturous it is to go back and forth—did he or didn't he?" I said. "Could he have done something or should I not even be thinking such thoughts? I can't believe this has happened, but I'm not blind. I see his behavior. We haven't even had a real one-on-one conversation. I tried Saturday, but we were constantly interrupted when Susan kept knocking on the door, saying it was time to start that meeting. And I think, well, could he have done something to Laci? But then I think about them, how they were so loving with each other, and I go, no way. Oh my God, it's tearing me up."

Then I added, "And speaking of that meeting, I couldn't believe what I was hearing when Scott announced he hired a dog psychic. A dog psychic! What's up with that? Why would he hire a dog psychic instead of a 'people' psychic? Did he really think McKenzie would learn to speak and tell him where Laci is?"

I stopped talking when I noticed their shock. They hadn't been at the meeting and didn't know about the dog psychic idea, so they were as incredulous as I'd been. I let it sink in and Patty and Lissa must've realized I just needed to vent and they let me go until I ran out of steam. When Patty checked her watch, she saw that an hour had gone by. We were still in her car. I put on lipstick, and we went into the restaurant's back room.

On December 31, some 1,500 people poured into East La Loma Park at dusk for a candlelight vigil that highlighted the potential of love and goodness in the human heart. Kim Petersen, Betty Williams, and Shelly Streeter from the Carole Sund/Carrington Foundation organized the vigil to keep Laci in the public's hearts and minds.

I had no idea what to expect, and I was astonished when I got there and saw the number of people who'd come out on New Year's Eve to lend support and hope and love to the search for Laci. I noticed couples holding hands, families with babies in their arms, and so many looking downcast or in tears. Everyone carried candles that when lit turned the park into a sea of twinkling lights. While waiting in the command center with Ron, Brent, Rose, Amy, Sandy, and Chief Wasden, I realized I wasn't doing well. I didn't feel stable or strong as I watched the behind-the-scenes ranks grow with the arrivals of Amy's mom, Nancy, Gwen's daughter Kasandra Kemple, Dennis's cousin Addie Hansberry, and my friend Linda Wilson. I kept to myself.

Then Jackie and Lee arrived with Susan. The lack of sleep and food along with the worry and the conflict I was trying to work out had caught up with me. I didn't have any energy left. I glanced out at a poster of Laci. She seemed to stare right back at me. I felt a connection, her presence, and I drew strength from her.

"I'm here for you," I whispered.

All of these people had come out for Laci. Actually, we were waiting for one person—Scott Peterson. None of us had seen him or knew where he was, and Kim didn't want to start without him. She kept asking, "Where is he?" Eventually, her patience worn, she asked Susan to find him. When Susan returned, she explained that her brother didn't want to be on stage. It was "too hard" for him.

"He said to get started," Susan said.

Brent got a similar response when he called Scott on his cell. Scott told him that he wanted to stay in the crowd with his friends.

The event itself was intensely emotional. It featured songs, prayers, and testimonials from Laci's family and friends. I'd never experienced anything as strong and moving as when I looked out from the stage and saw more than a thousand people holding candles, photos of Laci, some with their arms linked, singing, swaying, listening, crying. The spirit there was powerful. That said, it was bittersweet for me. My heart filled with hope but also with sadness, and when it came time for me to speak, I was fighting back tears.

"Laci would be amazed at all the people here tonight. She wouldn't believe it. We're so grateful for everyone who has helped look for her and prayed for her. Thank you. Just keep looking for her. Don't give up."

Brent said much the same thing, and afterward Dennis waded into the crowd, shaking hands and personally thanking people. Throughout the whole vigil, I never saw Scott. One volunteer later told me that she'd seen him giggling with his nieces as people openly sobbed on their way out and set their burning candles on the ground. The local newspaper got a photo of him smiling. Kim saw him in the crowd, and asked, "You must be feeling incredible support right now?"

She tried to hug him, but he pulled back, and she saw him try to squeeze tears from his eyes in response to her question, but he couldn't get a single one to fall. Patty witnessed that, too, and later said Scott looked as if he'd been unfazed by the whole event. It seemed impossible. Was he human? According to Patty, he looked "as if he was fighting back on his stupid grins."

For me, it was a watershed night. I left sensing a new reality. Laci might not come back home.

Afterward, Joan Faria, Amy's former boss, announced that she'd made a batch of spaghetti and insisted that everyone meet at Laci and Scott's for dinner. Ron didn't go; he wanted no part of it. I reluctantly said yes, and only because Brent and Rose had been pressured into going and I wanted to see my grandson, Antonio. As it turned out, he'd gone home with Rose's parents, as I wished I had done, too.

The evening's tone was inappropriate from the start. Scott behaved as if he were hosting a party. As I entered the house Joan was hurrying everyone to sit down at the table and eat, so I didn't get past the dining room, and thus didn't know that Brent, Rose, Amy, and Amy's mom, Nancy, were in the family room. I wasn't aware they were even there until I asked about them. Then I got up from the table and talked to them.

I returned to the dining room where Sandy sat at one end of the table and Lissa and I sat on each side of her. Lee and one of Scott's brothers were next to me. Scott sat at the head of the table, with another brother on his right. Jackie sat next to him, then Lissa. Scott had picked out a bottle of red wine and poured it into a decanter.

"I'm impressed," Lee teased. "You serve wine out of that fancy little decanter? At home, we pour it right out of the bottle."

The two of them laughed. Lee then told a joke and Jackie encouraged him to tell another. Lissa, seated across the table next to Jackie, caught my attention and rolled her eyes. Sandy made a similar face that said, "I can't believe this." Neither could I. It was awkward.

It only got worse. After more wine and food, Scott looked directly at me. Grinning broadly, he pointed to the two white chairs where several coats had been laid in a big pile.

"Laci would be really upset if she saw those coats on her nice white chairs," he said.

Scott laughed as if he found his observation funny. I found all of it strange and upsetting. If he knew Laci would've been mad, why didn't he get up off his ass and take the coats off those chairs?

At that point, I had to get out of there. Brent and Rose had left shortly after we arrived and Amy and her mother had just gone home.

I caught Sandy's and Lissa's attention and told them I was ready to leave, and Sandy drove us to my house.

I was bothered by Scott's lack of concern for Laci. It wasn't just obvious; it was disturbing. The more time I was around him, the more doubt I had of his innocence. Yet I somehow continued to deny it.

Lissa sat up with me until 3 or 4 a.m. We talked about Scott. I said I was bothered by his lack of concern for Laci, which had been so apparent by his behavior at dinner. Lissa agreed. He could say one thing, but his actions said something else. Again, Lissa agreed. She made me feel less guilty for thinking this way.

At my suggestion, we made a list of Scott's pluses and minuses, describing what he was like before December 24 and how he had changed after it.

When all was said and done, we didn't see how Scott could've been involved with Laci's disappearance. We probably convinced ourselves not to see the obvious. I don't know. I wish I'd saved those lists.

Deep down I knew something wasn't right and I didn't know what to do about it. After Lissa left, I once more covered my face with my hands and fell apart.

"Scott knows she's not coming home," I said out loud to myself. "He knows it. Or else he would've gone over there and taken those coats off that chair."

Chapter Thirteen

On January 1, 2003, I was in the car with Sandy, searching the outskirts of town for Laci. As I did every time I was in a vehicle, I looked along highways, behind trees, along riverbanks, at anything that caught my eye. If I could figure out what happened, I knew I could find her, but even if I couldn't figure it out, I still had to try. More than a week had passed since Laci's disappearance and the massive effort by police and volunteers didn't seem as if it was getting us any closer to finding Laci or figuring out what happened. I read that the police had received nearly one thousand tips, but I didn't know what, if anything, was panning out. As I've said, we didn't know what their investigation was uncovering, which by this time included Amber Frey, who was recording her conversations with Scott. To me, the first day of the new year didn't promise anything more than those that had preceded it.

But I remember one moment as we drove when I looked up at the sky—large billowy clouds floated in the deep blue—and thought it was beautiful, something Laci would've admired. *Gee, Mom,* she would've said, *look at that. Isn't it pretty?* I wanted it to be a positive sign. I was desperate for one.

Sometime in the late afternoon, before heading home, Sandy and I, exhausted, stopped at the volunteer center. We entered through the back door and found it relatively empty. There were a handful of people talking, checking computers, and picking up posters. I was surprised by one of those present: Scott Peterson. He was standing not doing anything, not seeming to be connected to anything or anyone. Since I'd come in the back door, he didn't see me.

I stared at him for a moment, collecting my thoughts. The only recent face to face we'd had were those too brief minutes on December 28, before Susan hurried us into the meeting where he introduced the idea of bringing in a dog psychic. Since then, I'd called him about getting together to exchange information, but he always had a reason he couldn't make it, promising to set something up, which he never did. Two days earlier, I'd talked to him about picking up their video camera since I wanted to look at their most recent tape for footage of Laci. The police had taken the camera during their search, presumably to do the same, but Scott said they'd given it back without the cords and charger. I offered, and he accepted, to use mine, which was similar to his, to charge the battery. But when I arrived at the agreed-upon time, he wasn't there. Scott and I also talked about watching their wedding video together, and we even set a time. But, as usual, he canceled; something else came up, he said.

Now, though, he couldn't escape. Quietly, I walked up behind him and took his arm. He turned suddenly and looked surprised to see me. I said, "Hello, Scott, we need to talk," and led him into a room where we could be alone. We sat facing each other on the beds, our knees almost touching. My first instinct was compassion. As conflicted and confused as I was, I wanted to reach out and hug him and be hugged back. Eight years of history weren't easily rewritten. I tried to convey that in what I said.

"Do you know other than those few minutes last Saturday we've never talked alone?" I said. "We have never sat down, just you and I, uninterrupted."

If Scott would've agreed and said he felt horrible at not having spent any time together, if he'd have said he was angry, confused, overcome by pain, if he would've apologized for behaving so strangely and said he was also beside himself with worry and fear, I might have relaxed. I could've related, that's for sure. But he didn't say anything, showed no emotion, didn't seem real. What he did do was entirely inappropriate, but consistent with the way he acted. He grinned.

"Scott, we love you, and Laci loves you," I said. "I want you to know that. But I need to know everything that happened on Christmas Eve."

He didn't nod, agree, argue, say anything, or look at me with the sort of emotion one would expect from a distraught husband/future father/loving son-in-law. He just grinned.

If I could figure out what happened, I might be able to find her. I might be able to help her.

"Tell me again what were Laci's plans that day."

He repeated the same thing he had told me Christmas Eve: She was going to go to the grocery store, make gingerbread, and take the dog for a walk.

Personally, I don't know of anyone who would take the time to style their hair before going outside into the damp, drizzly, foggy air just to walk the dog and then go to the store. I was sure Laci wouldn't do that.

"When did you buy a boat?" I asked.

He shrugged his shoulders, smiled, and replied, "A couple weeks ago."

"Why didn't you tell us about it?" I asked. "Knowing Ron's an avid fisherman, I would think you would have mentioned it."

"I was going to surprise Ron and tell him on Christmas," Scott said.

If it had been me, I would've volunteered every bit of information I knew. I would've told of the decision to purchase the boat in the first place, the price, the time—anything that would allay guilt or suspicion. If it had been me, my life would've been an open book. Scott didn't willingly offer one detail unless I specifically asked.

What he *did* talk at some length about was his trip to the police station with Brocchini on Christmas Eve. Scott felt he was being set up. He complained that the detective had intentionally left his keys in the back of his (Scott's) pickup and his notebook in his (Scott's) boat at the warehouse so he could go back to each a second time. He also said Brocchini had checked his hands for cuts or scrapes, and then he made a point of showing me his hands. I looked at his hands quickly and I saw what appeared to be a line across the knuckles of all four fingers. This line, to me, looked like a cut or a slice that was almost healed.

I didn't say anything and he continued on.

Scott also told me that he wasn't speaking to the press so they'd focus on Laci, not him. He wanted to stay in the background, he said, explaining that if he sensed the press losing interest, he'd give an interview to rev it back up.

I heard every word of what he said, but it didn't stick. I didn't feel like we were connecting. Hoping to get some kind of reaction from him, I described what I wanted to do to the person who took Laci. I acted it out, too: I'm not a violent person, but I pretended to grip a knife, explaining how I was going to remove one chunk at a time up one side of the body and down the other. I was so raw and angry, I shocked myself. But Scott watched, impassive. He didn't say anything like good for you, indicate he wanted to do the same or worse, or that he'd help me. He merely continued to grin.

I returned to my questions.

"I thought she was in the park because you told me that McKenzie had his leash on," I said.

He said, "You asked me if McKenzie had his leash on."

"I did *NOT* ask you that question," I said. "You told me that you found McKenzie in the backyard with his leash on."

Scott refused to admit he'd said that. He tried to convince me that I'd brought up the leash and asked him if the dog had it on. There was no reason for me to have asked that question; he was the one who'd told me that Laci had planned to walk McKenzie that day. To my knowledge, she hadn't walked the dog since she became ill in the park in late October.

I finally let it go. He wasn't telling me anything that I didn't already know and he wasn't saying anything new. I got up, said good-bye to Scott, and found Sandy. When we were back in her car, I was depressed and disappointed; we still hadn't found Laci.

At a January 2 press conference, I continued to refute the idea that Scott had anything to do with Laci's disappearance. I still believed that, no matter how many times I went back and forth. But Detective Ridenour didn't let him off that easy, telling reporters that the police wanted more help corroborating Scott's version of events before ruling him out as a suspect. He also showed photos of Scott's pickup, boat, and trailer, and asked anyone having seen him between the twenty-third and the twenty-fourth to come forward. Asked if Scott had taken a polygraph test, Ridenour didn't say yes or no, and when pressed further, he said, "He's cooperating to *some degree*." This was the first public indication of how much more the police knew than they told us and where their investigation was headed. They were already checking in to Scott's trip to the marina, and, unbeknownst to me, the bag of cement he'd purchased for making an anchor (he claimed he'd made one, while they had found indications he'd made four others), and the boat cover soaked in gasoline (to mask any odors?) they'd found in the shed. They knew his alibi was sketchy.

They were also listening to his conversations with Amber. He called her constantly; you could say obsessively. They heard him complain to her one night about a barking dog, saying, "I want to kill it." They heard him tell Amber he was going to Brussels. They heard him tell her that he'd just sold his condo and car. They also heard him sweet-talk her. "You're wonderful," he told her. "Our relationship will grow—and know how beautiful you are."

We were all interviewed by detectives as if we were suspects, if only to rule us out. Brent and Amy even took polygraphs. I was told it was a formality since both were heirs, along with Laci, to their grandfather's estate, though they couldn't inherit anything until they turned thirty, and then only if there was an estate to inherit. Their grandfather was still alive at that time and he was using his money to live, including his significant medical expenses.

Anyway, it was a good example of how innocent people cooperated fully and without hesitation. Brent and Amy took polygraphs as soon as the detectives asked. They also told the investigators everything they knew. All of us did. Anything they wanted to know. Anything to help find Laci.

I received a call from Kim Petersen asking me about a basket that was supposed to have been picked up by Scott on Christmas Eve but, when he didn't show, Amy was called. I told her I didn't know anything about it, she needed to talk to Amy.

Kim's mom, who frequented Vella Farms, had stopped for coffee that morning and after she left she contacted Kim. She told Kim an employee told her that Scott was supposed to pick up a Christmas basket on Christmas Eve but didn't show up. They were ready to close so they called Amy, who had placed the order, and she picked it up instead.

I asked Amy, "He was supposed to pick it up?"

"He offered when I was cutting his hair," she said. "He said he would be playing golf near there so he would pick it up. . . . But I got a call from Vella Farms saying the basket was still there and they were getting ready to close."

"And?"

"I called him, but I didn't leave a message. Instead I left work and got it myself."

With all that was going on Amy had completely forgotten about this. She immediately called a detective and relayed this information.

The next day, January 3, it seemed, at least for a moment, that we had our answers. Right after the afternoon's press conference, my cell phone started ringing. Everyone wanted to know if the rumor they heard was true—had Scott been arrested?

I dialed Detective Grogan, who'd become my main contact with the Modesto P.D. I called him whenever I had a question, sometimes two and three times a day. Craig had heard the rumor, too, but it was false. What had happened was the police had apprehended the men who'd robbed the Medinas—Steven Wayne Todd and Donald Glen Pearce. The two had admitted to breaking in early on the twenty-sixth and dragging a safe out of the house right as the media parked along the street.

According to Chief Wasden, a recipient of some of the stolen property not wanting to get caught up in Laci's case actually walked into the station with a sack containing that stuff, dropped it on the counter, and ran off. I was disappointed at losing the best lead in the case, also one that pointed away from Scott.

That night Ron and I and Jackie and Lee did a remote on CNN's *Larry King Live* from the volunteer center at the Red Lion. Jackie and Lee were already there when Ron and I arrived. I asked if they'd heard any news during the day. They hadn't. I warned them not to be alarmed if they heard that Scott had been arrested, then explained the rumor going around and said it wasn't true.

"But the police arrested the two men who burglarized the Medinas' place across the street," I said.

"Really?" Lee said, surprised.

"No connection to Laci, though," I added.

"Too bad," Lee said.

"Where's Scott?" I asked.

"He went to the police station to pick up Laci's car," Jackie said.

As for the interview, Nancy Grace, who sat in for Larry King, seemed to have already formed strong opinions about the case. As a former prosecutor and a victim of crime she doesn't mince words when she feels strongly about a case. When she asked if we suspected Scott, we said no. His parents rejected such speculation, too. Lee emphatically termed it a nonissue. When asked about the ongoing search efforts in general, both families expressed equal frustration at the lack of results, most likely for different reasons. For my part, it wasn't frustration as much as fear.

Just before we went on the air, something happened that brought forth my worst fears, fears that I spent considerable energy keeping in check. As we'd waited our turn, I'd watched Nancy interview her first guest, Brenda Van Dam, the San Diego mother whose adorable seven-year-old daughter, Danielle, had been abducted, tortured, and murdered by her neighbor David Westerfield. Earlier that day, Westerfield had been sentenced to death, and Nancy was discussing Brenda's Victim's Impact Statement—her emotional face-to-face address to the court and her daughter's killer.

They played a tape, and I heard Van Dam, in a broken, tear-choked voice, say, "Why didn't you just let her go?" I didn't tell anyone of the effect it had on me, and it wasn't something I wanted to share on air, but I pictured myself in her place, and it made me ill. I didn't know how she'd done that. I hoped to God I didn't have to do the same.

After the interview, Joan had everyone over for dinner again. As before, I didn't want to go. I appreciated everything she had done, but Laci was missing and I wasn't in the frame of mind for socializing. Once I got there, the atmosphere was, as I'd feared, uncomfortable for me. I didn't feel like I should be there.

"Do you know where Scott is?" Joan asked me.

"No," I said. "I haven't seen him."

"He said he was going to pick out the wine," she said. "He wanted to bring the wine."

Laci had been missing for over a week. How could he even think about volunteering to bring the wine? Why wasn't his every thought focused on Laci? I was lucky I could bring myself to her house, let alone contribute to dinner. I hated the denial, the attempt to pretend anything mattered other than finding Laci.

Scott showed up about thirty minutes later and as he had promised, he brought several bottles of wine, handed them to Joan, and then visited with his family before he came to the table with Brent, Rose, Amy, Lissa, and me. At dinner, he explained that he was late because Detectives Grogan and Brocchini had kept him at the police station when he'd gone to pick up Laci's Land Rover. He said he'd been fingerprinted and photographed.

He complained that the detectives had asked him about the bruises on his hands. As he'd done on several occasions already, he held out his hands for us to see, a whole table of witnesses, and he turned them over, front to back. Scott pointed at one hand and said he'd told the detectives, "Those aren't bruises. That's ink from the fingerprints you just took." I looked for the marks I had seen two days earlier, but he flashed his hands too quickly. I kept trying to catch a glimpse throughout dinner, but between the lighting and where I was sitting it wasn't possible without staring.

If that was ink, I thought, why hadn't he washed his hands?

"It's all part of the investigation," he said, trying to sound nonchalant. "They even showed me pictures they got from the Internet that are supposed to be me and some girl."

All of us gave him the same questioning look.

"Yeah," he nodded. "I have to say, they did a really good job, because the guy actually looked a lot like me."

Of course now we know that it *was* him.

The picture was from a Christmas card that Amber Frey had sent out, which her mother had forwarded to the police. On December 30, Amber herself had called the Modesto P.D.'s tip line and said she had been seeing Scott Peterson. Questioned by Detective Brocchini, the Fresno massage therapist revealed that she'd been involved with Scott since November 2002. She gave them documentation, photos, gifts, dates, and an entirely different perspective of Scott.

It had been Craig Grogan and Al Brocchini's hunch from the beginning that Scott was lying, but it was confirmed when they showed Scott the photo and he denied being the guy with Amber. Since the detectives knew better, they urged him to admit any extramarital affairs, but Scott swore that he hadn't been with another woman since marrying Laci. From then on, I think the detectives knew their job was to uncover the extent of his lies.

I'm amazed whenever I think about how much happened around us without us being aware. I spoke to Craig almost every day and I couldn't get much out of him. He told me as much as he could, but it was never enough.

I added that bit of information to the larger puzzle, still without seeing anything definitive. Again, I stayed up with Lissa and made more Before and After lists—how Scott treated Laci before December 24 and how he acted after then. The Scott from the Before list was considerate, thoughtful, and loving. But the Scott Peterson who emerged from the After list was different from the Scott I'd known for eight years. This Scott Peterson hadn't come to me and said, "Where can Laci be?" He hadn't said, "I can't believe this is really happening." He hadn't said, "Mom, I'm desperate. I'm worried. I can't eat or sleep. What are we going to do?"

He hadn't shown any emotion around me at all, except for the grin.

I'm surprised when I look back at how hard I tried to deny that he could be responsible for Laci's disappearance. But if Scott was involved, there was only one conclusion: Laci wasn't coming home alive. And I couldn't allow myself to go there.

In November 2002, Laci had taken her wedding ring to a jeweler to have it remade using stones from a wedding ring she'd inherited from her grandmother, but she never saw it finished. On December 27, the police asked me to call the jeweler and give permission for them to take the rings as part of their investigation. Apparently, the jeweler told investigators he wouldn't release the jewelry without my permission. He had known Laci's grandparents for years and was being protective. I forgot about the rings until January 4. Before I gave permission to release them, I decided I should see what I was allowing to be released. Sandy drove me to the store, where I was told investigators had already been and had photographed the rings. After I left the store, I told Craig that I had the rings and put them in my safe-deposit box.

On January 4, the day I was at the jeweler, the police closed down Highway 132 leading out of town while bloodhounds keyed on Laci's scent continued to follow her trail. Scott, driving Laci's Land Rover, had taken a different route, then approached officers and asked for directions to Modesto. What was he doing out there? Was he trying to throw the dogs off by driving Laci's vehicle? The officers recognized Scott, but didn't let on they knew his identity.

From GPS tracking devices they'd planted in his and Laci's vehicles, detectives also knew Scott spent January fifth and sixth watching the search efforts at the Berkeley Marina. They never asked what he was doing, but they knew.

His parents started to seem more concerned than previously. One day Jackie and Lee asked if they could attend the daily meeting we had with Chief Wasden after the press conference when he gave us any updates. Of course I said yes, and I told Ron that I was surprised they hadn't joined in sooner.

We sat at a table in a small conference room on the first floor of the police station—me, Brent, Amy, Jackie, Lee, Kim Petersen, Captains Savelli and Aja, and Chief Wasden. After the chief's update on the search effort, Jackie asked a question: Could the authorities prosecute a homicide if they didn't find a body? I was offended and shocked by her callousness. That body she referred to had a name—Laci. And why, I asked myself, was Jackie thinking that Laci wasn't going to be found, alive or not? We'd never discussed it among ourselves.

Despite her insensitivity, I understood the implications of her question. The chief told Jackie it could be done. Lee asked the chief when the investigation of Scott would end.

The chief's face was stern as he looked directly at Lee. I thought it was a look meant to tell him who was in control as well as the reality of the situation.

"This investigation will take us to wherever it leads us," he said. "We're hoping to have answers very soon."

"Thank God," Lee said. "Then we can finally go home."

I couldn't believe what I heard—or didn't hear. They made me feel as if this was an inconvenience and wanted it over so Scott could go back to his life and they could return to San Diego. I don't know how I kept my mouth shut. I think it was because I was in shock. When asking these questions Jackie and Lee never expressed concern about Laci. They never acknowledged that she was their son's wife. In fact, they never mentioned her name. To them, she was "the body." How was I supposed to respond to that kind of talk?

I was giving an interview on the morning of January 7 when I said something along the lines of "the Scott we know" would never harm Laci. *The Scott we know.* The phrase just came out of me. I was shocked to hear myself say that. It was a subconscious slip, but it was true.

That night we were supposed to have dinner together. Joan had made reservations at a restaurant, but when I said I wasn't going— enough with the party atmosphere—some of the others also declined. When Scott heard about the cancellation, he suggested that he and his parents come to our house for dinner. Though I wasn't up to having people over, I still thought it might be good for all of us to be together.

Arrangements were made to have food delivered. The more I thought about it, the better the idea seemed. This was the first time since Laci's disappearance that we'd all sat down together, alone, as a family. Lee said he was glad to be out of the hotel and in a "real home atmosphere." Jackie also sounded tired of being at the hotel, particularly when she reiterated that Scott didn't want Lee and her at his house, which I took as a jab at Scott.

"He says he needs his privacy," she said, sounding annoyed.

Her emphasis of the word *privacy* caused Scott to grin and I thought he might say something in response, but he kept his composure. I noticed he kept his eyes fixed on his plate, but he had that huge smirk on his face.

I was mystified by his ability to control his emotions. I hadn't seen him show any real concern about Laci's disappearance, genuine or otherwise. But then something happened that changed that. After dinner, we turned on Fox News's *Hannity & Colmes* show. I knew they were going to talk about Laci, and their guest turned out to be an expert who said that experience in similar cases as well as statistics would likely show that the husband, Scott Peterson, had murdered his wife.

Is that what happened, Scott?

Scott leapt from the table and stormed around the room, pacing back and forth, ranting about this guy's idiocy.

"I want their number!" he said. "I'm going to call them right now."

Scott stalked back and forth and continued to say he wanted the phone number so he could call them, yet he made no attempt to get the number, and to my knowledge, he never did. He was all bark and no bite. I watched Jackie as she watched her son with what looked to me like growing concern.

"Just sit down and try to calm yourself," she said.

Minutes later, Scott finally sat down, refilled his glass with wine, and muttered something to himself.

After dinner I told Scott and his parents about being asked to release Laci's rings and told them that I had picked them up. I offered to give Laci's wedding set to Scott, explaining that all he had to do was ask and I'd go to the bank to get them out of the safe-deposit box. I thought he'd want his wife's wedding ring, if not immediately then someday, for sentimental reasons. But I was wrong; Scott didn't utter a single word. And he never asked for, or mentioned, Laci's wedding rings to me; never.

They stayed a bit longer, then left. I was still thinking about the expert we'd seen on TV.

Is that what happened, Scott?

If we knew what happened, we could find Laci. Why don't you tell us, Scott?

Early the next morning, January 8, Scott, Lee, Jackie, Terri Western, Kim Petersen, Rene Tomlinson, and I met at the center to address a few issues. Our Web site, created and maintained excellently by volunteer Jonathan Smith, was overloaded. We never anticipated getting hundreds of thousands of hits. Either we upgraded it or we lost our connection with all those people around the world who shared their concerns and prayers, which—and I say this from the bottom of my heart—kept us going when the days were their bleakest. We agreed to make whatever adjustments were necessary to keep it up and running.

The next issue we tackled was money. As donations started to come in, we opened a special fund at the bank and agreed that Scott, Brent, and I would be the signatories on the account. All three of us had to agree before a check was written. (Scott never signed the paperwork.) Lee asked if it would be possible to use some of the money for mortgage payments on Laci and Scott's house.

"People are donating this money for the search effort," Kim said. "It's supposed to help find Laci. They don't want to pay Scott's living expenses. So I don't think it's a good idea."

Jackie started to say something, but Scott quickly put his hand out in front of her. His gesture was abrupt and harsh, and, frankly, rude. He'd already given me the impression that he didn't have much respect for his mother, and this showed it all too clearly.

Afterward, Jackie and Lee left town for a few days. They didn't tell us where they were going; Jackie had just said they needed a break (it turned out they went to Carmel).

I couldn't sleep. I couldn't eat. All I could think of was Laci, what she might be going through, where she might be, what I could do to find her. There were no time-outs.

They needed a break? We needed a break in the case, not a vacation.

Chapter Fourteen

In 2002, the Modesto Police Department dealt with 1,400 missing persons cases, and nearly all of those people had been found. That's what I read in the *Modesto Bee* on the morning of January 9. Needless to say, after reading that story, I didn't start the day feeling hopeful.

That same day the police continued to search the Berkeley Marina, with scuba divers and sophisticated sonar equipment. Thus far, days of searching the bay had yielded no results. Fourteen hundred missing person cases, I thought as I waited for an update, and only two people were not yet found, one of whom was Laci.

Late that afternoon, Sergeant Cloward called and said they'd discovered something on the bottom of the bay. Although I didn't think Laci was *there,* I still got a clutch in the pit of my stomach as I thought, *What if.* I took a deep breath before asking the obvious questions. Was it Laci?

Sergeant Cloward said the sonar equipment didn't differentiate between a body or an object, and that they'd sent divers down to investigate, but strong currents and bad weather had prevented them from getting a close look.

"It looks like they'll go back down on Saturday," he said. "The weather is supposed to be bad tomorrow. They want to give the divers time to rest."

I called Ron, Brent, and Amy with the update before they heard it on the evening news. Like me, they desperately wanted a break. All of us were hoping against hope, trying hard to ignore the bad news that seemed more inevitable each day. That said, I cautioned against jumping to any conclusions.

"I just don't feel like it's her," I said.

On January 10, I was up at 2 a.m. and at 4 did the morning news shows—*Today, Good Morning America*—from the police station, followed by radio show interview that was broadcast from the volunteer center and devoted its entire three-hour block to Laci's search.

Later, at the volunteer center, I watched the *Today* show. It was the first time I'd stopped to really look at myself, and I was shocked by my appearance. I looked dreadful. I had no idea of the extent that constant worry, lack of sleep, and not eating had taken on me. It scared me—but not for myself. If I looked that bad, what about Laci? What did she look like? At some point that morning, Scott's half sister Susan Caudillo asked Ron and me if we thought the person who took Laci could've put her in the bay following all the publicity about the search there. Ron looked at her with raised eyebrows, as if to say, "Come again?" Well, she figured that by this time everyone, including her possible abductor, knew Scott had been fishing in the bay on the twenty-fourth, and discarding her body there would be the perfect cover-up, a convenient way to throw off investigators. Ron shook his head and turned to me. Because I was so tired, I thought her theory might be possible. But later I applied common sense.

"Of course not," Ron said. "Why on earth would someone take the chance of being caught putting her there when the place was crawling with police?"

"To frame Scott," she said.

I didn't have a response. I changed the subject instead.

"Where's Scott?" I asked.

"He had some business to take care of," she said.

"Well, where is he?" I asked more forcefully.

"He had to go out of town," she said.

Susan never said where he went, and I never found out if he actually did go out of town, but months later, when I looked back on this conversation, I didn't think it was a coincidence that Scott may have left town on the same day that police found an object in the bay.

On January 11, I saw the note I'd made on my calendar two months earlier—Laci's baby shower. It was supposed to have been that day. Per Laci's instructions, I was supposed to have brought a cake. Instead I checked the weather as soon as the sun began to come up and thought it seemed good enough for police to resume their search for the object they'd found at the bottom of the bay.

Indeed, a little later that morning, I received a call confirming that the divers were back in the water. I waited for word, anxiously checking the clock every fifteen or twenty minutes. Even though I didn't feel like they were going to find Laci there, I was afraid they might.

And then what?

Shortly before one, the phone rang, and it was Sergeant Cloward with news that he wanted me to hear before it was all over the media. The search had turned up an anchor. I needed a moment to process that information. *An anchor. Okay . . . it wasn't a body. It was an anchor.* I asked what their discovery meant, but Sergeant Cloward didn't elaborate, implying that at this point it was just an anchor. But to me, it was more. It meant I could still hope Laci was alive.

After hanging up, I phoned the volunteer center and asked for Jackie or Lee. They weren't there, but Susan picked up, and I gave her the good news. I also told Terri Western and she passed on the information to the volunteers. The reporters there also heard it, and it had reached the airwaves before the divers got back to shore.

I was anxious to tell Scott the news, so I called him. When he didn't pick up, I left a message: "Hi, Scott. This is Mom. It's about a quarter to one. Just wanted you to know I just got a call from Ron, Ron Cloward. He's at the marina and it was a boat anchor. Of course we knew it wasn't Laci, but I just wanted you to know."

Within a minute, he called back. I could tell he was in his truck. He sounded normal as he said, "Hey, Mom."

"Did you get my message?" I asked.

"I did, yeah," he said.

"See, we knew it," I said.

"Big old boat anchor or something, huh?" he said.

"Yep, but thank goodness at least it wasn't another body and it would just postpone everything else and take longer at that."

"Yeah, I know. Yeah."

"So your mom and dad know and Susan knows. Because I was try-ing to reach you."

"Yeah."

"And so now we're just trying to call everybody to tell them that it was an anchor and everybody can breathe and get on with finding her."

"Yeah."

He said he was taking care of business in Bakersfield and planned to hand out some flyers before driving home. However, I know from evidence revealed in court that earlier in the day he'd told his mother that he was in Fresno; when we spoke, he was around Gilroy; and by afternoon, just outside of Modesto—nowhere near Bakersfield.

A few minutes later, Scott called his father. You'd think the first thing out of their mouths would be the anchor. Instead they spoke about business ("Everything's working real smooth right now," Scott said) and dinner that night ("Did you know Joan's having cioppino tonight?" Lee asked).

Eventually Scott asked, "How stinking big was this anchor?"

"I don't know. That's what I'm wondering," his father said. "Susie said, 'Gee, what a surprise to find in a marina, an anchor.'"

About twenty minutes later, Scott called his friend Guy Miligi and said the chief of police had called to tell him "they pulled up an anchor . . . a big ol' boat anchor." In point of fact, I'd called him, not the chief, and I wondered why he sounded almost boastful. Ten min-utes later, he called his friend Mike Richardson's wife, Heather, who'd been Laci's maid of honor. "I just got a call from, uh, the chief, or not the chief, the sergeant up at Berkeley," he said. "Did you hear the news?"

"No. What's up?" Heather asked.

Scott went over the story, mentioning a "big ol' boat anchor." Within the hour he was on the phone with his friend Rob Weaver, boasting, "They just called me up, the chief of police did." His buddy suggested someone could make money selling the anchor, and Scott got a kick out of that.

"Ha," he chuckled. "Excellent."

On the afternoon of January 12, I was told that Scott had been at the volunteer center and told people that he was emotionally drained. From what I heard in the courtroom, he may certainly have been drained, but it was most likely from keeping an impossibly busy schedule of activities that included daily calls to Amber, spying on police search efforts, golfing, working out, keeping up with his family, and dodging efforts by detectives to get him to confess.

I didn't know then the pressure the detectives had started to put on him. He'd retained local attorney Kirk McAllister, and I was shocked months later in court to learn that the DA's office approached McAllister soon after searching the marina about getting Scott to confess. McAllister refused. On January 13, I went on *Larry King Live*—along with Ron, Amy, Lee, Kim Petersen, Scott's sister-in-law Janey, and Chief Wasden—and continued to defend Scott.

We never wanted to believe Scott had anything to do with Laci's disappearance. Why would we? That would only bring more pain and heartache. And, even though I would have doubts at times, I tried to rationalize those doubts away. Lee said sadly that Scott was totally shattered, losing weight, and barely able to manage daily life. He was, said Lee, "just what you'd expect from someone who is missing their wife and baby."

That wasn't the Scott Peterson I'd seen, and it wasn't the Scott Peterson who came to our house for dinner the next night.

It was January 14, exactly three weeks since Scott had called me and said those fateful words, "Laci's missing." His parents had returned home. Only his sister-in-law Janey was still in town. A little before five, he called and said he was on McHenry Avenue, putting up flyers, and that he hoped to come over with Janey for dinner.

I wasn't up for having anyone over for dinner that night. Susie had made a stew and brought it to my house so I could share it with Scott. I was tired and I thought about dropping off the dinner at his house, but then he'd called, so I told him to come at six.

"They're doing a different story tonight on Greta's show," I said.

"Oh yeah?" Scott replied.

"It's about a fisherman who goes fishing in the bay for sturgeon with that kind of boat," I said.

Scott had told police that he'd been fishing for sturgeon.

"What?" he said.

"Yeah."

"Seriously?"

"Seriously."

"Did you hear the uh . . . what they found in Oakland today?"

No, I hadn't. Scott said something about dredging a channel near the boat launch ramp.

"And they picked up a car with two dead people in it," he said.

"Ahhh," I groaned. "No kidding."

"I mean they know who they are," he said. "They're two guys that disappeared after a fishing trip."

"Really?"

"Yeah. They got drunk and I guess drove into the bay."

"Oh my gosh! How long have they been missing?"

"Since November," he said.

"Wow!"

"That'll be an interesting story for Greta, huh?" he said with a chuckle.

But there was an even more interesting story about to break. The first indication was when Scott called to say he was running late. Later, I learned he was at the police station, where Detectives Grogan and Buehler informed him that they knew about his relationship with Amber Frey.

I don't know how Scott reacted, but as soon as he walked into our house everything was just wrong. I didn't know he'd just met with the detectives, but I had a bad feeling about him. I wished he wouldn't have come over. There was a definite change in his attitude. Still, more out of habit than anything else, I went to give him a hug, but he stopped a few steps inside the door and turned toward me:

"You know, someone asked today how I was doing," he said with a smile on his face. "I said, 'I'm doing fine.' It really surprised me when I said that, because *I really am doing fine.*"

I stepped back, not believing what I had just heard. I was shocked and appalled at what he'd just said. I thought, What do you mean you're doing fine? Laci is gone. We don't know where she is. She's been missing for three weeks. What do you mean you're doing fine?

The evening went downhill from there. Ron couldn't stand being around Scott and went into the bedroom as soon as dinner ended, leaving me with Scott and Janey. Scott talked about someone who he wanted to work on updating our Web site. In an unusually insistent tone, he said the guy would have access to the Web site for only about ten minutes, make the necessary changes to prevent it from crashing, and be done with it.

This irked me. We'd already discussed this person at our meeting. Something about the guy didn't sit well with me, and I'd told everyone that I personally knew a couple of people who might be able to resolve the problem, and to let me know and I'd put them in contact with Rene Tomlinson, who kind of oversaw the site. Since I hadn't heard from anyone, I assumed the problem was resolved.

Obviously not. Scott handed me some papers, e-mails from this guy to Jonathan, our webmaster, in which he essentially said he was volunteering out of the goodness of his heart and we must be idiots for not wanting him to help us. He wondered why we didn't trust him. Were we stupid? Scott kept trying to sell me on the guy.

"Why on earth would you want someone with an attitude like this involved with the Web site?" I asked Scott.

He abruptly snatched the papers from my hand, something he'd never done, and something so out of character that it startled me. Something, though unspoken, had been revealed. I'd seen straight into him, deep down where the truth was buried, and I think he'd felt it. I felt a slow burn beginning to rise.

He quickly picked up the argument about the Web site, claiming it "will fail tomorrow" if we didn't let his guy help. Because I was tired, and against my better judgment, I relented. Although Scott promised the guy would be involved for only ten minutes, he ended up staying for a few months.

A few minutes later, Kim called and Scott wanted to talk to her. He took the cordless phone and walked into the kitchen, standing by the sink. Though he stood with his back to me, I still heard him clearly.

"We need to let the media know that Laci's due date is February sixteenth, not the tenth," he said.

What? I'd never heard that.

But he repeated it. I felt my breath catch in my throat and a knot begin to twist in my stomach.

"Conner was going to be born on the sixteenth, not the tenth, which is what everyone's reporting."

I sat down and waited for him to hang up.

He sat across from me. "Scott, when did Laci's due date change?" I asked. I know from being pregnant twice that anytime you're that close and your due date gets pushed back, you're going to complain about it; you're not happy about having to wait even longer. But Laci didn't say anything to me that night I talked to her. She said everything was fine with the doctor. If there'd been a change, I know she would've told me.

Scott didn't answer. He just stared at me.

I stared right back.

"Scott, when did the baby's due date change?" I repeated more sternly. I wanted to be sure he heard me.

I got the same reaction. Nothing. He looked at me as though I wasn't even there, as if he was looking through me, as if I had somehow vanished from his life. I wonder, Was that how he looked at Laci before he murdered her?

I let it drop, both of us did, and turned on *Greta*. I was seething and my mind was going a mile a minute trying to process what I'd just heard.

It was strange to watch these shows at night and listen to them talk about *us*. Of course the media had been a fantastic help in getting out the message about Laci's disappearance, but none of us expected it to turn into something so large and have such staying power. Of course we didn't expect Laci to be gone this long.

Laci was the topic almost every night on the cable news shows as well as most morning shows, and often there was something reported that we didn't know, or something mentioned that added a new way of looking at the situation, and this night was no exception. Greta had on a San Francisco fisherman who talked expertly about fishing for sturgeon in the bay. He said the preferred bait was live shrimp. I looked at Scott to see his reaction. He was walking to the computer on the opposite side of the room, so I couldn't see his face.

"So, Scott, what kind of bait did you use?" Janey answered for Scott. "He didn't use bait. He used lures."

"Well, was it at least shaped like a shrimp?" I asked.

He looked over his shoulder at me and chuckled, but didn't say a word.

I got up and walked toward Scott, who was standing at the desk. He spied the stack of local newspapers I'd saved and stored alongside the desk since the first story about Laci appeared. I glanced down and saw that day's headline—"Peterson Effort Spreads to L.A." (The Red Lion manager Brad Saltzman was going to L.A. over the weekend and offered the use of a Red Lion room there to hand out posters and information.)

Scott waved his hand toward the stack of papers and said, "I'm not keeping any of those."

"Why?" I asked.

"Laci wouldn't want to see it," he said.

"Why wouldn't Laci want to see that people have been looking for her?" I asked. "I think she'd love to know how many people have been concerned about her."

He shook his head, but didn't say anything. A few minutes later he and Janey left. I was so relieved.

I went in the bedroom, where Ron was still up, watching TV. I told him that I was dumbfounded by what I had witnessed in Scott's behavior; I thought his attitude was rude, nonchalant, uncaring, and cocky and I felt the same about what he had to say. I looked at Ron and said, "I think this is the first time I can say that Scott *really* pissed me off." I was scared to death that everything was about to change.

That was also the last time I saw Scott in person as a free man.

Chapter Fifteen

Detective Buehler wanted to talk to us at five o'clock. It was January 15, early afternoon, when Ron told me that he'd called. I assumed it would be a phone conversation, but as it got closer to five Ron spoke to Buehler again and then said the detectives wanted to see us at the station. I reminded Ron that we'd agreed to go on Greta's show that night so we needed to cancel, but he thought we could still make it.

We didn't know why Buehler wanted to talk. But in the car, I had a premonition that something significant was about to happen. They wouldn't have had us come down otherwise. They would've just talked to us on the phone. Ron shrugged, as if to say, "We'll see."

Buehler met us at the door of his downtown office and took Ron and me into the same private conference room where he and Craig had interviewed us on December 29. Al Brocchini was seated at the table. I didn't know Al was going to be there. They were all business, as always, and nothing about them hinted at the bombshell they were about to drop.

Since January 2003, I've heard some people say we "turned against Scott" after the police told us he was having an affair and that "having an affair doesn't mean he murdered Laci."

I haven't addressed those critics before, but I want to make it clear that we're not so naïve as to believe an affair equates murder. We were never hell-bent on blaming Scott for Laci's murder. We loved the Scott we knew before December 24, 2002. But after this meeting, we had more information than the public had. We didn't know everything, but we knew enough to come to a conclusion.

Buehler began the meeting by explaining that, despite daily reports in papers and television and constant coverage in magazines, most of their work had taken place without being revealed to Scott, the family members, or the media. It was true, and we understood why it was done this way. Then he said he was merely preparing us for what they were about to tell us next, and it was pretty tough stuff.

I shut my eyes, held my breath, and wondered how much I could take. Something terrible was coming, and I didn't know if I could handle it.

Buehler looked at Brocchini, and then at us. He told us that on Thursday the *National Enquirer* would be publishing a story about Scott having a girlfriend. He said she was a massage therapist in Fresno, and her name was Amber Frey. He said Scott had been having a relationship with her since November 2002. He said the police had known about their relationship for two weeks. In fact, Scott was still involved with her, calling all the time, talking about a future together, and even about the two of them living in Europe.

I started to shake; I couldn't breathe.

The detectives continued to talk. I couldn't take any more. I said that I needed to call Kim Petersen and cancel our interview with Greta. I didn't care about the interview; I needed a distraction from the information we'd just been told and what it clearly implied. I didn't want to be there, in that room. I didn't want to hear anything more either. But as I reached for my purse to get my cell phone, Buehler said it had already been handled.

God, please, get me out of here, now!

Buehler said Scott had purchased a boat on December 9, which, he further explained, was the same day Scott had told Amber that he'd lost his wife and would be spending his first Christmas without her.

His first Christmas without her?

The room started to spin. It seemed as though the air had been sucked out of it. I felt like I was gasping for air. I was sick. I wanted to run away but I couldn't move.

"I think I'm going to throw up," I said.

I tried to stand up to leave but my legs wouldn't hold me so I sat back down.

"He didn't have to kill her," I sobbed.

Ron put his arm around me, but he too needed comforting. I heard him sob as he slumped in his chair and stared straight, dazed.

I just wanted to go home. Most of all, I wanted Laci home and safe and alive. I've said that a lot, but that's what I thought over and over again. I wanted Laci home, safe, and alive, and I wanted our lives back to normal.

We weren't finished. Buehler opened the folder that had been in front of him the whole time, pushed it toward Ron and me, and spread out three color photographs of Scott and Amber. One showed them at a Christmas party, the other two were of them in Amber's apartment. Scott and Amber were obviously a couple. I couldn't take my eyes off them—especially Scott. I studied him intensely, his face, his eyes, his smile. Suddenly he looked like a stranger.

He looked like a murderer.

"He killed her, didn't he?" I said, still looking at the pictures, not at the detectives.

Buehler and Brocchini didn't say he did kill her, but they didn't refute it either. The information was on the table.

We asked if Scott had had other affairs, and they said yes and told us about his affair with Cal Poly student Janet Ilse during his final semester at Cal Poly. I asked if Laci knew, and they said yes, Janet had walked in on her and Scott while they were in bed.

"It would've been difficult to not know," said Brocchini. "His roommates had to drag her [Janet] out, kicking and screaming."

Buehler explained they hadn't planned on revealing any of this information to us at this point, and they would've preferred to wait until they'd tied more of the evidence together, but the *National Enquirer* forced their hand. In the end, they didn't want us to be surprised.

"We don't know the extent of their story," Buehler said. "They may also have more pictures. We just don't know."

"Are you telling the Petersons?" Ron asked.

Brocchini said they were, and he explained that Detectives Grogan and Phil Owen were in San Diego telling Lee the same things we were being told. They were telling Lee and letting him break the news to Jackie because of her fragile health. (I heard that Lee told Jackie that the photographs the police had of Scott and Amber were from a party that Laci and Scott had attended together.)

Despite what he told Jackie, I know from reading the transcript of Craig's conversation with Lee that Lee asked if it was a girl from Sacramento. He also said that she must have known Scott as someone else. What parent reacts by saying she must've known him as someone else?

Our entire meeting with Buehler and Brocchini lasted 15 to 20 minutes. I left sick, crying uncontrollably, weak, and wiped out. Basically, I was destroyed. It wasn't Scott's affair that did it as much as it was the implication of his affair, his deceit, and the assumptions I was left to make. These weren't rumors. There were photos and tapes. They implied what happened, but more, I now knew Laci wasn't coming home.

That was the first time I really had to imagine her dead. I had to think about Scott killing her. I had to think about all the questions that went with that—how, when, did she suffer, did she fight, did she plead with him?

I had to be helped out to the car. My legs were gone and I was crying so hard I couldn't see—just full body heaves. "He didn't have to kill her," I wailed as they put me in the front seat.

I couldn't stop the wailing:

He didn't have to kill her.
He didn't have to kill her.
He didn't have to kill her.
He didn't have to kill her.

On the way home, Ron called family and friends and had them come to our house. He was most comfortable working out the toughest moments by himself along a riverbank or driving in his truck. But he knew I hadn't wanted to be alone since Laci disappeared, and he made sure I was always in the company of a friend or groups of friends and family, my circle of love, as I referred to them.

They arrived just after we did: Gwen and Harvey, Kim, Sandy, Patty, Lin, Lissa, Susie, and Gil. They gathered in the living room and listened as Ron explained the latest news and I went into the bedroom and laid down on the bed. But I was way too agitated to stay still and soon got up to join everyone else. Halfway down the hall, I impulsively slammed my fist into the wall, but unlike the movies, the wall didn't give and I thought I'd broken my hand. But that pain was minor compared to the pain that was raging inside of me. Not to mention the feeling of helplessness that came over me. I had the sense that I was spiraling down, down, down a bottomless pit and there was nothing to grab onto to stop my fall.

Sometime that night I said we should close the volunteer center. What was the point of keeping it open? Scott had murdered Laci. How would it look to have him wandering through the center? Once the media got ahold of the *National Enquirer*'s story, nothing would get done. Kim agreed and relayed the information to key people as well as to Buehler, who passed it on to the department.

Then I sat in the living room and I thought, Now what? Where were we supposed to go from here? Where was all the oxygen in the room? I could barely breathe.

Laci wasn't coming home.

Before that point, I never in my life thought about murder as something that might touch my life. I didn't know anyone capable of taking a human being's life, and I didn't want to. My neighborhood was filled with good people. We didn't lie, had nice friends, went to work, paid our bills. We raised responsible, nice children. They did their homework, got good grades, went to college. They married. They were making us grandparents. Why was I now thinking about murder? What had happened in the universe? Why Laci? I didn't want to know such a crime intimately. Not my flesh and blood. Not my baby. And her baby.

What kind of animal killed his pregnant wife?

I kept thinking about her. About him.

He didn't have to kill her.
He didn't have to kill her.
He didn't have to kill her.
He didn't have to kill her.
My baby was dead. And her baby was dead. It was incomprehensible.

Early the next morning, Craig Grogan called and apologized for not being present when Ron and I were told about Scott and Amber. We'd grown close, so I appreciated his concern. He said that now they wanted to focus on Scott. He asked if I'd wear a wire to secretly record my conversations with him. After hearing what that entailed, I refused. I didn't want to get that close to Scott.

"I'm afraid of him," I said. "If he could murder Laci, he could do that to me. *I don't want to be in a room with Scott Peterson,*" I said.

Craig understood. He said he didn't want me to do anything I didn't feel comfortable with. Then he asked if I'd be willing to record phone conversations I had with Scott. That I was okay with, but to be honest, I didn't expect to ever hear from him once he knew that we'd found out about his affair with Amber Frey. Still, I was up for trying to help and wanted to do whatever I could to find out where Laci was and bring her home. *She needed to be home.*

Overnight, the situation had changed. A day earlier, I had my doubts about Scott, strong doubts that weren't easily addressed, but I was still flip-flopping. Something wouldn't let me come right out and say he was responsible for Laci's disappearance. If he'd been a stranger, no problem. But Scott was my son-in-law; my daughter had loved him, I'd loved him, and I didn't want to believe he had done it. If I believed that, then Laci wasn't coming home.

But he bought a boat on the same day he told Amber he had lost his wife and this would be his first Christmas without her.

When Grogan and Buehler came over to wire our phones, the house was full of people, as usual: my mother; Brent; Amy and her mother,

Nancy, and half-brother Nathan; and also Sandy, Gwen, and Lissa. Brent had called Scott earlier and left a message for him to call back. He'd also brought over the new *National Enquirer*, which we read with a fine-tooth comb.

The story reported details from the police investigation, both information we knew and didn't know. We showed it to Grogan and Buehler and asked them questions, but they wouldn't comment on anything.

Craig was in the process of attaching the listening device to the phone in the bedroom as I expressed concern about how helpful I could be since the last thing I wanted was to speak to Scott Peterson, "if he called," I said.

But then, amazingly, he did. I looked at Craig, shocked by Scott's timing. Sandy, who'd picked up in the kitchen, brought the cordless phone and said he wanted to talk to me.

I wasn't ready for him. I hadn't prepared myself mentally. Deep breath. Several more. Now that he was on the line, I didn't trust what I might say.

"What do I do?" I asked Craig.

"Go ahead and talk to him if you want," he said.

I took another a deep breath. And another. Then I picked up the phone and said hello.

"Hi, Mom; Scott," he said. "Hey, um, why are there signs at the center that we're supposed to close today?"

"I don't know. Is it closed?"

"I was down there . . . and, um . . . but we just found signs on the doors and it says closed."

"Huh," I said. "Did you call Terri or anything?"

"I don't have Terri's number," he said. "Do you?"

"Yeah. I didn't know it was closed."

"I didn't, either," he continued. "I'm trying to call Kim Petersen. She's not available."

"She's—oh yeah—she's going to be in Sacramento today."

"Oh, is she?"

"Yeah. We'll see."

"You don't know why?"

"No, I haven't talked—nobody's called me. I haven't heard anything."

"Hmm," he said. "How are you doing?"

"Not very good today," I said, wanting to get to the real issue but not knowing how. "Not having a good day."

"Well—"

"It's been a real rough day today," I said.

"Yeah."

"Just thinking—are you out there right now?"

"Yeah."

"Did you ask anybody out there why it's closed?"

"No, we just noticed the signs on the doors say closed today," he said.

"You mean like when you get in there they have signs on the door?"

"Yeah. I didn't notice 'em coming in the back way, but then people came in and—hey, there's signs that say you're closed."

After chewing the same thing for another minute, I decided to stop wasting time. I wanted to ask a real question.

"Scott, we've seen some photos of you with another girl. Is there somebody you've been seeing?"

"No. Yeah. The police are, ah . . . have a very"—he stammered, clearly unprepared to answer even though it was in print across the country.

"Well, we've seen the photos, and it's you with this other girl," I said.

"U-huh," he said.

"So what's that all about?"

"Well, I'll sit down with you and talk to you about it."

"Well, are you seeing somebody else or not? Is that why you're not coming forward or—"

"No," he interrupted me.

"You're not seeing anybody?"

"No," he said.

"Um. So . . ."

"Is that why Brent called me this morning?" he asked.

"I don't know," I said.

"Have you seen him today?"

"No, I haven't seen Brent today. Haven't talked to him."

"Okay."

"But I mean, in the photos, you're by a Christmas tree, Scott, and—"

"Yeah." He again interrupted me.

"You guys are kissing and . . . and you're trying to tell me you're not seeing somebody else?"

It was so hard to ask him these questions.

"We'll sit down. Okay, Mom?"

"When are we gonna sit down and talk?"

"Well, I'll see you today. Definitely."

"Are you coming over here?" I asked.

"Yeah," he said.

My heart pounded.

"No," I said.

"Well, as soon as I figure out why the center is closed—"

"Let me find out and I'll get back to you."

"Okay, thanks."

"And don't—don't come over here because—yeah. It's—that's not a good idea to come over here."

"Okay," he said.

"Okay. Bye."

After I hung up, I heard Buehler tell Craig that Scott appeared to be on his way to our house. I asked how he knew that, but I didn't get an answer. They were monitoring him via GPS, something I didn't know, and the information was being relayed to Buehler over the phone. Hearing that Scott was on his way over scared me to death.

I put my hand over my heart and felt it race. I thought, My God, I told him not to come but he's doing it anyway.

A moment later, the doorbell rang. I nearly jumped out of my skin, anticipating Scott. I waited for the detectives to say something when

Sandy opened the door and let in my friend Bonnie Hearst. I told her to hurry and get inside because we thought Scott was on his way over. She thought I said to hurry and get *outside* because without pausing she walked straight through the living room and went right out the back door onto the patio.

It was actually a funny moment amid all the tension.

But as time passed, Scott didn't show up. We figured he drove by, saw the cars out front, and kept going. What if the detectives hadn't been there, though? What if he'd stopped and forced his way in? He scared me. I told the detectives that I didn't like the way he'd behaved at dinner two nights earlier, the way he grabbed the papers from me, the look we'd exchanged. I was surprised he'd even come after they'd just confronted him about Amber. He was unpredictable, not normal, couldn't be trusted. And now he said, "Hi, Mom"?

It was all too much.

"You don't have to talk to him," Craig advised. "You don't have to pick up the phone and call him. We're not asking you to do that. But if you want to talk to him, or if you get mad enough and you want to say something, and if you want to record it, go ahead."

"Okay," I said.

"We're not ever going to tell you what to do or what not to do," he said. "It's all up to you."

"Understood."

Once the detectives had left, I spent the rest of the morning and early afternoon on the bed. I was a wreck. I cried and wailed, "I can't believe this. It's unreal." Ron tried to comfort me, but I couldn't calm down. But by early afternoon, my emotions underwent a dramatic change, and all of a sudden I was extremely angry, and I wanted to confront Scott.

I leapt out of bed so fast it startled Ron.

"Where are you going?" he asked.

"I'm calling Scott," I said.

I walked into the dining room, where my mom sat at the table. Normally I vacillated between wanting to shield my mother from this nightmare and wanting her around to support me. But at that moment, I had no idea what I was going to say, no idea what might come out of my mouth if I actually got Scott on the phone, and I didn't want my mother to hear me. She understood and gave me an approving nod as she went outside.

I tried to stay calm as I dialed Scott's number. I told myself not to scream or yell right away if I got him. I didn't want to begin the conversation by asking the questions I really wanted answered, how he killed Laci and where she was. I just wanted to get him going and keep myself together—and I did for a few minutes.

"Scott?"

"Yeah."

"Where are you?"

"I just loaded up all the stuff for the LA Command Center."

"Oh."

"Just left the volunteer center. I gave a couple interviews to the press and then—"

Enough with the lies, I thought.

"Well, since you've managed to lose all my confidence in you, what I want to know is, where's my daughter at, Scott?"

"I wish I knew, Mom. I wish I knew where she is."

"Yeah, you do know," I said. "You do know where she is, and I want you to tell me. Where is Laci and her baby? Where did you put them?"

"Where is my wife and our child? I don't know."

"You killed my daughter, didn't you?"

"No, I didn't, Mom."

Something about the way Scott said that was wrong, it was too light, and it made me even madder at him. Why, I wondered at that point, was I holding back? I really didn't care what he thought or felt. Laci wasn't coming back. I didn't have to worry about her being upset with me for thinking Scott was responsible. I could be as blunt as I wanted.

"Yes, you did, Scott," I said. "And I want to know—just let me bring my daughter home, okay? That's all I want. I don't want anything else from you. I want you to tell me where my daughter is. I want to be able to bury my daughter. Now would you tell me where she is, Scott?"

"Don't know where she is," he said. "I want my wife."

"Stop lying. I'm tired of your lies. You have looked me in the eye for weeks and been lying to me. You have looked me in the eye for years and been lying to Laci and me. Now where is she?"

"I wish I knew."

"You do know! Stop lying! For once in your life, take some responsibility and tell the goddamn truth. Where is my daughter?"

"I want her home, Mom, and—"

"Shut up! Don't tell me such stupid things. You tell me where she is. Where did you put her? Scott, tell me where she is!"

"I'm sorry—"

"And you can run away. You can go do whatever the fuck you want. But you tell me where my daughter is." From that point on, I gave up any pretense or propriety. I was never going to see my Laci again. And it was his doing. If I said the F-word or any other curse words, so be it. He deserved it and so much more.

"I'm sorry—"

"I have every right to know where you put Laci."

"We all have a right to know where Laci—"

"Quit lying to me. Don't bullshit me. You tell me where she is."

"We all want her home."

"Shut up. You are such a fucking liar. You make me sick, Scott. Where is Laci? Tell me where Laci is. I want to be able to bury my daughter. Now you tell me what you did with her."

"I want her and our child home," he said.

"Oh shut up. You're disgusting. Do you know there's not a person in this town who wants to see your face? Now you tell me where she is and then you can get the hell out of here. Tell me where she is. I want my daughter, Scott. That's all I want from you. I don't care what happens to you."

"We all want her back."

"Oh God, you're disgusting," I said.

I was shaking uncontrollably, that's how mad I was, and if I could've reached through the phone and strangled Scott, or worse, done what I'd acted out for him in the room at the Red Lion, I would've done it. He'd murdered my daughter, and he'd lied about it. He was still lying.

Out of the corner of my eye, I saw Ron watching me. I asked if he had anything to say to Scott. He took the phone.

"If you've got anything left in you, Scott, you better tell us where she is," he said.

"I wish I knew, Ron," he replied calmly. "We all want her back."

"The police are going to be seeing you before long, Scott," he said. "And your world is crumbling."

"My world is done without Laci and my child," he said. "We all want her back. And I'm sorry that you guys feel I had something to do with it. But the only important thing is getting her back."

"Scott, I don't know how you can just—I don't know how you can do this. Just keep saying—We've seen pictures. . . . We've seen other things. You're in trouble. We want her back."

"We all want her back. There's no question to that," he said. "We're—we need to find her and Conner."

I shouted something in the background, something to the effect that I wanted her back, too.

"I've had enough of this," Ron said. "I don't want to talk to you anymore. You tell us where Laci is."

Scott didn't, and Ron hung up abruptly.

We didn't expect a confession from Scott, we never have, but we had to ask, and both of us felt a small amount of satisfaction because we'd needed to scream at Scott for some time. Yet when we finished, Ron and I were no closer to any kind of resolution than before. We didn't have Laci, and the man who'd murdered her was free.

We stared at each other, spent. Instead of anger, which had consumed me moments earlier, I was overwhelmed by grief, intense grief, that hit me like punches one after the other.

I don't know how I kept going. I'd lost my daughter and her baby. I'd also lost the son-in-law that I loved. The Scott that walked among us since December 24 was a complete stranger to me, a man I didn't know.

Brent had said that he'd spoken to Scott, who admitted his affair with Amber but denied harming Laci, and we sat around the rest of the night fuming at his lies. The next day's *Modesto Bee* reported that we no longer supported Scott, and our change was accompanied by new facts: he'd had an affair (Amber's name, even in the *National Enquirer,* was not yet public) and he'd taken out a $250,000 life insurance policy after Laci got pregnant. It also noted the volunteer center had shut down.

Chief Wasden, speaking for the police, refused to comment on the investigation. Ironically, Scott talked to a reporter on the record.

"I really don't care what people think of me as long as it continues to keep Laci's picture, description, tip line in the media," Scott said. "Make me the biggest villain if you want to, as long as it keeps her picture in the press. They can think anything they want of me. Let's find Laci."

Shortly after noon that day, I called Scott. I desperately wanted Laci home. I had to keep trying to get him to tell me where he put her. Despite such an awful conversation the previous day, I called and ended up leaving a message. I don't know why, but he phoned back at one thirty.

"Where are you?" I asked.

"Trying to get this volunteer center thing to happen in Los Angeles. Can't believe they canceled it."

"What do you mean you can't believe they canceled it?" I said, amazed at the level of his denial or deception, I didn't know which.

"Why can't we have it?" he said. "We need to keep her picture out there and the volunteer center in Modesto—"

"You know, when are you gonna give up the charade, Scott? You know, when are you gonna call it quits and admit what you've done?"

"When I find my wife and child," he said.

"Well, you're the only one who knows where they are, so why don't you fill the rest of us in so we can go get them?"

"Mom, I didn't call you to—"

"Well, that's the reason I called you."

"Okay. Well—"

"I want you to tell me where Laci is," I demanded. "I'm tired of your lies. I'm tired of your conniving. I'm tired of your manipulation. You know damn well they're not opening a stupid center down there because you've embarrassed your family and everybody else.

"You've shamed this world, Scott," I continued. "You've had people out looking for Laci and somebody else when you've known all along where she's been. So tell me where she is. I want her back."

"I know you won't believe that I want her back also. That's all I—"

"Oh, I'm sure you want her back, too," I snapped sarcastically. "Yes, you're brokenhearted. I know that, Scott. So now, just be honest with me, and tell me where she is."

"I can't listen to you tell me—"

"And I can't listen to your fucking lies anymore."

Chapter Sixteen

Once we learned about Scott's affair on the fifteenth, everything changed. It was such a traumatic shift. In hindsight, denial had been such a comfortable place to hide from the truth. I didn't want to believe Scott would hurt Laci. At that point, our search efforts intensified. When I was out driving, I looked even harder. I wanted to know what Scott had done to her, and how he did it. I tried not to pay attention to the details that were out there. They weren't substantiated, and they were so grisly. But I couldn't stop from imagining different scenarios. I couldn't think of anything but my poor daughter, my helpless Laci.

At night, I didn't—and couldn't—sleep. (I still hadn't returned to my bed.) In the daytime, nothing mattered except the search for her. As much as I didn't want to, I thought of ways he might've murdered her. In each case, I wondered how I might have been able to help her. I had so many questions.

Did he poison her?

Did he hurt her?

Did she know that he was murdering her?

Did she call out? Fight back? Struggle?

On the night of January 17, I couldn't stop thinking about Laci and what Scott must have done to her. I was crying uncontrollably. I was having horrible images of Scott murdering her. I couldn't get these images out of my head. I hated not being able to find out what had happened to Laci. I was tortured, despairing, and feeling so help-less. Kim was with me and saw what I was going through. She called Craig and told him how upset I was. At 9 p.m., he and John Buehler came over. They talked to me. They believed, based on their experi-ence, that Laci was probably killed while she was asleep.

"We haven't found any signs of a violent struggle," Craig said. "I don't know if that's any comfort."

From what I could tell, even a veteran cop like Craig had a hard time discussing this with me. But it helped put my mind at ease—even if only temporarily. I appreciated that he and John dropped whatever they were doing and came over. Then Craig did something I'll never forget. He knelt beside my bed, took a small package out of his jacket pocket, and gave it to me.

"Someone wanting to remain anonymous gave it to the chief, and he asked me to pass it on to you," he said.

Inside the package was a ribbon-shaped gold pin set with blue sap-phires. It was beautiful. To me, it represented Laci and Conner—their lives, the hope we might get them back, the love I had for them. I still don't know who gave me that gift, so I've never been able to say thank you or explain how much it meant to me, and how much it continues to mean, but I wear it all the time.

We decided that we needed to address everybody who'd worked and prayed to find Laci. We couldn't suddenly close the volunteer center without providing an explanation and saying thank you. On January 24, Laci's immediate family—Ron, Dennis, Brent, Amy, and myself—addressed volunteers and reporters at the Red Lion.

"The past few weeks have been the most painful time I've ever ex-perienced," Amy said before breaking down and stepping away from the microphone. Brent stepped up next and acknowledged that Scott had admitted his affair with the woman in the *National Enquirer*'s story. He also revealed that we'd changed our opinion of Scott's involvement in Laci's disappearance. "Because we have so many questions that he has not answered, I am no longer supporting him," he said.

Fighting back tears, Brent pleaded for Laci's return. I listened, crying myself, as he tried so hard to stay composed but couldn't, as he tearfully described the past month as "the most disturbing and emotional time of my life." Then, speaking directly to his sister, he said, "I miss your beautiful smile and your fun-loving personality. Every time we were together, I could feel the unconditional love between the both of us."

I was brokenhearted for him. He was in such pain.

"As your older brother, I only wish that I had the opportunity to be there to defend you from the person that decided to take you away from me. We talked about our children growing up together and spending summers at each other's house."

My daughter was dead and my son was devastated. Why? Because of Scott—his cruel, selfish, murderous act.

"Now that you and Conner have been taken away from me, I realize that my children will not have cousins to grow up with. And family events will feel very lonely without you and Conner. Wherever you may be, I hope you know how much I love you and how important you are to me. My search for you will never end."

When it was my turn to speak, I was already emotionally drained. I didn't have anything left, no energy whatsoever. But that's when I thought of Laci and how it was up to me to keep her alive in front of the world, and as always, that was more than enough to help me find the strength to step up to the microphone. And then it wasn't as difficult.

"Since Christmas Eve, our one and only focus has been to find Laci and bring her home to us," I said. "I love my daughter so much. I miss her every minute of every day. I miss seeing her. I miss our talking together.

"I miss listening to the excitement in her voice when she talks to me about her baby. I miss not being able to share with her the anticipation of her approaching delivery date. I miss listening to her talk about her future with her husband and her baby.

"I miss sharing our thoughts and our lives together. I miss her smile and her laughter and her sense of humor. And I miss everything about her.

"Someone has taken all of this away from me and everyone else who loves her. There are no words that can possibly describe the ache in my heart or the emptiness in my life.

"I know that someone knows where Laci is, and I'm pleading with you—please, please, please, let her come home to us. . . ."

We got home around four, and moments later Craig called, informing us that Amber Frey was giving a press conference at six o'clock at the police station. In my naïveté, I seriously didn't understand why Amber was speaking to the press, why now, a week after the news had broken. Craig explained that her identity, which till that point wasn't public, had been revealed by an acquaintance of hers to a radio talk show. The media was camped outside her Fresno apartment. To protect the safety of her daughter, she wanted to come forward.

Word spread quickly. Rene Tomlinson called to say that she and Stacey and Lori—Laci's girlfriends—were attending the press conference. They were curious about this other woman and wanted to see her in person. The press conference was broadcast live on TV, and I watched it with several friends at Lissa's house. I found it trying, one more layer of torture, and my friends knew how difficult it was for me. But as hurt and repulsed as I was, I had to watch it. I had no choice.

My reaction was mixed. On the one hand I couldn't help but compare Amber to my daughter. Knowing that Scott was promising her a future at the same time he was plotting to end Laci's life, that was painful. Was her existence a reason to murder Laci? Amber looked scared to death. I knew she'd been unwittingly caught up in this tragedy. I knew she was cooperating with the police and I felt sorry for her as she gave her side of the story.

"Okay, first of all, I met Scott Peterson on November 20 of 2002. I was introduced to him. I was told he was unmarried. Scott told me he was not married. We did have a romantic relationship. When I discovered he was involved in the Laci Peterson disappearance case, I immediately contacted the Modesto Police Department. . . ."

When it was all over, I was angry, confused, and grateful that this woman had stepped forward. I felt the urge to thank her. I went into Lissa's living room for privacy, called Craig, and told him that I wanted to talk to Amber. He asked if I was sure. I heard that questioning tone in his voice, but I assured him I merely wanted to thank her.

He said he would make the arrangements. I called back two more times before Amber and I finally spoke. I think Craig was concerned that I might rip her to shreds. He needn't have been.

Once I got her on the phone, I thanked Amber for coming forward. I told her that I felt bad that she'd found herself in this situation. Learning that she was spending the night at Lori's house, I suggested meeting before she left town, and she accepted. That night Laci's girlfriends told Amber all about Laci and then Rene brought her to my house in the morning.

It was strange having her there. She was my daughter's husband's lover, and I couldn't help but feel she'd been a contributing factor in Laci's disappearance (though I knew Amber personally didn't have anything to do with it). I sat on the sofa and Amber took the love seat across from it, but once she started to talk about her relationship with Scott, the calls, their dates, and so on, she didn't stop. I tried taking notes, but she spoke so fast that I asked for a time-out.

"Wait a minute," I said. "Let me get a calendar."

By this point, I was keeping my own records and wanted to compare the dates I had to what she was telling me. As she described some of her and Scott's activities, I checked them against entries on my calendar and saw how many times Laci thought he was out of town on business when he was actually with Amber.

Amber told me that her friend Shawn had told her about Scott. She told me about their first date and then gave me the dates that Scott had spent, days and nights, with her. She gave me dates and times that Scott called her, usually at night, which made me think he called when Laci was asleep. She gave me several examples of what he said to her, how he cried and sobbed when he had said he'd lost his wife. With each revelation I felt myself sinking: my heart, my soul, my mind. My poor Laci. She loved him so much. My heart ached for her. I felt sick. Suddenly, I was unable to listen to another word; I excused myself, went into the kitchen, and quietly signaled to Rene to get Amber out of the house.

I'd heard more than enough. I was done.

That evening we did a segment on the *John Walsh Show*. We were scheduled to meet with John Walsh early that afternoon. The taping was delayed several times during the day due to flight delays. A producer called regularly with updates, but I didn't care. After listening to Amber, I didn't have any more patience. On top of that, I was exhausted from nearly a month of not sleeping, and was basically just in a foul mood.

Fortunately Kim was with me when the producer called with the final update, because by then I was on the verge of canceling out of the show. I told Kim that if we didn't start soon, I wasn't going to participate. That was so out of character for me, she asked if I was all right. Truthfully, I wasn't, which I told her. But I thought if anyone could understand how I was feeling, it would be John Walsh. I didn't know what was happening exactly, but I was in the midst of something serious. And I didn't even care.

Around six, we taped our segment from the Doubletree Hotel. Ron did most of the talking, something he ordinarily left to me, but I wasn't able to participate as I normally did. After the interview, as we walked to the car, I realized that I couldn't take another step. I wanted to lie down on the sidewalk and go to sleep. I was shutting down. Somehow Ron got me to the car.

When we got home, just after 8 p.m., I opened the door and stepped inside.

And there was Laci, sitting on the sofa, with her back to the door. I recognized the back of her head instantly. There was no mistaking her; that was Laci, waiting for us. Then, she turned around so she could see me, and smiling like she always did, I heard her say, "Hi, Mom!"

I couldn't move. I stopped in my tracks and Ron bumped into me. *Oh my God. Laci has come home. I'm looking right at her.*

"Hi, Mom," Laci said again.

I blinked. The sofa where she'd been was empty. Ron asked what was wrong. I told him I'd just seen Laci sitting on the sofa. I walked down the hall and got into my own bed for the first time since December 24. I slid down, pulled the covers up, and cried till I fell asleep.

The next day, January 26, was Brent's birthday and Super Bowl Sunday. I couldn't get out of bed. I remember being awake and lying motionless under the blankets, curled up in a fetal position, with half my face buried in the pillow.

At one point, Ron came in and stood next to the bed. "Aren't you going to get up?" he asked.

I heard him but didn't respond. I didn't want to. I didn't want to "come up to the surface."

Later he found me in the same position. When I didn't respond to questions, he got scared. But I knew I was okay. I didn't want him to worry about me. I wanted to let him know I was okay, but I couldn't, wouldn't. It was incredibly selfish of me, but I was desperate. I knew if I spoke, I was going to *feel* again, and that meant I was going to be in unbearable pain again, and I didn't want to hurt anymore.

For the past month, I'd been consumed by fear, confusion, desperation, rage, and helplessness. Most of all, though, there'd been pain, and I was tired of the pain. I no longer wanted to feel anything. I thought if I stayed in the same position, I wouldn't feel anything. I thought if I closed myself off from everything, maybe I could avoid the pain. I thought if I simply stayed under the covers and didn't move . . .

It made perfect sense to *me*.

Ron was frantic. He called Sandy and asked her to come over. She sat next to me on the bed and held my hand and cried. Although I didn't break my silence, I felt bad for making her so concerned. Kim also came over, as did Patty and Lin, a former nurse. All of them sat on the bed, offering comfort and support. Yet I didn't move or say a word.

At some point, though, when I was alone with Sandy, I said, "I'm okay." I mumbled the words so she'd know. I hated that I was making her and Ron and everyone else worry so. But I desperately wanted to stay in "that place." And the instant I opened my mouth, I came to the surface and I could feel again and started to cry—exactly what I didn't want. I wept steadily, until I closed my eyes and managed to return to that place where I didn't feel.

Kim had the police department's psychologist, Phil Trumpter, come over. By that time, I could no longer get myself all the way back to the depths where I didn't have to deal. I was already beginning to "come up to the surface" and it hurt so much to do so. Phil sat on the bed next to me and asked what I was feeling. I told him how I'd seen Laci, spoken to her, heard her say, *Hi, Mom,* and how, while he might think I was crazy, she was as real as he was sitting on the edge of the bed.

He nodded knowingly, sympathetically, and explained that she had been real—to me. But she really hadn't been there. He continued explaining that what had happened next was normal, that my brain, overwhelmed by stress, had gone into a protective, shut-down mode. By going to bed and not moving, speaking, or acknowledging the outside world, I'd simply put myself in a more comfortable place.

"If you stayed like that for a couple of weeks, we'd have good reason to be concerned," Phil said. "But this is normal. You're regrouping."

"And seeing Laci?" I asked.

"The mind is an extraordinary thing," he said. "You probably needed to see her. You love her very much."

"Why did Scott kill Laci?" I asked him. "I don't understand. I thought he loved her."

"He probably did love her," Phil said. "But there are times when people do things that can't be explained."

Part Three

Coming Home

If you met her in kindergarten, third grade,

seventh grade, high school, college, or beyond,

it didn't matter, because she never changed.

Her smile may have gotten bigger and her laugh

louder but Laci was always the same bubbly,

energetic, spontaneous, ambitious, creative, and

fun-loving daughter, sister, aunt, niece, cousin,

and friend that we loved so much.

Each day we need to remember that she loved us.

LACI'S FRIEND RENE TOMLINSON
AT LACI'S FUNERAL, AUGUST 29, 2003

Chapter Seventeen

At a little after 3 p.m. on January 27, Scott left a message on our answering machine, inviting us to join him in TV interviews he planned to do that week, including one with *Good Morning America*'s Diane Sawyer.

Scott clearly needed a turn on the airwaves to counter all the stories about his affair with Amber. He'd taken a beating in the press and lost our support. But he was still denying everything, and promoting himself as innocent, misunderstood, and intent on finding Laci.

I didn't think he really wanted us to join him in interviews. I simply think he wanted to be able to say, "I tried to get them, but they didn't return my calls." But he made no real effort.

At 6:55 a.m. the next day, Scott called the house again. Ron answered. Scott said that his interview with Diane Sawyer was airing within the hour on ABC and he wanted us to know that he'd told Sawyer that he had admitted his affair with Amber to Laci in early December.

"There's no way!" I exclaimed to Ron. "We had dinner with them within two weeks after he says he told her about Amber and everything with them was hunky-dory. Laci may not have wanted to say my husband's screwing around, but if she'd known about his affair, even if she didn't say anything to us, we would've noticed it in her attitude."

During the actual interview, Sawyer asked if he'd killed Laci, and

Scott dismissed that notion with a rather unconvincing "No, no, uh, I did not," with a smile on his face and a chuckle.

He said he took McKenzie for walks in the park and described that as his private time to communicate with Laci; as he said that, he actually cried.

"I've never seen those tears!" I said to Ron.

Scott said that he didn't want to think of Laci as dead, but sometimes at night he couldn't help himself and the thought crept into his head.

"What did you do to her?" I said. "Tell us what you did to Laci. Tell us where she is!"

He claimed to have told the police right away about his affair with Amber—a complete lie, as they didn't find out until December 30 when Amber contacted them.

I wanted Diane Sawyer to come down harder on him, and she finally did when he said Laci wasn't angry about his affair. That was such BS. I almost cheered when Sawyer asked if he really expected people to believe that an eight-and-a-half-month-pregnant [sic] woman was fine with her husband having an affair?

"Good for you!" I said.

"What about Laci's family?" Sawyer asked.

"They're wonderful people," Scott said. "They're obviously upset with me about the romantic relationship with Amber. They have little trust as they've expressed in the media to date. But I believe that they're still looking for Laci and I would like to work with them. . . ."

Not likely. In private, Ron and I, in our naïveté, were frustrated the police hadn't already arrested Scott when his guilt was so patently obvious, and we fantasized about what we'd do to him if we had a chance. We talked about holding him hostage, tying him up, drugging him, and torturing him—whatever we could do to get him to tell us where Laci was.

In reality, we didn't want to do *anything* that could jeopardize the case against him when it was finally made. We wanted to let the police conduct their investigation, make the arrest, and then do everything within our power to see him convicted.

Naturally, the press wanted to know our thoughts about Scott's interview. By 8 a.m., reporters filled the front yard and driveway. I didn't want to talk, but Ron went out and fielded a few questions.

"It's his word against Laci's," he said. "And she's not here to defend herself."

As for Scott's family, they appeared on *Good Morning America* the next day, part two of Scott's interview, and they continued to defend him. I wasn't surprised. I hadn't spoken to Jackie for a while, and though she'd called several times, I hadn't felt like talking to her. I already knew how the conversation would go. She'd say Scott was innocent, or she'd give me reasons why she thought he was being framed.

She talked *only* about Scott; rarely did she talk about Laci.

Sure enough, when I finally did speak to her, she said, "I don't know why you think he'd have done this to Laci. It was just a one-night stand."

How can you say a one-night stand? I thought. *You were on* GMA *when Diane Sawyer asked him if he was still seeing Amber and he said yes.*

"Well, he must've been drunk," Jackie said.

I had no response, she was his mother, and ended the conversation. I thought about Jackie and how critical she was of Laci. At the same time, it seemed Jackie was willing to excuse anything Scott did. I'd hoped she would see Scott for what he really is, Laci's murderer. That's not to say she should stop loving her son, or turn her back on him.

On January 29, Scott gave a lengthy interview at home to local TV reporter Ted Rowlands. Since we didn't get KTVU2 in our area, we didn't watch. We heard it covered the same ground as his interview with Diane Sawyer. I remember hearing several TV analysts, including prominent Los Angeles attorney Harland Braun, saying, "This is a case where the guy should keep his mouth shut."

An e-mail sent around the world asked people to stop on January 31 at 7 p.m. Pacific time and light a candle for Laci and Conner. We had close to fifty people at our house that night. All of us went out front and lit candles. My friend Rita Keller said a prayer. It was a very nice, simple, peaceful moment, and I was told the flame actually made it around the world.

Scott apparently didn't see the light. Earlier that same day, Craig Grogan told us that Scott had traded Laci's Land Rover in for a Dodge Ram pickup. Scott claimed it was because his Ford truck was still in police custody. We got the car back, though. Four days later, Dennis bought it for one dollar from Doug Roberts of Roberts Auto Sales, who was reeling from the negative PR that came with his purchase.

Privately, we didn't want the car anymore. It was immaterial compared to getting Laci back. Getting rid of Laci's car was clear evidence to me that Scott knew she wasn't ever coming back, as was the fact that he'd already made two inquiries about selling their house. I didn't know what more the police needed.

I asked Craig almost every day, sometimes two or three times a day.

"We're gathering evidence," he said each time. "We're working through the case."

At the start of February, I couldn't help but think that Laci's due date was the tenth, and we should've been planning for that special day. Instead we were still looking for her. We held a press conference at which Brent announced plans for a series of three searches that he organized on the first three Saturdays of the month. Sergeant Cloward had given his approval to the efforts to go back over the wetlands beyond town.

In hindsight, the police probably liked the idea of something that would distract the press from the department's continued search of the Berkeley Marina and Bay and also keep us occupied. Plus, there was always the chance something was missed during the first search. But the cops were on the right track.

I called Craig one day and I told him that I found it particularly odd that Scott had never asked how the police got involved in the case. Nor had he ever sat down with us and cried. He wasn't with us at the candlelight vigil. He didn't help participate in the searches. He mainly kept to himself.

Craig had me watch a videotape the police had taken inside the house when they searched it on December 26 and 27. I made a couple of observations. I noticed the three large patio umbrellas that Scott had reportedly loaded into his pick-up and taken to his warehouse on Christmas Eve morning were still leaning against the back fence. I thought he'd taken them to the warehouse on the morning of December 24. What were they doing back at home? He said he was taking them to the warehouse to protect them from the rain, yet he drove them to Berkeley, where he claimed it rained, and left them in the back of the pick-up. I couldn't keep up with his lies.

I also spotted the blue pool cover, which was a relief to me, since, after hearing so much about a blue tarp in the press, I'd convinced myself that Scott might have wrapped Laci up in the pool cover before loading her in his truck.

To be honest, I didn't know what to make of Scott. He seemed to have gone off whatever script he'd intended to follow. I think he was shocked at the attention Laci's story continued to get. I think he planned on police giving up by this time. He probably thought he'd have moved on to his new life.

But no one was giving up. In fact, I was trying to hang on to my daughter. Several weeks earlier I'd asked Scott if I could get some of Laci's belongings. It was the first of numerous requests. I also asked Craig to relay the same message. I wanted her wedding dress, photo albums, cheerleader outfit, and other things that he didn't need but held meaning for me. They were a way I could still keep her close.

It should've been easy, but it wasn't. On February 3, Scott sent me an e-mail. It was a rambling response that mentioned my request for some of Laci's belongings but also covered other issues that seemed more important to him.

Mom,

I have never taken the opportunity to apologize to either Ron or yourself for lying to you about my infidelity to Laci. I am truly sorry that I was not forthcoming with you immediately. I know that both our goals is to find Laci and Conner, I am hoping together we can do more than separate.

The next paragraph struck me as key. Most disturbing, he seemed to be trying to stop people from searching in the water.

> *I understand you are organizing a search this coming weekend, and you know that we are trying to put together a national search day this Sunday (I have attached the rough draft of the press release). I am wondering if you want to keep the two separate or try to combine them. Have you spoken with Sergeant Cloward, and has he given you an idea on where to search? I am hoping that any search is one that directs people's efforts toward finding her safely, targeting medical institutions, houses and the like, the only possible end to this is them back in our arms.*

The rest was typical Scott.

> *I received the change of address form for the fund and obviously will not contest this.*
>
> *I also received a message from detective Grogain [sic] regarding the lamps and photos, of course I am willing to share any photos with you, Laci loves her lamps and they should be in our home when we bring her home.*
>
> *For all of us, and more important for Laci we need to find her and bring her back where she belongs, among us, we can do this if we can communicate and work together.*
>
> *Scott*

That e-mail left me frustrated and angry. If Laci loved her lamps so much, as he wrote, and he wanted to have them when "we bring her home," why had he inquired into selling their house *furnished* when she'd been gone less than a week? And why was he thinking we would "bring" her home as opposed to her "coming" home alive and well?

The first search that Brent organized showed how many people had refused to give up hope of finding Laci. More than five hundred volunteers on foot, horseback, motorcycles, mountain bikes, and quads met that Saturday, February 8, at the Orchard Restaurant in Vernalis, outside of Modesto where I-5 and Route 132 converge. They scoured the vast area of farmland, orchards, and waterways till late afternoon.

Nothing was found. I went home drained, depressed, and angry. We were putting out so much effort when in reality the person with the information I wanted was right among us. I called Scott and left a message. I think he heard the desperation and sorrow in my voice. I practically burst into tears on the phone. I begged him, "Scott, please, tell us where you put her. She needs to come home. Monday is her due date and I want her home. You loved her once. Don't leave her out there all alone." I told him to call me or Brent and tell us where she was or make an anonymous call to the police, disguise his voice, and then leave the country if he wanted. Just tell us where she is.

Then, amazingly, he returned my call. I didn't waste time getting to the point. I said I knew he was lying and we wanted Laci home and I wanted him to tell me where she was.

"I loved her," Scott said. "I love my son. I want them home."

"I'm having a hard time believing any of that," I said. "'Cause you're not showing it. . . . You've shown us nothing like that at all."

"I've . . . had . . . looking . . . everything I can and I'll continue to," he stammered.

"No, you're not. You're never in Modesto anymore. You're not out looking for Laci. We're out looking for Laci. I need to have her home, Scott."

"We need her home," he said. "There's no question about it."

"She is part of me," I said. "I have to have her home."

"She is my joy and my happiness," he said.

"Then why did you kill her?" I was so mad at that point.

"I did not hurt her," he said.

"Maybe you didn't hurt her. But you killed her."

"I did not."

"Yes, you did. Yes, you did, Scott."

"Why do you think that?" he asked. "I can't understand how you could ever think that's even a possibility."

"Well, it's about time you said that because you certainly didn't say that the first time I said this to you. When I said, did you kill her, you just said no."

"I—"

"I mean you just asked it," I continued.

"I never hurt her."

"You have been totally unemotional about this whole entire thing."

"That is not true," he said.

"Yes, it is true, Scott. The only time you've shown any emotion is—"

"How do you think I could ever hurt Laci? Ever hurt my wife and my son?"

"Well, you're the one who made us believe that."

"By lying to you—"

"Not by before, but by your actions afterwards. By everything you've done afterwards, you've convinced every one of us that you killed Laci. All I want from you, Scott, is to have her back. That's all I want from you. Like I said, you can call the police department anonymously, disguise your voice, whatever it is. Just tell us where Laci is so we can go get her."

"I . . . she . . ."

"I have to have her back."

"Right now, we, yes, we need her back. There's no question. I have nightmares every night about what could be happening to her. We need her back—"

"Oh, we can tell you're having nightmares. Yes, we know you're having nightmares." I could no longer mask my sarcasm. "It's obvious. I . . . you know, cut the bullshit, okay. Please don't insult us. Scott, we know—"

"How could you think I could have anything to do with this?" he asked.

"Because you act like you did."

"No, I do not."

"That's how—that's how we think it. Because you act that way. You haven't shown any remorse whatsoever."

"I don't have any remorse," he said (an amazing comment, maybe the only time he was honest). "I didn't do anything. I'm out here look-ing for my wife."

"No, you're not looking for her. Do you know, Scott, you didn't even talk to me—it was a whole week afterward, and the only time you talked to me was when I actually took you into the room to talk to. You avoided me every chance you got."

"That's not true."

"You never looked at any of us."

"No, that's not true at all."

"Oh, yes it is true. . . . You would think me, being Laci's mother, would have been one of the first people that you wanted to tell every-thing to . . . and explain everything to and . . . and . . . that I would see you out there in front of the camera saying bring my wife home to me, somebody took her . . . but no, instead you've been hiding out since day one."

"Do you really believe the media crap?" he asked.

"I don't have to," I said. "I'm not talking to the media. I'm not get-ting my information from the media."

"Well, they—"

"It's you, Scott. It's you. It's your behavior that has caused people to think this. Or lack of behavior . . ."

"My behavior—searching for my wife and not wanting to be dis-tracted by media following me around and getting things done—that behavior about the thought we had to keep them involved by me being in the media immediately? How—how is that behavior that you could think I'd ever have anything—"

"Because most people would be out there, begging to have them bring their wife home. And you've never once done that. So, look, Scott, I don't want to have this conversation. Like I said, the only thing I ever want from you is to tell me where my daughter is. I need to have her back. I need to take care of her."

"I could never hurt her. I have no idea where she is. And I want her back just as bad as—you know that."

"Well, you know what? You're the one that's going to live with this. You're the one who's going to burn in hell for doing this and lying to everybody. So if you have any compassion, any soul at all, for any redemption at all, Scott, you've got to tell us where she is. Don't leave her out there all by herself."

"I want her back."

"Would you think your mother would want to go through this if that was your body that had been thrown away someplace?"

"She's still out there," he said, changing the topic. "Someone told me. We're gonna find her. I had nothing to do with her—"

"I can see this is going nowhere. If you ever get, uh, a heart and a soul, Scott, and a conscience, like I said, call us and tell us where she is. Or call the police department. Otherwise just don't even bother us. Because we know you did it."

I slammed the phone down. The tears would come again, but at that moment I was so angry. I'd asked him everything, tried pressuring him, and received nothing.

I dreaded the dawn of Laci's due date, February 10. Laci and I had talked a bit about the trip to the hospital, and I could hear us making a checklist of things to put in her bag so she'd be all set to go to the hospital. This should have been such a happy time and full of anticipation.

But the opposite was true. I would've preferred to skip those days altogether.

Knowing how I felt, Patty arranged for a few of us to spend the ninth and tenth at her cabin in Strawberry, a gorgeous pine- and lake-dotted hamlet in the Sierra Nevadas. I thought it was a good idea. Before leaving, I made a batch of oatmeal–chocolate chip cookies. I hadn't worked in the kitchen since Laci disappeared, and it was hard. I cried the entire time.

But it felt good to be at Patty's cabin. The crisp mountain air had a rejuvenating freshness. We spent the afternoon putting an outdoor heater together. That night we sat on the deck, staring at the stars and trying to talk about everything but Laci. But I woke up the next morning feeling an inescapable sense of loss and sadness. My grandson Conner was to have arrived on this day and Laci would've been so happy. I couldn't think of anything else.

After a while, though, my mind started playing tricks. What if Laci wasn't dead? What if she was giving birth somewhere and someone recognized her?

A thousand what if's ran through my brain. I couldn't think of anything else. I cut short the trip. I had to get home.

Chapter Eighteen

We kept up the PR effort on February 11 and 12 by doing TV interviews. Brent, Amy, and I were determined to keep the focus on finding Laci. We wanted her home. That's the message we wanted out there. Of course, some members of the media were more interested in getting us to discuss our declining faith in Scott.

CONNIE CHUNG: *I'm wondering, Amy, when did you begin to doubt Scott Peterson? Was it before or after you learned about this affair?*

AMY: *It was more after I learned about the affair. . . . He had a chance to tell our family the truth in the beginning about that and he didn't. So, yes, my family has changed after that.*

CHUNG: *Sharon, Scott Peterson did a number of interviews. He acknowledged the affair, but he also said that Laci was okay with it. Do you think that was true?*

ME: *No, I don't think that Laci knew about the affair. . . . Laci was the kind of person that—she was a happy, upbeat person. We would have noticed a difference in her attitude, in her behavior. Whether she said anything to anybody or not, there would have been a definite and obvious difference in her attitude. And if she had known about it, I truly feel that she would have told somebody. If not have said something to me, she would have said something to at least one of her friends. And nobody was aware of it.*

CHUNG: *Sharon, if Laci happens to be listening out there, what would you like to say to her?*

ME: *I'd like to tell her that I love her very, very much, and I miss her tremendously, and I want her home. And we're looking for her and not to—not to give up, that we're still searching. We'll never give up looking for Laci.*

On February 13, I was talking to Gwen at about 10 a.m. when I heard another call come in and clicked over. It was Scott—the last person I expected. I felt a clutch in my stomach as soon as I heard him say, "Hi, Mom." He didn't mention the Connie Chung interview or sound upset. Instead he said he and his family were holding a press conference that afternoon in San Diego and he invited us to participate.

"I know geographically it's not possible for you to be there," he said. "But I wanted to let you know about that."

"Okay," I said.

Caught off guard, I didn't ask why the press conference was in San Diego when the search effort was still centered in Modesto and the Bay Area. I called Craig Grogan, who compounded the mystery by saying that if there was a press conference in San Diego, Scott wasn't going to make it, either. Since Craig didn't elaborate, I had to read between the lines. I guessed that Scott was nowhere near San Diego (which turned out to be true).

That afternoon, several members from Scott's family faced the press in San Diego and reaffirmed their commitment to finding Laci. Susan, assuming the role of spokesperson, noted the passing of Laci's due date as an emotional time for everyone, but stated "there are no new developments." She urged people to remain hopeful Laci was still alive and keep looking for her.

I think if it had been up to the Petersons, the press conference would have ended at that moment, without a single mention of Scott. But his absence, along with the lack of any new information, was too conspicuous for reporters to ignore, and they wanted to know where he was and how he was doing. Jackie said he was looking for his wife. Susan said he was in Modesto. And then they left.

I watched on TV and thought it was a futile if not strange effort to provide some positive spin for Scott Peterson. *Let's think of Laci as alive. Let's not look for her killer. No one wants her returned safely more than me.* But why wasn't he there?

That afternoon, I managed to get Scott on the phone. I was still amazed he took my calls, but I didn't pause to ask him why. I had questions, and on the surface he was amenable to answering them, or so he said.

"The last night you talked to Laci—"

"Uh-huh," he interrupted.

"What was going on?" I continued. "What happened after eight thirty that night? Were you at home when she called me?"

"Yeah, I was there," he said. "We, um, we watched a movie. We had got a haircut—Amy, earlier that night."

"Yeah, I know earlier. But I'm talking about after eight thirty. After I talked to her."

"We picked up a pizza and watched a movie and went to bed," he said.

"What movie?" I asked.

"Uh, *The Rookie.*"

"And then you went to bed at what time?"

"Oh, I don't know. Probably ten thirty or something."

"What was she wearing when she went to bed?"

"Um, my pajamas. The blue ones."

"Your blue pajamas?"

"Yeah."

"How come she was wearing your blue pajamas?"

"Because they fit her."

"And she went to bed about ten thirty?"

"Think so."

"Was she feeling okay—when she went to bed?"

"Yeah. Yeah. She looked fine."

"Did you guys have some other plans, some tentative plans, for Christmas Eve?"

"No, just coming to your place."

"Because it took her—I asked a couple times before she decided—or before she told me that you guys were coming over."

"Uh-huh."

"So you didn't have anything else planned for Christmas Eve—before?"

"No. No. I think the question in her mind was who was gonna be over there."

"And she was feeling all right when she went to sleep?"

"Yeah. Definitely. I mean she was, you know she was feeling a little more tired the last couple days. That week. But she was fine. She wasn't sick or anything."

"And then how was she feeling when she got up in the morning? What time did she get up?"

"She got up before I did. About seven. You know. And you know how, ah, she is—she has to eat right away or else she felt sick. So—her breakfast. Then I got up and—cereal again together."

"You ate cereal again together?" I asked.

"Yeah."

"So she got up and had breakfast and then ate breakfast again?"

"Well, had a little bit—piece of toast and I had some cereal," Scott said.

"No, I mean her."

"Yeah, she got up around seven, I think."

"And then she—"

"Had her bowl of cereal—"

"Yeah."

"I got up later. And had cereal and she had a piece of toast," he continued.

"And what was she wearing when you left?"

"She had on her black pants and like a white top with long sleeves."

"A pullover or button or what?"

"Yeah. Pullover. Like, ah, you know T-shirt-kinda sweater-kinda thing."

"And what shoes?"

"I don't know. She maybe had slippers on. I don't know."

"So you don't even know what shoes she had on?"

"No, not really."

"I just wanted to know. I mean I talked to her at eight thirty at night. I need to know everything that happened after that."

"Sure. Well—"

"I mean, what she—how she acted—if she was sick or if she was tired or—"

"No, she was . . . I mean, she was feeling good that morning. You know her. She was, you know, excited to be baking. She was into her gingerbread thing and going to—helping—and you know get ready for Christmas Day. She felt like she had—all her French toast stuff and she was gonna make French toast for Christmas Day."

"Well, how come you didn't notice when you walked—"

". . . set the table on Friday."

"How come you didn't notice when you walked in the door that she hadn't been baking or the lights were off or anything?"

"Because I was late and I was rushing."

"I mean, surely McKenzie came up to you when you walked in the back gate with his leash on."

"Yeah."

"But you didn't—"

"I took it off of him and I didn't—it didn't even register."

"Didn't even register that Laci wasn't in the house when you walked in? It was a dark house. Didn't smell like she'd been cooking? Everything was cleaned up and neat and tidy—and nothing even registered to you?"

"No, I—again—ah, I grabbed a piece of pizza out of the fridge and jumped into the shower immediately, and when I got out, then I looked at the messages. I assumed she was over at your place."

"I mean, we've never even had this conversation after all this time."

"True. I know. And it wasn't until you asked about the McKenzie thing—and I—even if I remember I—you know mentioned to you—yeah, and he had his leash on, he—go to the park."

"I didn't mention it. You told me he had his leash on."

"Right. Well, you asked about McKenzie. If he was in the yard."

"No, you told me he was."

"Okay. I mean either way."

"I mean, that's how I knew all that stuff. There was no reason for me to ask about that. I didn't even know she was going for a walk until later that night when I asked you when we were standing in the driveway. I asked you what were her plans for the day, and that's when you told me—that she was—planned on going for a walk. So she was wearing your blue pajamas? Is that a blue top and bottom?"

"Yeah. But she was wearing the—"

"Is that what she normally wears to bed?"

"Oh, that whole past month. Yeah."

"Were they like flannel pajamas or—"

"No. Cotton."

"Okay, well that's what I wanted to know. I mean, these are questions that I've had and I've never had them answered. I mean, just what she was doing that night."

"Uh-huh. Yeah."

"She went to bed about ten thirty and everything was just fine?"

"Yeah."

"And everything was fine at seven o'clock when she got up?"

"Oh yeah. Great. She was excited about doing the cooking stuff."

"But you said she set the table."

"Setting it up for Christmas Day. Oh yeah, the table was set."

"No, it wasn't," I continued.

"Three or four days ago."

"All that was on there was the, um, the little cracker things. What did she set on the table?"

"Well, the cracker things and the candles and all that stuff."

"Because there wasn't anything on there but the crackers and the candles. There weren't any plates or silverware or anything else set out there."

"Okay. I mean—"

"Was that what you're saying? She did all that?"

"Well, I don't know. I don't recall if there were plates out there or not. I do remember the crackers and the candles and—obviously the presents and the tree and all the—"

"You just said she had the table set for three or four days."

"Yeah, it was like it was ready. She had those red berry things out there. All that. We were just ready to have people over Christmas Day. That's what she was excited about. Christmas Eve. Getting prepared."

"Like I said I just—it's odd that you didn't notice anything when you walked in the house. I mean, the dog had his leash on. The house is dark. She hadn't cooked. And you went ahead and took a shower and didn't bother to call until afterwards. I would've thought you would've called right away. There was no note for you or anything."

"No."

"Okay. Well, that's what I wanted to know for now. Unless I can think of something else."

"Okay."

"Okay. Thanks."

"Bye."

"Bye."

I'd caught Scott off guard. Angry, I thought of additional questions. I decided to call again—just not right away. I knew he wasn't going to admit he murdered Laci, but I needed to know as much as possible for my own peace of mind. And maybe, just maybe, he'd slip up and tell me something that would lead us to where he put Laci. I *needed* to have her home. She *deserved* to be home.

Around four, I called him again, and miraculously he answered. As soon as he heard it was me, his guard went up.

"I did have a couple more questions," I said, and before he was able to utter a single word, I continued. "What was Laci doing when you left that morning?"

"She was mopping the kitchen floor," he said in a snippy tone.

"She was mopping the kitchen floor?" I asked.

"Yeah."

"Why was she mopping the floor if the maid had been there the day before?"

"With the dog and the cats, you know her. She mopped all the time."

"Oh."

"I'd like to talk to you but—I mean you're—you know, still accusing me of doing the most disgusting thing."

"Well, Scott, you know what you told me?"

"Calling me and asking me—and I want to talk to you about finding her."

"Do you know what you told me that she was doing when I asked you this before? Do you remember telling me that—"

"She was mopping the floor."

"No. You told me she was sitting on her little bench in front of the mirror and she looked so cute because she was styling her hair like Amy had styled it for her the night before. Do you remember telling me that?"

"No, I don't remember telling you that."

"Hmmm. That's too bad you don't remember that because I talked—"

"Why are you asking me these questions?" Now he was angry.

"Because I want to know what happened to my daughter."

"If you're gonna call me up and accuse me of doing something to my wife—to my child—to your daughter—to your grandchild—it's the most disgusting thing that you could do. And you know me better than that."

"Well, then let me ask you this. When did you tell her about the affair? Exactly when did you tell her about the affair?"

"It was early in December. I don't remember the date."

"You don't know a date?"

"No. I don't know the date."

"And how did she react? What did she say to you?"

"If you want to talk about finding Laci, I want to do that with you."

"But you don't want to give me any details, do you?"

"You're accusing me of doing this and it's so disgusting. And it's unbelievable that you could ever possibly think [I had] something to do with her disappearance."

"Yeah, you're right. It's unbelievable, Scott, and I'm really disappointed. I truly am. But there are so many things that you've just— you know, like I said, you told me that she was sitting in front of the mirror combing her hair when she left. That she looked so cute sitting on her little bench."

"It is disgusting that you think I could ever have done something to my wife—my child."

"Then what happened to her?"

"You know I love her."

"What happened to her?"

"You know me. We spent, I mean, how long? Well, I've known you for eight years."

"What was Laci's reaction after you told her you had an affair? How did she react?"

"I'm gonna go. You're not gonna—"

"Scott, these are things that are important."

"Why don't we look for Laci? Why can't we be a family for that? Try to bring her home?"

"Because I don't think you've been doing that."

"Oh, I have been. You don't know what I've been doing."

"I need to know some other details here, Scott. Why won't you tell me what her reaction was when you told her about the affair?"

"Well, I mean, was she happy? No, of course not."

"What did she say? What did she do? How did she react?"

"I'm sorry. You know that's between her and I. We had a tough, you know, terrible talk and, and she didn't understand why and I don't know why I had an affair. But we made our peace with it and . . . we will always love each other."

"If you loved her so much, why did you have an affair?"

"I don't know why I had an affair."

"You even said on TV the other day that you were still seeing her after you told Laci."

"I did see her once after—"

"But you don't remember exactly when you told Laci?"

"No."

"But you do remember that you—"

"I can get a calendar and try to figure it out for you if you want, but I don't know the date."

"And she wasn't mad or upset or hurt or anything?"

"Of course she was upset. Hurt. Yeah. Of course. But you know we are—we're strong enough. We love each other enough to get through it."

"See, I have a really hard time believing all that because—"

"You saw us after I told her and how you know—I mean—you know her—we're the same."

"Well, of course she was the same because I really don't believe you told her. I know my daughter. She would have said something to somebody."

"I-I-I . . ."

"She would have been—"

"Would hope you would help us."

". . . crushed. She would've been crushed to know this, Scott. And you know that as well as I do. It would've broken her heart. She loved you so much."

"We love each other. There's no question. That's why we can get through it. Why we got through it."

"Or was it just a matter of a few days you got through it?"

"Well, I'm along the road to never thinking about it again. Absolutely."

"What was that? I didn't hear what you said."

"We're on the road to never thinking about it, you know, the affair, again. But it was still, obviously, fresh and—"

"It couldn't have been more than a week or two since you told her."

"What?"

"If she disappeared on December 24, and you told her in early December—"

"Right."

"It couldn't have been more than a week or two since you told her, and she's already over it?"

"Right. No, I'm not saying . . . you know, we still talked about it.

But I mean we were okay. You know. You saw us. We were happy. We are happy. And we will be . . . you spent time with us during December. You know how we loved each other."

"That's why all this is just so hard to believe."

"You should be—"

"Why did you tell me she was sitting on a bench in front of her mirror?"

"I don't know if I told you that or not."

"I remember it specifically because it was one of the very few times we ever spent any time alone at all."

"Okay."

"Because I told you . . . I wanted to know exactly what Laci was doing when you left that morning."

"Why did you call and ask me again if you have the—"

"Because I want to know exactly what was going on when you left that morning."

"So you're accusing me of doing something to my wife and son?"

"I'm just trying to find out what's going on here, Scott."

"That's what you're doing. You're saying I did something to my wife and son."

"Well? Did you?"

"That's disgusting. I did not. And I don't want to talk to you again today. I want to talk to you when you're ready to look for Laci and for your own daughter."

"Oh, like I haven't been?"

"I'm gonna go. I can't take this from you. You haven't been looking. I'm gonna go."

I heard a CLICK, then a dial tone, then nothing.

Chapter Nineteen

I was home, in bed, with the flu, when Brent led volunteers on another search, this time at Lake Don Pedro, on February 15. Some hundred people—fewer than the previous weekend—gave up their Saturday to search the reservoir and surrounding farmland east of Route 132 in Tuolumne County. I made sure that Brent and Ron informed everyone that if I'd been physically able to leave the house, I would have been there, helping, but I was too sick.

At the end of the day, Brent and Ron let me know the effort had yielded the same results as all the previous searches, nothing but lowered expectations, frustration, and a sense of growing futility as we wondered what to do next. But on February 18, I heard a report on the morning news that three men in suits were in the front of Laci's house, talking to Scott. The anchorman wondered if Scott was going to be arrested.

I called Craig on his cell and told him what I'd heard. He asked, in an atypically clipped tone, if he could call me back in a few minutes. He didn't. A couple hours passed before he finally got back to me, and then he explained.

"I was one of those three men in suits, and I was standing right next to Scott when you called," he said.

As I found out, Craig had been among the detectives who'd served Scott a search warrant, this one for the house, his truck, and a new storage locker he'd been renting since emptying out his original warehouse.

On that night's news, they showed Scott's pickup being driven away. They also showed Scott standing in the driveway, scowling. The next day the detectives carried several brown paper bags from the house and loaded them into a truck. I asked what was going on but didn't get an answer. I had to assume that detectives Grogan, Buehler, Brocchini, and the others involved in the investigation were going about their jobs methodically and thoroughly, as they promised. It made me feel as if they were making progress.

And they were. During their search, they found a number of things that raised more suspicions about Scott. For instance, they discovered Laci's dirty clothes stuffed into her dresser drawer with clean clothes (something she'd never do); a grocery bag containing, among other things, Scott's blue cotton pajamas; several thousand dollars in cash; and Scott's things strewn in Conner's bedroom (in a fairly recent interview, Scott had told local TV reporter Gloria Gomez that he hadn't been able to bring himself to enter Conner's bedroom).

I also undertook my own search. A week before, I had been reading some e-mails on our Web site and noticed a message from a self-declared psychic who said Laci was somewhere on the delta near Antioch, a town off Highway 12 toward the Bay Area. Our Web site had received thousands of messages from people offering thoughts and theories about what happened to Laci, including dozens from psychics, none of which I'd pursued till now. This one was different.

Amber had told me that Scott had gone duck hunting on Christmas Eve with his father, and there were duck ponds in the area described by the e-mail. Perhaps as important, Scott had now told one person he'd gone golfing on December 24, another that he'd gone fishing, and Amber Frey that he'd gone duck hunting. But I couldn't focus on these discrepancies now—I was desperate to go to Antioch.

I called Gwen and the two of us drove up there. As we drove, Brent called and it turned out he was headed in the same direction, taking time off work to look for his sister. I thought that was an interesting coincidence, both of us in the same area. We met up along the way and went together. Once in Antioch, the three of us got out of the car and in silence trudged all over the area, through tall grass, silty soil, and along the marshland, scanning every rock and ripple of water.

I didn't want to find her, because I didn't want her to be dead, but as I stared out at the watery landscape, it seemed like the whole state was water—particularly up in the Bay Area. We probably weren't ever going to find her, I thought.

After we dropped Brent at his car, I started to think about what Scott did to Laci, and it destroyed me. Gwen understood and tried to console me.

"She probably died in her sleep," she said. "She was probably sleeping and Scott probably suffocated her with a pillow or something."

I'd also thought of that many times. It didn't help.

"That doesn't mean she didn't wake up," I said. "That doesn't mean she didn't know what was happening. She would've been struggling, fighting to breathe."

I'll never forget that conversation. Poor Gwen couldn't say anything that would make me feel better. Words couldn't help.

When we got back into town late that afternoon, I wanted to see what was going on at Laci's house. I drove down Encina, the street perpendicular to Laci's, which allowed me to look without driving in front of the house. I was devastated by what I saw: Media trucks lined the street. Reporters stood outside. It was a spectacle, like a circus, and it broke my heart. Laci would've been appalled.

I picked up my cell phone and called Scott. I said I wanted permission to go into the house and pick up some of Laci's belongings. Without any hesitation, he said no.

"You're looking for a body," he said. "You think Laci is dead."

"You know what?" I said. "It doesn't matter what I think or feel. I just want some of my daughter's things."

I tried to reason with him. I said I'd already spoken to Craig, who explained I needed Scott's permission before entering the house and taking things. If he'd call Craig, I could go over to the house when the search was completed. After first saying no, Scott changed his mind and said he'd tell Craig.

That evening I spoke to Craig and, to my surprise, I was told that Scott had given permission for me to go into the house after the police search was completed. On February 19 I had several friends come over and wait with me until the police said they were done so that they could help me get Laci's belongings and keepsakes. But it didn't happen. Around noon that day, Scott called and said the search was running long and I'd better hold off on coming by the house till he gave the go-ahead. I let him know I was disappointed. In turn, he offered to bring Laci's Cal Poly sweatshirt by the house if I wanted something of hers to comfort me.

Even if I'd accepted his offer, I thought Scott would've come up with some excuse for not making it. It seemed he just wanted to placate me on the phone. The last thing I wanted was for him to come to the house. I didn't want to be anywhere near him. If he could murder Laci, his pregnant wife, the woman he loved, what would stop him from doing the same to me?

"It's not a good idea," I told him. "I have people over. I'll wait till the search is done."

Scott called a short time later and said he might not be at the house by the time the search was completed. I said that was fine. I'd wait for Craig to call and say the search was completed, then go to the house, and he'd stay there while I gathered Laci's things. Scott didn't have a response to that; after a second, he said, "Hmmm. Okay."

I was back in bed with a relapse of the flu, obviously brought on by stress, when the phone rang around three. I was too wiped out to answer, but I heard the message. "Hey, Mom, it's Scott," he said. "It's three fifteen, and they're gonna be done with the search warrant today, but it's probably not right that you come over with Grogan today just because of all the media. We should try to do it another day, of course. You know if you want something, a sweatshirt or anything else from the house to hang on to, just let me know. Talk to you later. Bye."

That message was the last time I heard from Scott. Despite getting two more messages from me over the next several weeks, he apparently decided not to return my calls anymore, and the two of us never spoke again.

The next time I spoke to him, or rather at him, would be in the courtroom during the penalty phase on November 30, 2004.

Around the middle of February, I heard that Amber was going to do the media circuit. Like all of us, she had been courted aggressively by the media elite. I heard Connie Chung, after campaigning hard for the first big tell-all, was about to get her.

None of us wanted Amber to talk and give away potential evidence. Even though Scott hadn't been charged with any crimes yet, we felt sure it was only a matter of time before he was. I'd stopped talking about him in the press. I honestly felt as if I didn't know him any longer, so what was I going to say? Plenty of other people emerged willing to talk about Laci and Scott, including Amber's father, sister, and former boyfriends. Someone claiming to know Scott had supposedly heard him say he was going to murder his wife. We heard rumors about his possible involvement in the death of a student.

It was like a feeding frenzy. People came out of the woodwork with outrageous claims. Strangers professed to be Laci's best friends. People identified themselves as hit men for Scott. I saw Laci-related items on eBay, some legitimate and some not. I learned of people soliciting money under the pretense of sending it to Laci's family, and then they didn't. T-shirts, hats, bracelets, and photos have been sold.

I called Amber myself, told her what'd I'd heard, and how I felt about it. At my request, we continued the discussion in person at my house the following night. Amber arrived with her daughter. She complained that the Modesto Police Department, despite all the calls with Scott she was taping, didn't pay her last phone bill and her service was disconnected. As she made clear, she was interested in exploring the opportunities being created by the media.

I said I'd talk to the police and try to get her phone bill paid. At the same time, I was clear that I preferred she didn't talk to Connie Chung or any other outlets about Scott or anything else she might know. I emphasized that what might seem like an opportunity to her was a horrible tragedy for my entire family and many others close to Laci.

I added that if she kept quiet, the media's offers would double and triple; in fact, they'd multiply in proportion to the times she turned them down.

To her credit, Amber agreed to put off all interview requests and opportunities until later, which I appreciated. I remember being curious about something else. I still wondered what Laci knew or didn't know about her, and I asked if Scott had a picture of her (Amber). She said yes, she'd given Scott a card with a picture of her and her daughter in it.

"If Laci found this card, would she have known that Scott was having an affair?" I asked.

"Yes," she said, and added, "But Laci didn't find that card."

The way she said that offended me, and I was blunt. How did she know Laci didn't see that picture? How was she so sure?

She said Scott told her that Laci never saw it. How could she possibly believe a liar like Scott? Suddenly I'd had enough. It was time for Amber and her daughter to leave. I thanked her and we parted decently.

On February 22, Brent led the last of his three searches, this one around Lake Tulloch. Like the two others, it failed to turn up any new evidence or clues. On February 25, we were interviewed by CNN's Larry King, and our frustration and fatigue were apparent. We were wearing out.

"Each day, the longer we go on, it gets a little more tiring," Brent told Larry. Ron admitted that sometimes, despite his best effort, he thought about life without Laci. And I simply said, "Our lives have been changed forever. Every day is—it's just minute by minute. It's very difficult."

February ended, and I couldn't believe Laci had been gone for two months. It felt like an eternity. Each day was excruciating for its seeming lack of progress. When would the police have enough evidence to arrest Scott? Where was Laci? Why couldn't they find her?

At the beginning of March, Craig warned me that the case was about to be reclassified as a homicide rather than a missing person investigation, and we offered a $50,000 reward for any information as to her whereabouts. Given the implications and the resulting attention, he wanted us to have advance warning. The official announcement was made at a press conference on March 5. Ron, Brent, and I stood to the side of the stage, our heads bowed. Although the change was described as a formality, the next morning's paper trumpeted the new reality: "**LACI IS DEAD**, POLICE BELIEVE."

Even though I was prepared, the words jumped off the paper and into my chest and ripped my heart out.

LACI IS DEAD . . .

I immediately picked up the phone and dialed Scott's number. He didn't answer. After it beeped, I screamed, "ARE YOU HAPPY NOW? THE BIG BOLD LETTERS SAY '**LACI IS DEAD**.'"

As the days passed, I came to terms with what the police had done, and why, but being Laci's mother, until she was found, I publicly and privately clung to the slimmest chance that she was still out there someplace, alive. I told Ron all the time, trying to convince myself, and in fact I can still hear myself say, "Maybe, just maybe she'll come home."

Though no one said anything to the contrary in front of me, I know they were losing hope. But on March 13, there was a development that momentarily rekindled the dream. Elizabeth Smart was found. The Utah teenager had been missing since June 5, 2002.

I was leaving my sister's house when I heard the news on the car radio. I jumped out of the car, leaving it running in her driveway, and ran back in the house screaming, "Elizabeth Smart has been found. She's alive!"

When I got home, I called Craig at the station, thinking if she came home after ten months, there was hope for seeing Laci again. Craig picked up right away. I said, "You knew I would be calling, didn't you?

"Is there any possibility whatsoever that these people who had the Smart girl are connected to Laci?" I asked, listing some of the reasons I imagined there might be a link, namely that the Smart captors were nomadic and in San Diego around Christmas, and the woman carried a doll as if it were a baby. "I have to ask. I'm a mother."

It wasn't just a job for Craig and the others working the case. I could tell how much it pained him to say that they'd already checked and ruled out a connection. With that "no," I lost my last thread of hope, and I honestly think he did, too.

It wasn't just a job for anyone involved. One stormy day, we were meeting with Sergeant Cloward at the police station. Because of the bad weather, the search at the bay had been put on hold and one of the Tuolumne County Sheriff's divers was there, as were the couple supervising the side-scan sonar search. Sergeant Cloward introduced us, and the sonar couple showed me their boat with the scanning equipment in the parking lot and explained how it worked. I realized what a massive undertaking it was to try to find anything or anyone in that bay. I thanked the diver for going out on the bay almost every day to search for Laci.

When it was time to leave, Sergeant Cloward and I walked together to the parking lot, and he told me something I'll never forget. Solemnly, as if revealing a secret, he turned over his clipboard and showed me a picture of Laci that he'd attached to the underside.

"She's the reason I go out there every day," he said. "Every single one of us has this picture on our clipboards. We look at her every time we go out on the bay to search for her." Then, with tears in his eyes, he said, "We won't stop looking for Laci until she's found."

Chapter Twenty

One Saturday night in mid-March, Ron and I reached our lowest point since Laci's disappearance. Scott hadn't been arrested, we didn't know where Laci was, progress seemed slow, and we didn't know what else to do.

"You know Scott knows," I told Ron.

"I know," he said.

"I can't get anything from the police, either," I said. "They aren't going to tell me anything."

"They can't," Ron said for the hundredth time. "They can't tell us a thing because we're potential witnesses."

I could've clawed the walls, that's how anxious and restless I felt, but instead I sat down at the computer and checked the Web site. I read messages in the family section, and then, perhaps because I was desperate for something to happen, I checked the section for messages left by psychics. I didn't know what I'd find. I'm as skeptical as you can get. But for no apparent reason, a specific e-mail caught my attention.

The e-mail, titled "Did EVP Solve The Laci Peterson Case," was from a Northern California woman named Sandra who described driving home one day when she became curious about what happened to Laci. Apparently when she had such questions, she turned to spirits, asking them questions and getting answers in return. The answers were sometimes cryptic, sometimes garbled in code, but they made sense to her.

According to what the spirits told her, Scott had strangled Laci with a lamp cord. There'd been a brief struggle, but Laci didn't have a chance against him. Then he'd wrapped her in a tarp and loaded her in his truck. Scott took her to the marina and either tied her to or dumped her body near the fifth buoy off the Albany Bulb, a point north of the Berkeley pier. The divers hadn't looked there, and the spirits urged another underwater search, only deeper.

Reading this message turned my skin hot and my stomach into a giant knot. I printed out all twenty-five pages, reread them umpteen times, and then I e-mailed it to Craig. I said in my note to him that I knew he was going to think I'd lost my mind, but I wanted him to read it anyway as I thought it was full of excellent information and wanted his opinion.

I also knew that I had to go to the Berkeley Marina and check it out with my own eyes.

I wanted to go the next day, Sunday, March 16. When I got up in the morning, Ron had already left the house to go fishing. He didn't know it, but I'd wanted him to drive me to Berkeley. I'd always been independent, but I hadn't driven much since December 24, the trauma having shattered my confidence, and other than short jaunts around town I didn't feel capable of driving. I certainly didn't trust myself to get to Berkeley.

Then my sister Susie called and invited me to her house. She could tell I'd been crying and asked what was going on. I told her about the e-mail and wanting to go to Berkeley. The next thing I knew, she and her husband, Gil, picked me up and we were speeding up the freeway toward the bay.

As we pulled into the marina parking lot in Berkeley, we were determined to keep a low profile. I definitely didn't want to be recognized and end up in the news. I pulled up the hood on my coat and put on my sunglasses. However, Susie forgot to remove the "Missing" Laci button from her jacket, and a woman in the parking lot noticed it and asked if she was part of the search. Susie said no, she was merely concerned.

Once the woman had left, we looked at each other and started

Divorce is always an option, not murder.

McKenzie, Laci's dog, as a puppy.

Barbara Lee, Tammy DeGrasse, Lisa Braden, me, and Sandy Rickard, at the New Year's Eve vigil. *(Courtesy of Richard Costa)*

Chief Roy Wasden, Modesto PD. *(Corbis)*

Jim Brazelton, the then Stanislaus County District Attorney. *(Corbis)*

Doug Ridenour, the then public information officer of Modesto PD. *(AP/Wide World Photos)*

Lt. Mark Smith, prosecutors Rick Distaso and Birgit Fladager, Lt. Bill Grogan, prosecutor Dave Harris, Lt. Kevin Bertalotto, and Det. Craig Grogan. *(Courtesy of Lisa Harris and Meagan Distaso)*

Det. Al Brocchini. *(Courtesy of Mark Smith and Kevin Bertalotto)*

Det. John Buehler. *(Courtesy of Mark Smith and Kevin Bertalotto)*

Defense attorney
Mark Geragos.
(AP/Wide World Photos)

Jackie and Lee Peterson,
the parents of the
convicted murderer.
(AP/Wide World Photos)

Kim Tyler, Lori Ellsworth, Rene Tomlinson, Stacey Boyers, and Renee Garza—Laci's wonderful friends having Christmas with Laci, 2003. *(Courtesy of Rene Tomlinson)*

Stacey Boyers and Terri Western.

BACK: Harvey Kemple, Ron Grantski, Ricky Rickard;
MIDDLE: Lissa McElroy, Lin Pereira, Patty Amador, Gwen Kemple,
Sandy Rickard, me; FRONT: Marlisa Ferreira and Kim Petersen.

My sister, Susie,
and her husband,
Gil Aquino.

Me and Ron.

Attending the signing, by President G. W. Bush, of the Unborn Victims of Violence Act, aka Laci and Conner's Law. *(Courtesy of White House Photographer Paul Morse)*

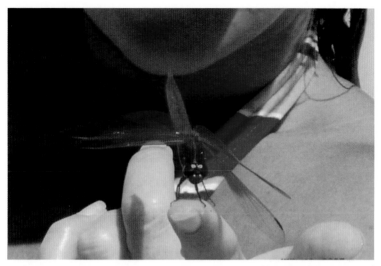

IN·LOVING MEMORY OF
LACI AND CONNER

laughing. I shook my head and said, "So much for being incognito. Way to go, Bucko." But I blamed myself. If I'd paid attention, I would have seen the button.

We walked along the path at the shore of the bay and followed it around Cesar Chavez Park. I had binoculars with me and we stopped every few yards so I could gaze out toward the bay, but it was so cold and so windy I was unable to hold the binoculars still. The water was an ugly, threatening gray-black, with white caps breaking on the surface. I didn't like the way it made me feel, and it was so windy I struggled to stand.

It wasn't just the wind I struggled against. The longer I was there and the more I looked, the more I knew in my soul that Laci was out there. I felt it so strongly. I'd like to say that I don't necessarily believe in that sixth sense, extrasensory stuff, but too much has happened in my life for me not to believe in it, at least to some degree. And this was a time when I definitely believed.

I stared out at the buoys and tried to find the fifth buoy the spirits had spoken of in the e-mail, but I had no idea which one of those bobbing things was the fifth. We stayed there a couple of hours, the three of us, just staring at the water, waiting for something to break the surface. It was such a desperate scene, but I was desperate. I needed to find Laci.

After I had my fill, we drove around to the marina and walked to the boat dock. I kept telling Susie and Gil that I knew Laci was there. I couldn't bring myself to leave. I stared out into the water some more from the dock. I kept expecting to see something that would lead us to her, if not Laci herself. Finally the bitter cold and fatigue got to me; we decided we'd looked enough.

I put $5 into the machine and bought a boat launch ticket, the same as Scott did on Christmas Eve. Mine read "Time: 2:44 P MAR 16 Expires: 11:59 P SUN MAR 16 03." I still have the ticket.

We left there and drove north to the Albany Bulb, the next point up from the Berkeley Marina. The psychic had written that if you stood at the tip and looked out, Laci was put into the water in the direction of 11 o'clock. We didn't walk to the tip because there were too many people and I didn't want to be recognized. So I looked through the binoculars, focusing intensely on a couple of buoys in that direction, while Susie and Gil scanned the surface up and down the shore.

We spent a long time staring at the water. As farfetched as it sounds, I really expected to see something, and when I didn't, I felt so helpless, so hopeless. It was getting late. I knew it was time to go, but I still didn't want to leave. I knew Laci was there.

I can't explain it, but I felt her, and in the moments before we left, I told God that I wanted to see something, some kind of sign, that would help me find her. I was ready to handle it, I thought. I stared out at that place where water and sky converged and I felt an umbilical tug between me and my daughter. She was there, I was certain. I had to force myself to walk away.

As we drove away, I felt guilty, like I was abandoning Laci. The psychic had relayed a sense of urgency, saying that storms and shifting tides were moving her body around and she needed to be recovered quickly. Knowing Laci was there gave me a very small sense of relief, as if I'd finally found her. I no longer thought of her as lost. From then on, I thought it was a matter of time before I got her back.

Months later, I learned two facts that explained why I was so compelled to go to Berkeley and why I felt Laci's presence there. First, around the time I had been at the marina, the side-scan sonar used by the officers searching the bay had detected what they thought was Laci's body. But the currents were too strong and they were unable to get to her then and she was gone when they returned. *The storms? The shifting tides?*

Also, during the trial, Dr. Ralph Cheng, a research hydrologist with the U.S. Geological Surveys, testified that, based on where Conner was found, he would've been put in the water at a specific location, which, when he calculated it, was almost exactly where the psychic had predicted.

I knew going to the marina had been emotional, but I didn't know the extent of it until a few days later when Ron and I sat down for dinner. I took one bite of food but couldn't swallow. Picturing the churning ocean and thinking about the details the psychic had written about the way Scott had murdered Laci, I had a sudden meltdown, then stood up in a rage. "I have to take care of Scott now!" I screamed. "I can't wait any longer."

Ron jumped up and grabbed me, making sure I didn't bolt out the door, where it seemed I was headed.

"I don't know if he'll ever be arrested," I continued. "He doesn't deserve to be free a minute longer. He murdered Laci!"

Eventually Ron calmed me down, but I had frightened myself that night. If Scott had been within my reach at that very moment I could've killed him. That was the one and only time I felt anger and rage so strong that I might've given in to it.

A week later, I caught up with some of Laci's girlfriends at Terri Western's house as they sent thank you notes to people who'd donated to the Laci Peterson Fund, and one of the girls said she'd heard that Scott had been kicked out of Del Rio Country Club. Shortly after that I heard the decision might have been mutual. Whatever the story, he had few supporters in town. Interestingly, Ron also heard from a couple friends who golfed at Del Rio that Scott had actually sold his membership.

In early April, Brent and Rose had their second child, a boy, and while I was with them at the hospital, Craig called with an update on Scott. He'd been staying with his sister Anne Bird in Berkeley. One day, in fact, Scott had called the Berkeley police to report some fresh graffiti and then told officers that the Modesto police were harassing him.

"Oh, Mr. Citizen," I said sarcastically. "Why on earth is he calling the Berkeley Police Department?" I wondered. "Does he want them to know he's there?"

"I have no idea," Craig said.

Scott's motives remained a mystery. I spent every day for months trying to make sense of it all, but there was no figuring him out.

On a beautiful springlike Monday, the biggest pieces of the puzzle emerged, answering the questions we'd feared. It was April 14, and Ron had left the house early to work on some problems at a shopping center he'd helped build in Los Banos, about fifty miles south of Modesto. By early afternoon he was finished, and on his way back he stopped at a favorite fishing spot at the San Luis Reservoir. He didn't even take his fishing pole out of his vehicle. He just sat on the bank, enjoying the quiet and sunshine. This was how he dealt with the sadness and stress, and at one point, he looked up at the clouds and started talking to God.

"God, I don't ask for much, but I know Laci's dead," he said. "I want you to give her back to us. Sharon has to be able to mourn. If she doesn't get Laci back, I don't think she'll ever get better. If you could help, I'd sure appreciate it."

A short time later, he got back in his truck and saw the message light flashing on his cell phone. It was his friend Frank, asking if he'd heard the news. Ron called him back immediately and asked, "Have I heard what?"

"They found a body washed up on the shore in the Bay Area," Frank said. "I think they found a baby yesterday."

Ron's eyes were blurred with tears as he looked up at the sky and said, "Thank you, God." Then he called me.

That morning I was under the weather. I had tossed and turned all night and I got out of bed with less energy than I had the night before. I had a premonition that the world was going to come crashing down. I turned off the phones, closed the drapes, and shut off the computer. I turned on the TV to A&E and got under a blanket, feeling I needed to shut out the world.

It was pretty much the first time since Laci's disappearance that I wanted to be alone. After about an hour, I heard footsteps on the front walk, followed by a knock at the door. I didn't answer it. The knocking continued. I heard voices outside but couldn't make out who they were or what they said, and I didn't want to know. I knew, whoever it was, I didn't want to hear what they had to say.

I couldn't explain it if I had to. I felt it in my bones the way I'd felt her presence in the bay. This was it. Whoever was outside was going to tell me about Laci.

It's ironic. For four months I'd wanted nothing more than to know where she was. Every breath I'd drawn since December 24 had been directed to finding her. I'd *needed* to know more than I'd ever needed anything in my life. But now that information was on my doorstep, literally, I didn't want to hear it. I wanted whoever was out there to go away. I already knew Laci wasn't coming back.

Finally the knocking stopped and I heard the footsteps recede.

Good, I thought, they didn't get me.

Then out of the corner of my eye I saw Kim Petersen and Sandy Rickard at the back door. That was it. I couldn't hide any longer. Without saying a word, they knew that I knew. Kim said that Craig had called me several times earlier, but no one answered. I admitted to turning off the phones. Sandy shook her head sadly.

"They found a body," Kim said.

I closed my eyes and I felt the warm tears fall down my face.

"It was on the shore at Point Isabel in Richmond," she said. "Just north of the Berkeley Marina."

That was the next point up from the Albany Bulb. The psychic had been pretty accurate. Kim went on to tell me that a baby boy had been found the day before about a mile north of Point Isabel.

"Chief Wasden is going to give you more details as soon as he has them," Kim said. "He's going to call."

"Is it Laci?" I asked.

"No identity has been made yet," Kim said. "I don't have any more information."

I remembered an awful conversation I'd nonetheless had a while ago with the chief. He'd explained that when Laci was found, they should be able to get an immediate identification by using dental records. I figured that was what they were waiting for, and it wouldn't be long before we heard. But I knew it was her—a mother knows.

Anticipating the barrage of media that would arrive once news broke, we went to Patty Amador's house and waited there for the chief's call. In the interim, I spoke to Ron, Brent, and Amy. Patty made sure the television was turned off so I didn't have to hear the nonstop media reports about the bodies.

When Chief Wasden called, I was in the upstairs bedroom and braced for the news. Instead, he said they weren't able to make any identification yet. I brought up our prior conversation about using dental records to make a speedy ID. The chief paused.

"Sharon, there was only a torso," he said.

I didn't understand.

"What does that mean?"

And then he told me her head was missing.

I wanted to throw up. Not once did I give any thought to what condition her body would be in when she was found. The new imagery made it unbearable. Did Scott do that to her? How much of a monster was he? My poor baby. A strange sound rose from my gut, more primal than a groan. "Nooooo," I cried. "No, no, no." I dropped the phone on the bed, leaned against the wall, and slid to the floor, bursting into tears as the world ended.

Later that afternoon the chief drove out to Patty's to tell us more. By this time, Ron had also arrived, and the whole bunch of us—Kim, Sandy, Patty—went back into the upstairs bedroom and connected Brent via speakerphone so everyone could hear at the same time. I was more composed now; I just wanted information.

According to the chief, they had to do DNA testing in order to identify the body, and that required a few more days. I said I knew it was Laci, and he didn't disagree. The chief also confirmed reports that a baby, an almost fully developed fetus, had been discovered the previous day on the shore in Richmond. Because it was in a different police jurisdiction, there was a delay in passing on news of the discovery, but after Laci was found, the Richmond authorities realized there might be a connection and notified the Modesto police. It wasn't long before Craig tried calling me, so I'd know before it reached the media.

From this point, it was all about process and procedure. DNA tests, autopsies, whatever they did. But we knew, everyone in the room knew Laci and Conner had been found. One detail from everything the chief told me stood out above all else. Conner had been found about a quarter-mile north of where Laci washed ashore, and from that, I realized that Laci had made sure her baby had gotten to shore. She had tried to protect him until the very end.

Chapter Twenty-one

We hadn't seen Scott Peterson for weeks. I felt like giving him a piece of my mind. The morning after we heard about Laci I called him. Nothing—so I left a message.

"Scott, this is Sharon. You need to call me immediately."

After three hours went by without hearing from him, I got ahold of his mother and asked if she'd heard from Scott and if she knew where he was.

"No, I don't," Jackie said. "And I'm really getting worried about him. He calls every night, and he didn't call last night."

I didn't care about that. By this time, after all the crap we'd gone through, I was barely civil. Her son had murdered my baby daughter and her baby son. I had a hard time controlling my anger as I gave her the news.

"They found two bodies—a female and a baby," I said.

"Well, Sharon, I'm ninety-five percent sure that isn't Laci," Jackie replied.

"Well, Jackie, I'm one hundred percent sure it is," I said.

"The coroner said that the body they found wasn't wearing maternity clothes," she said.

"Well, that's odd," I said. "You must've been listening to a different coroner than I listened to because he refused to answer those questions."

There was no use continuing our conversation. Jackie didn't tell me where Scott was. Even after bodies were discovered near where Scott said he went fishing, Jackie still refused to see the obvious, just as she'd refused to acknowledge his relationship with Amber was anything but a one-night stand.

On Friday the eighteenth, the chief called and said he would like to come by and talk to us. A short time later, about eleven thirty, he and Captain Savelli came over and told us that Scott had been arrested in Torrey Pines, a suburb north of San Diego. All of us exhaled, relieved. We'd waited months for this to happen and we got satisfaction from what it meant.

"Thank God," I said. "It's about time."

The chief filled us in on as many details as he could. Department of Justice officers had been watching Scott for a few days, but he'd recently slipped away from them, then turned up a couple days earlier in San Diego. He'd been in contact with his family, and from conversations that came out in court, I believe his mother was trying to help him plan an escape to Mexico before Laci's and Conner's bodies were identified.

Once authorities found him, they kept him under tight watch, fearing he was a flight risk. In anticipation of DNA results, detectives Grogan and Buehler went to San Diego. Early that morning, the DOJ agents tailing Scott reported that he was driving in an erratic manner on the freeway, and they worried he was a danger to other motorists, if not himself. Interestingly, he was driving an older-model Mercedes, which he'd purchased six days earlier, paying in cash and putting it in his mother's name, Jacqueline. When the seller questioned Scott about his name, he said it was "like a boy named Sue thing."

Around 11 a.m., Grogan gave the word to arrest him. Within minutes, Scott was stopped, cuffed, and put in the back of an unmarked police car. Grogan slid in next to him, and so began their ten-hour drive back to Modesto. It was the end of Scott's road and the start of a new one for those of us seeking justice for Laci.

The news was bittersweet. On the one hand, as I've said, I felt relieved by what the arrest meant, but at the same time I also felt the onset of a new set of worries and anxieties. We had to bring Laci and Conner back home, arrange a funeral, say good-bye, deal with the finality of months of searching, and then, of course, go through a trial, whatever that entailed.

The whole time the chief and the captain were at our house, they were on their cell phones, checking on the DNA test results, which they'd expected by then. They left around one, without hearing anything, but returned later that afternoon with confirmation that the remains were, as we knew, Laci and Conner. At that time, the living room was packed with family and friends. Chief Wasden gave me a hug, and all of us cried and hugged one another.

Laci and Conner were identified on Good Friday. As news spread, people left candles, stuffed animals, flowers, poems, and photos outside Laci and Scott's home, turning it into a shrine to sorrow.

Both the DNA test results and Scott's arrest dominated that night's local and national news, and I watched the coverage as if in a trance, as if I still hadn't come to grips that this was my life. Occasionally the news flashed on those leaving flowers, but mostly the reports focused on the progress police were making in bringing Scott back to Modesto, where he was going to be booked.

The local TV stations cut to a shot of dozens of people outside the downtown police station with signs reading BABY KILLER and MURDERER. I got tremendous satisfaction from seeing that. I could've easily gone down there and joined them. I thought about it, in fact, but I didn't want to be seen like that on television. I was curious, though. I wanted to see Scott's face close up. I wanted to know if he showed the tiniest bit of remorse.

"I don't have any remorse," he'd said to me on the phone. *"I didn't do anything."*

It was just after midnight when the gates to the parking lot at the downtown County Jail office opened to let in the car ferrying Scott. I was riveted as Craig got out of the car and then helped Scott, whose hands were cuffed behind him. Dressed for golf, he wore white shorts, a white knit shirt, and a blue sweater. I knew that clean-cut look well; the rest I didn't recognize. Scott's hair and a goatee he'd grown were dyed yellow-orange. Scott claimed that his hair turned that color after he swam in a friend's pool. The truth was that he'd had it done in a salon in San Diego.

When I first saw his dyed hair, I thought Scott was probably headed to Mexico and wanting to slip over the border unrecognized. A police search of his Mercedes turned up, among other things, almost $15,000 in cash, three credit cards (including one in his sister Anne Bird's name), outdoor survival gear, and numerous changes of clothes. Anyway, Craig and Scott stood quietly beside the car as if Scott was taking a last bit of fresh air and bidding good-bye to life without walls and bars. Indeed, once inside, Scott began his new life as a criminal, albeit he was, at this point, still only accused of murder, but the change had to have been traumatic. In a small room, he was read his rights, fingerprinted, and photographed. Some of that was shown on TV, the cameras looking through the windows, and I couldn't take my eyes off the screen for one second. I didn't know whether to rejoice or feel repulsed. I was just glad they got him.

Thank God, I said to myself, just as I had to the chief when he told us of the arrest. *It's about time.*

I watched the scene replayed on TV throughout the night. I saw it dozens of times. Each time, I got angrier at Scott, until finally everything boiled into a single emotion: **HE WAS GOING TO PAY.**

I have no idea how Scott spent his first 48 hours in jail, but over the weekend his mug shot was all over the news. His arraignment was Monday morning. Family and friends wanting to attend the proceeding were told to be at the courthouse one hour before it was scheduled to begin.

On Monday morning, April 21, Deputy District Attorneys Rick Distaso and Dave Harris, the two lead prosecutors, briefed Ron, Brent, Amy, Dennis, and me about the proceeding. We entered the courtroom and took seats in the front. I sat on the end so I could be closest to Scott when he walked in.

Others from our family had arrived early to be assured a seat in the courtroom. They were told to wait in the hallway and someone would seat them. While they waited, they saw members of the media filing into the courtroom, and when they finally approached the bailiff he said there wasn't room for them. That wasn't right. After they asked if four media people could be removed so they, Laci's family, could attend the arraignment, the bailiff immediately seated them in the empty jury box. But this issue of not enough seating for family and friends of the victim recurred throughout the trial, and I didn't think it was fair. In my opinion, family and friends of the victim should be seated first, then the media and public.

Moments before court started, Scott's mother swooped in on me from behind, gave me a hug, which I returned, and then whispered in my ear, "I'm sorry about Laci."

Why was she saying that now? I've always believed it was for the benefit of the media seated nearby. Scott wore a prison jumpsuit and his arms were shackled. He'd shaved his goatee. To me, he looked remote and scared. It was the one time throughout the entire proceeding I saw fear on his face.

And the sight of him like that shocked me. I was overwhelmed with emotion and against my expectations, I cried. Scott had murdered Laci. She was gone and never coming back. Scott had murdered his baby. I couldn't come to grips with the heartbreaking reality sitting right in front of me.

I also had a hard time grasping that all of this was real as the Stanislaus County Superior Court judge read the charges against him—two counts of first-degree murder, one for Laci and one for Conner. It seemed surreal, unreal. But then, the sound of Scott's voice snapped me back to the present.

"I am not guilty," he said.

In the hushed courtroom, the judge explained that because the murders were premeditated, Scott was not eligible for bail. According to the law, he could also face the death penalty.

I have no remorse.

What a waste of lives, I thought. What a horrible waste of lives.

After the hearing finished, we held a press conference at the police station. Dennis and Rene Tomlinson thanked everyone for caring so deeply, and Ron, fighting back tears, talked about moving to the next phase.

"We started this nightmare with one purpose in mind—to find Laci and bring her home," Ron said. "While this is not the way we wanted to bring her home, it will help us to begin the long process of healing."

I didn't want to cry again in front of TV cameras, but I felt obliged to speak to everybody who'd put Laci in their thoughts. So many people had shared the experience with us, and I felt the connection. To me, it was like talking to an extended family, and so I started with thank-yous to everyone from our webmaster to the Red Lion Hotel to the Modesto Police Department and their families.

"If Laci were here now, she would be absolutely amazed at the outpouring of love and concern for her and Conner," I said in an unsteady voice. "I know, in my heart, that she is fully aware of the love we have for her."

I paused. I knew this part about Laci was going to be the hardest, and it was. My composure disintegrated and every word became a struggle. I hadn't wanted to cry, but I couldn't help it and let myself go.

"On December 24, 2002, shortly after five fifteen p.m., I received a phone call and heard the devastating words that would forever change my life: Laci's missing. I knew in my heart that something terrible had happened to my daughter and my grandson. My world collapsed around me. Since receiving that phone call, we have been living a terrible nightmare.

"The search for Laci began that night. The questions were always there: What has happened to Laci? Where is she? Is she safe? Who took her from me? I made a plea to the person or persons who took her to please, please let her go and send her home to us. We heard nothing.

"As the days passed, I made more pleas to take her to a hospital or fire or police station, or tell us where she is so we could come to her and bring her and her baby home safely. Still, we heard nothing. We searched and searched and searched but still no Laci."

At this point, Ron was standing behind me and literally holding me up because I felt my legs going. But I'd worked hard on this statement, staying up till three in the morning for the past three days honing my thoughts and getting what I wanted to say just right, and I was determined to finish no matter what.

"I love my daughter so much. I miss her every minute of every day. My heart aches for her and Conner. Without them, there is a huge void in my life. I literally get sick to my stomach when I allow myself to think about what may have happened to them. No parent should ever have to think about the way their child was murdered. In my mind, I keep hearing Laci say to me, 'Mom, please find me and Conner, and bring us home. I'm scared. Please, don't leave us out here all alone. I want to come home. Please don't stop looking for us.'"

Here, I had trouble again. I looked out and saw Laci's friends and some of my friends in the front row, sobbing. I took a deep breath and continued.

"I feel that Laci and Conner could no longer wait to be found. So last week they came to us.

"Laci and Conner left us on Christmas Eve. I know that God has been watching over them. He sent them back to us on Good Friday. Now we can bring them home where they belong.

"Laci and her unborn child did not deserve to die. They certainly did not deserve to be dumped in the bay and sent to a watery grave as though their lives were meaningless. Laci meant the world to me. She was my only daughter. She was my best friend. We miss her beautiful smile, her laughter, her kind and loving ways. I miss seeing her, talking to her, and hugging her. We have been deprived of meeting and knowing Laci's son, our grandson and nephew. We will miss them and mourn them for the rest of our lives.

"Soon after Laci went missing, I made a promise to her, that if she had been harmed, we will seek justice for her and Conner and make sure that the person responsible for their deaths will be punished.

"I can only hope that the sound of Laci's voice begging for her life, begging for the life of her unborn child, is heard over and over and over again in the mind of that person every day for the rest of his life. The person responsible should be held accountable and punished for the tragedy and devastation forced upon so many."

Afterward, several of the detectives, Chief Wasden, and District Attorney Jim Brazelton accompanied us to the parking lot. We talked for a while about the transition from one stage of this tragedy to the next. Al Brocchini, in particular, let me know that my statement had moved him and he gave me a hug.

"I want you to know that my wife actually pushed me out of bed in the mornings if I didn't feel like getting up and said, 'Go find Laci,'" Brocchini said. "She wanted me to find her as much as I did, as much as all of us did."

When Brocchini left, several of his colleagues told me that Brocchini never hugged people or showed emotion in that way. But when I looked around, all of them were emotional. I don't know if Laci was an exception, but many of the people involved took this case personally. I could see it wasn't a job. It was about finding Laci, and now that they'd found her, it was about justice.

Just what justice entailed was yet to be decided, but the arraignment was step one on the long, difficult, slow, and emotionally draining road to a trial. On April 25, Ron, Brent, Amy, Dennis, Kim Petersen, and I met with Dave Harris and Craig Grogan and discussed calendaring hearings and various issues requiring our opinions, most important whether or not the district attorney would seek the death penalty.

The first time it was brought up, I let out a large sigh. Again, as I had so often in the past, most recently when I saw Scott at the arraignment, I thought of the waste, the tragic waste of lives. I asked myself, *How could it have possibly happened that my daughter was murdered and I was listening to a D.A. and a detective talk about my son-in-law receiving the death penalty?* I've said it over and over, but I didn't get it. It couldn't be my life—our lives. Yet there we were, the family, listening to Dave Harris and Craig Grogan tell us that if Scott was found guilty and sentenced to life in prison, he'd be led from the courtroom and locked up for the remainder of his days. And if he got the death penalty, he'd get an automatic appeal. When I heard that, I thought, My God, we haven't even approached the first trial and I'm already hearing about a possible second one. Would this hell ever end?

As for the death penalty itself, we'd talked about the issue as a family, though that was the first time we'd discussed it with outsiders. But the decision wasn't up to us, which was fine. That enormous burden was up to the district attorney, Jim Brazelton. If he felt the death penalty was justified, we weren't going to protest. And Brazelton seemed to have made up his mind, because later that day he told Larry King that "this was the kind of case that cried out for the death penalty."

Personally, all I wanted to hear was guilty. After that, I didn't care what happened next.

Either way, Scott Peterson's life was over.

Chapter Twenty-two

After Laci and Conner were found, I felt like Laci needed me more than ever and I wanted to be with both of them. But I was reminded of the grim realities of their condition, as well as the forensics that needed to take place, and so, as tough as it was to ignore the powerful maternal urges to go to Laci and her baby, I focused instead on planning a memorial.

I set it for May 4—what would've been Laci's twenty-eighth birthday. I made only one declaration: I wanted a celebration; this wasn't to be a funeral. I drew on everyone in Laci's and my circle of love for ideas and help. Laci's girlfriends insisted we play Van Morrison's "Brown Eyed Girl," a song Laci belted out every time she heard it, and they provided several funny imitations as proof. Police chaplain Donna Arno also arranged for use of the First Baptist Church, Modesto's largest, with 3,000 seats.

There were no formal invitations, but I sent an e-mail to Jackie and Lee to let them know when the memorial would be held. They chose not to attend.

To make the point that this wasn't a funeral, the program was titled "Celebrating the Life of Laci Rocha Peterson." I wore a white suit, and even the three limousines, which were so generously donated for our use and escorted by the police, were white. I told Brent that I was having a hard time comprehending this was all for Laci.

"I can hear her now," I said. "She'd be looking around saying, 'Nah-ah.'"

Brent said exactly that when he spoke at the crowded church: Laci wouldn't have believed it. Every seat in the church was filled, and at least another thousand people watched outside on monitors. I felt confident that Laci would've appreciated the service. Brent talked about a time after her grandmother's funeral in 1999 when she said, "When I die, I don't want people to be sad. I want them to be happy." Given the circumstances, that hers was a life cut tragically short, it was impossible for any of us to be happy. But the service combined music (Josh Groban's "To Where You Are" and Bette Midler's "Wind Beneath My Wings") with prayers, remembrances from friends and family, and a video of Laci's life from babyhood to the present that had everyone smiling and crying at the same time. For the closing, Laci's friends had chosen the song "Brown Eyed Girl" and everyone in the church, including the massive choir, stood, clapped their hands, and sang with a spirit to Laci. *Nah-ah, Mom.*

The memorial service captured her spirit. I was overwhelmed. I had no idea it would be so absolutely beautiful. People came back to the house afterward and spent a few more hours talking about the service (like me, everyone had been impacted by the choir's massive sound) and reminiscing about Laci's life. We weren't happy, as Laci had wanted, but we tried desperately not to be sad.

The next week was Mother's Day, and it was miserable. The previous Mother's Day, Laci had entertained me, my mother, Ron's mother, and Jackie at her house and talked excitedly about wanting to get pregnant and starting a family, so hopeful for the future, and all of us had assured her that we knew she'd get pregnant soon. I thought back to that and how this year's Mother's Day should have been a party like no other as Laci would've been celebrating her first as a mom. The sadness was too much for me, and at some point I laid down on the floor in my bedroom, then spent most of the morning there. I finally pulled myself together because Brent and Rose and my grandchildren were coming to visit.

That night, I noted on my calendar, "It was an ugly, ugly day." And it was.

On May 1, following days of speculation in the press, Scott's family hired defense attorney Mark Geragos to replace the court-appointed attorney that Scott had requested at his arraignment. Geragos, based in Los Angeles, had represented Susan McDougal in the Whitewater case and actress Winona Ryder on shoplifting charges, a case he'd lost. I was shocked when I heard about Geragos. Two days before Scott's arrest, Geragos had been on Greta's show and declared that, given the affair with Amber and that the bodies were found where Scott had gone fishing, it would be hard to find a prosecutor who couldn't get a conviction.

Once hired, Geragos spun a different story, promising to clear Scott, who, he said, was innocent and desperately wanted to find Laci's real killer. He filed a flurry of motions, including one to allow Scott to attend court unshackled and in his own clothes rather than the orange prison jumpsuit. At a May 5 hearing, he criticized the police investigation, describing it as "voodoolike."

Aside from just rubbing me the wrong way, he also got involved in my battle to go inside Laci's house and get some of her things. Though I didn't go into the house itself, I regularly watered the outside, ensuring Laci's gardens stayed green and in bloom. One day, while on my way to the house, I called the alarm company to see if the alarm was still activated because Laci and Scott had given me the code and a key to the house when the alarm was first installed. I was concerned about security to the house, which had strangers driving by all the time.

The girl answering the phone at the alarm company recognized my name and gave me a familiar, "Hi, how are you doing?" We'd spoken on previous occasions as my name had always been listed as the person to contact if Laci and Scott were unavailable, which had happened. The girl said the alarm was on, but added that Jackie had recently changed the code and given instructions that she be the only one authorized to use it.

This was news to me, but I realized that Scott, following his arrest, had given power of attorney to his parents. After all, it was Laci's house, too. The death certificate hadn't been recorded and Scott was in jail charged with her murder and the murder of their son. Jackie proved as evasive and uncooperative as Scott when it came to letting me in the house to pick up some of Laci's things. She either ignored my requests or found a reason that it was inconvenient for her to meet me. I called and sent e-mails, like this one from May 1:

```
Hi Jackie and Lee. I called you this morning and
left a message on what I hope is your recorder. If
you didn't receive the message, will you please call
me today after 4:00 pm. I will be out most of the
day. I would really like to talk to you. Thank you,
Sharon.
```

When Jackie finally responded, she said that she didn't know why I wanted to go into the house since there was nothing left of Laci there—those were her exact words, nothing left of Laci. She said the police had taken everything. *Everything?* I didn't believe that. Why would the police have taken all of her things, including her clothes? It didn't make sense, and I would've heard about it, too.

I pressed Jackie further, but she told me the same story two more times before I discovered it wasn't true. I assume that in case I was thinking of forcing my way in, Jackie also said they'd changed the locks on the door. (That proved to be untrue, too.)

I handed the matter to our family attorney, Adam Stewart, who contacted Geragos on May 14. Geragos, in turn, asked for a list of items I wanted. The list, which I submitted the next day, included furniture and Tiffany lamps given to Laci by her grandmother; her clothing, jewelry, and china; a picture Laci had painted; Conner's baby clothes; Laci's rocking chair, wedding dress, and diplomas; and watering cans that said "Laci's garden."

Through Geragos, Jackie said she felt that I wanted too many household items, and then on May 25 I got a response from Jackie herself to my nearly month-old e-mail.

"I just got my e-mail back," she wrote. "I just read your note of May 1. I called you last night and left a message. I am sorry that everything is taking so long, but we will get through this. Scott will be happy to share Laci's personal things with you—*weren't they supposed to be gone?*—although this is not the time. Scott feels the same loss you do and knows how painful this is for both of you and all of us. We think of you and your family every day and pray for you often. Take care of each other. Love, Jackie."

On May 27, I was told that Geragos was meeting with some of the prosecutors that afternoon and he was going to ask if they were finished with the house. If they were, according to the message I got, I'd be able to gather Laci's things. The prosecutors had previously told me they were finished, but I guess Mr. Geragos or the Petersons needed to hear it directly from the prosecutors, not me.

Once again I had friends poised at my house to help me move Laci's things. When my attorney hadn't heard from Geragos by four, I called Dave Harris, who'd been at the meeting, and he said that Geragos never even brought it up. That was at least the third time I'd been told I could go into the house and didn't receive a phone call to tell me they'd changed their minds.

After more back and forth with Geragos, our attorney Adam Stewart told me the Petersons had placed some of the belongings I'd requested in front of the house and left additional items with Modesto defense attorney Kirk McAllister, Scott's first lawyer, who was helping Geragos.

I was told they'd packed a box with two Tiffany-style lamps, three unopened Christmas gifts—two for my grandson and one intended for my mother—and a salt and pepper shaker set for me. I was further insulted at having to pick up Laci's belongings at Scott's attorney's office.

The instructions I received specified that only Amy could pick up the Tiffany-style lamps, not me. The Petersons left some plants in the front yard for me to pick up. But when Ron and I drove by the house early that night on our way downtown to guest on Greta's show, we didn't see anything in front of the house. We looked carefully. The yard wasn't that big. Nothing was there.

We revealed some of our frustration to Greta on air, but kept the vitriol to a minimum, saying merely that we didn't really understand why the Petersons were being so difficult when what we wanted was so simple—our daughter's things. On the way home, we stopped at Laci's again. Someone had been there in the interim, because this time we found a handful of potted plants and topiaries—most of them dead—sitting out front. I left them.

After all, I'd given Jackie and Geragos a list of the belongings I wanted. And per Jackie's request, I'd even revised the list. I couldn't have been any more clear as to what of Laci's things I wanted for purely sentimental reasons.

The next day I went by the house to water the plants, and when I got there I noticed that the gates had been padlocked. Jackie knew that I'd been taking care of Laci's potted plants, so I had no choice but to assume the locks were another message from the Petersons on the chance I had any ideas about going inside the house on my own, which, at that point, I didn't.

I also saw an SUV parked in the driveway and two men exiting the courtyard. They were getting into the SUV as I approached the house. At first, I wasn't going to stop, but I decided I had as much right as the Petersons did to be there. One of the men confronted me as soon as I got onto the walkway.

I'd never seen him before, but he seemed to know me and asked if I wanted to know why they were there.

"No. Who are you?" I asked.

He said his name was Matt Dalton, with the defense team.

I told him that it was obvious to me the Petersons were attempting to lock me out of my daughter's home (as I nodded toward the gate with the padlock) and I felt that I had as much right to be there as they did. He said he understood. I disagreed, emphasizing that I didn't think he or any of them understood.

That same night, Jackie went on Greta and acted unaware that I wanted to go into Laci's house to get her belongings. "Greta, I'm just really surprised at this," she said, knowing, of course, that she and I had exchanged phone calls and e-mails and she'd even received a letter from my attorney discussing all of this. I couldn't believe what I heard.

"Can she go in the house?" Greta asked. "I mean, because that's what she—"

"Of course," Jackie said. "I will serve her tea."

Tea? I didn't want tea!

On Wednesday afternoon, I received a phone call from Alex Loya, the senior advocate for Victim Services with the DA's office, saying that Geragos was going to work it out with our attorney, Adam Stewart, so I could get into the house the following Tuesday. He added that Geragos and his partner would be there to videotape me while I was in the house. Even though I'd asked for privacy to be alone in my daughter's house one more time, it didn't matter. I told Alex that I wouldn't be available on Tuesday because we'd already scheduled an interview with Katie Couric. Why should I believe that I would really be allowed in the house on Tuesday? They had already reneged at least three times. I'd been polite, respectful, and gone by the rules.

Then I called my attorney, who said he hadn't heard anything from Geragos about this so-called Tuesday meeting. I told Adam I wanted to go into the house tomorrow (Thursday) or Friday. I wasn't available the following Tuesday. He called Geragos and left a message per my conversation with Alex, requesting the alarm code so I could go in Thursday or Friday.

Adam and I spoke several times on Thursday, but Geragos had never returned any of Adam's calls. Thursday night, I called Adam and asked, "Am I going in with or without the alarm code?"

He said Geragos never returned his calls.

As far as I was concerned, that was it. I'd reached the end of my rope. I didn't believe the Petersons were ever letting me into the house. No matter what they said, they hadn't given me a single reason to trust them. So at that point, I made what I called an executive decision. With or without the alarm code, I was going inside that house and taking some of Laci's things.

I arranged for family and friends to meet at my house early the next morning. Everyone showed up at the appointed time. I gave each person—there were fifteen of us—a list with items by location in the house and each person was responsible for getting only the items highlighted on his or her list. We caravanned to Laci's in five trucks and then gathered in the backyard for last-minute instructions. I got everyone's attention and held up a photo of Laci.

"This is who we're doing this for," I said.

Then I held up a photo of Scott and Amber from the *National Enquirer.*

"This is why we're doing it," I said.

Everyone nodded. All of us were of the same mind.

I phoned the alarm company and got ahold of the girl I normally spoke to. I warned her the alarm was going to go off momentarily, but not to worry because it would just be me.

"I'm going to have to call Jackie Peterson," she said.

"That's fine," I replied. "Tell her it's me."

Then I looked at everyone and said, "Get ready, because when this alarm goes off, it's going to be loud." I took out my old house key, stuck it in the lock, and it worked! Clearly the locks hadn't been changed, as Jackie had claimed, but the alarm did go off, and sure enough it was loud. All of us ran around looking for the alarm box so the wires could be disconnected to shut off the alarm. After locating and disconnecting the wires, everyone fanned out, lists in hand. We found Laci's wedding dress, boxed up her china, and put everything else on the list in boxes, then loaded them in the trucks. Lori Ellsworth was limited physically from recent surgery, so she alerted the neighbors to what was going on at Laci's. I learned later that Lori, who has a great sense of humor, had also brought several boxes of doughnuts to give to the police if they arrived.

By the time police arrived we were almost finished loading the last boxes into the trucks. Someone stepped forward and explained that we'd taken only things belonging to Laci and we'd documented everything we took with videotape. They termed the situation a civil dispute rather than a burglary and let us go. The press showed up just as we were pulling out, too. As a photographer snapped pictures, I hid beneath a box in the backseat of a truck, and so they didn't know I was involved. The next day a picture of Patty (actually her butt) was in the papers with a caption stating Laci's family was breaking into her home. That was incorrect. We were leaving and Patty was applying a new padlock in place of the old one.

Maybe an hour later, by which time we'd unloaded everything in the garage, a captain, a sergeant, and a detective arrived at our house. They wandered around, asking questions, and eventually said they had to take everything to the station.

"Why?" my friend Patty asked, almost in tears. "None of this stuff is Scott's." She opened up Laci's cedar chest and pointed to the cheerleader outfits. "Scott isn't going to wear this. He's not going to wear her wedding dress."

I finally had almost everything I wanted; seeing them take it away would have been too much to handle. The officers didn't want to take it away, either. They understood. I got Adam on the phone, and he and the captain quickly worked out a compromise, allowing me to keep everything after the officers inventoried it.

The press, of course, had a field day. We watched the news at noon and saw defense attorney Matt Dalton thundering to the media about the burglary. A few days later, Dalton insinuated we'd taken a pair of shoes that were key pieces of evidence. We didn't have them and if the shoes were evidence, investigators would've taken them long ago. (In fact, Dalton was fired in August and Geragos later apologized to me for his behavior.)

In the end, I kept Laci's things and have them stored in her old bedroom. Authorities dropped the issue after determining that no crime had been committed. Only Jackie didn't let it rest. She called a few days later to complain. She was arguing about who paid for a crib and the cost of a plate. I was trying to hang onto things that would allow me to continue to feel Laci. I wanted to smell her again. I wanted to keep her near me. To me, these things were priceless.

On May 19, Kim Petersen and I flew to Washington, D.C.—she for National Missing Children's Day and I to lend support to the Unborn Victims of Violence Bill, which was coming up for a vote in both

Houses. The law, if passed, would make murdering a child in the womb while committing a violent act against the mother a separate offense. I obviously felt strongly about it, but I shuddered at the thought of myself as a lobbyist, walking the halls of the Capitol. Who was I to be speaking to the nation's leaders?

Sadly, I was painfully aware of the reason I was on the flight. My pregnant daughter had been murdered, and I thought that my presence could help other parents like me. Scott had been charged with a double homicide because California already had a law like the Unborn Victims of Violence Bill. When I heard that Pennsylvania Republican Melissa Hart wanted to make it a federal law, I wrote her a letter saying I'd be available to help get it passed.

Once in Washington, I was led from one congressional office to another, where I told Laci's story. Some lawmakers already referred to the legislation as "The Laci and Conner Bill." Whenever I heard that, I felt as if Laci was there giving me the strength to do whatever was necessary to help other families caught up in tragedies like ours.

The meetings were my one chance to influence the lawmakers. But by their voting for the bill, they had a chance to help so many other people, too. So they wouldn't forget, I left each one with a poem that had been sent to me:

LACI'S BABY

It had a beating heart,
two arms and legs,
a beautiful face,
a perfectly formed body
and a personality yet unseen.
It was Laci's baby.

It had a loving Mother
a warm place,
a promising future.
With the wonder of nature,
a giggle, a cry

a hope to go to kindergarten.
It was Laci's baby.

It had a plan, a life,
a million things to see and do.
It had a strong kick,
and dimples like Mom.
It was Laci's baby.

It had a family,
it had a home,
it had lots of gifts waiting,
that will now go unopened
and are stained with tears.
It was Laci's baby.

It had a connection,
It had Laci,
It had a name,
It was Conner.
It was Laci's baby.

Two lives together,
two people linked forever,
two angels who took their last breath in unison,
torn from their happiness,
taken too soon,
now together forever.

It was Laci's baby.
It was Conner's mother.
It was two tragedies,
not just one.
Not just one, not just one.
After all,
He was Laci's baby.

The whirlwind trip also included a thousand-person dinner attended by President Bush as well as a National Missing & Exploited Children breakfast for law enforcement officers across the nation who'd worked to rescue or recover missing children. Before I knew it, Kim and I were on a plane back to Oakland.

Prior to driving back home, we stopped for lunch, and while in the restaurant, I told Kim that I wanted to visit the site where Laci had been discovered. I'd wanted to go other times but feared the media might be there. This seemed like an opportunity to do it in private. Kim phoned Craig, who put us in touch with Det. Phil Owen, who happened to be working at the time near the site with divers. Phil was receptive and said to meet at Treasure Island, a Coast Guard base on the far side of the Bay Bridge.

There, we climbed aboard a Coast Guard boat and I wrapped myself in an orange jacket and cap—protection from cold, wind, and any chance encounters with reporters or photographers with long-range lenses. As we cruised into the part of the bay where the divers were searching, I stared at the water and imagined what had happened out there on December 24, 2002.

A short time later, Phil pointed at a spot on the shoreline and explained it was where Laci had been found. Tears were flowing down my cheeks. I'd long ago abandoned any inhibitions about showing emotions, and I cried when I needed to. He also pointed to the place where Conner had been found, just north from Laci's spot. I couldn't help but think of their final journeys, Laci making sure Conner got to shore before she did, and it just broke my heart that I couldn't have helped them.

But Scott had made sure she couldn't be helped, rescued, or easily found. As I looked around, I saw that the water was saturated with boats carrying divers who were still searching the floor of the bay for more evidence. I was told that the water in that area was only two or three feet, and churning with strong, dangerous currents. There was also about two feet of silt that made it so divers couldn't see more than a couple of inches in front of them. They had to literally feel their way through the dark for pieces of evidence.

The excursion wiped me out physically and emotionally, but I stuck around after we got back to meet a group of divers who'd worked the case for months. These were my heroes. Despite the rigors of dangerous currents, icy water, and long days that began at 5:30 a.m., each one said that they wanted to be there. I was moved by their dedication. I thanked each person individually, told them I appreciated it more than I could express, and said Laci also thanked them for working so hard. Somehow, I thought she knew.

One day, Stacey called, excited. She said that she'd been in her boyfriend's pool, floating on a raft like the one she'd given Laci for her birthday the year before, when two dragonflies began circling her. One seemed to take a special interest in her.

"It was dive-bombing me," she said. "Like *pay attention to me*! So I held up my finger and the dragonfly landed on it. And you know what I thought?"

"Laci," both of us said at the same time.

"Right. I just started talking to her," Stacey said. "It was funny. If I didn't pay attention, the dragonfly would dive-bomb again. Until I held my finger back up."

"That's Laci," I said.

Others felt her presence, too. Maybe it wasn't as personal as Stacey's experience, but it was no less profound. Our Web site posted evidence daily. Take this e-mail from a soldier in Iraq that I found one day:

```
Dear Friends and Family of Laci Peterson,

I have been in Iraq since January and am currently in
a place called Al Hilla, which is located in south
central Iraq. It takes some time for us to get mail
and magazines out here but today I read an article in
the June 2 issue of People. I don't know what made me
want to write and tell you all how sorry I am for the
loss of such a vibrant young person and her child.
Maybe going through this war has made me realize how
precious life really is and how I have sometimes
```

taken the people who are closest to me for granted.
Reading about your daughter helped me realize that I
need to make sure that the people who I love and
cherish know that. Although there are no words that
can express the grief you all have felt over the past
few months, please know that even in a place as
distant and harsh as Iraq, there is a sailor praying
that both Laci and Conner find peace and that you find
peace in your own lives the way she would have wanted
you to. Again please accept my deepest condolences
for your loss.

HMC (FMF) Matthew Lubold

Despite serving in Iraq, he thought about Laci and about us. He is one of the thousands of people who gave us strength.

On June 3, *Today* show host Katie Couric came to Modesto to interview Ron and me and other family members. She wanted to do a special about Laci. It turned out to be our last interview before a gag order was placed on everyone connected to the trial.

We spoke with Katie at a friend's house. It was an unusually hot day for the time of year. We were in our sixth month—it was, we told Katie, hard to believe we'd gone from planning a baby shower to waiting for the start of a murder trial. As she questioned us about Scott's arraignment and the press conference that followed it, I noticed that one of the cameramen kept wiping his brow.

After that segment, Katie talked with her producers while I went into the kitchen for some water and Ron walked around the backyard. The cameraman I'd noticed joined me in the kitchen. As he took some water, I commiserated with him about the heat, mentioning that I'd noticed him working so hard and that he'd probably had to put up with all types of conditions.

But he said it was us, not the temperature. He'd been crying. He said he'd shot the April 21 press conference at the police station, the one after Scott's arraignment, and said that in his many years of covering stories he'd never seen as many professionals crying openly the way they had that afternoon. After he left the room, the second of the two cameramen came in and told me that his sister and her one-year-old son had been murdered by her husband. But they were more fortunate, he told me, because her husband had killed himself.

"So we didn't have to go through a trial," he said.

I noticed his eyes were filled with tears.

"How long has it been?" I asked.

"Twenty-five years," he said.

I thought, Oh man, is this what I have to look forward to? Will it be this painful for the rest of my life?

"After my sister was killed, someone told me that whenever you see the numbers 11-11, it means there's an angel in the room," he said. "I'm telling you this because when I started to roll the camera, I looked at the clock and it said 11:11." He paused. "I wanted you to know that Laci was there with us."

Chapter Twenty-three

I don't know how I did it, but I showed up at almost every hearing, even though I had to listen to the defense going on and on at different hearings about Scott's innocence. Laci needed to be represented, and Scott needed to be reminded of what he'd done.

Geragos was intolerable at times. Unlike the prosecution, which was bound by the facts, he seemed able to say whatever he wanted. As I learned over time, that's the difference between the prosecution and the defense. Geragos didn't need hard and checked facts to make a point; he could pretty much say anything he thought might raise doubt. In June, for instance, he claimed a satanic cult was responsible for Laci's murder. The next month Geragos told the judge that he wanted the preliminary trial closed to media because he was going to present evidence that would clear Scott and he didn't want to tip off Laci's *real killers.* I wanted to stand up and ask Stanislaus County Superior Court Judge Al Girolami why he allowed this in his courtroom. For me, the worst was when Geragos petitioned to have defense experts do their own examination of Laci and Conner. That was like letting Scott have one more go at them, and it sickened me. What more did they have to do? What more were they going to put her through?

By August, though, it appeared that enough progress was being made that I could finally plan a funeral. On the eighth, Judge Girolami gave the defense a date and time limit for their examinations. On August 11, Geragos had his forensic experts conduct their tests, and within days graphic details from the autopsies leaked into the press. So much for the gag order. We didn't want to hear or know any of that stuff; they added more scars to our memories of Laci. It was impossible to avoid those reports and then impossible to forget them. As the prosecutors explained to the court, we didn't want those to be the last images we had of our daughter and grandson.

At least with the tests finished, we knew that Laci and Conner would be coming home soon. I'd never arranged a funeral before. Truthfully, I'd never thought about it. My mother had taken care of my father's funeral. And, of course, I never imagined burying one of my children. No parent thinks about a child's death, especially from murder. Just the idea is an affront to the gift of life and the promise of the future. I should've been choosing baby clothes with Laci, not picking her casket and arranging her burial.

Ron didn't think he could handle the funeral home, so I took my mother, sister, and Alex Loya for support. Until then, I'd tried to shield my mother from as much as possible as she'd recently battled some health problems. But this was different; I wanted her with me at the funeral home. I didn't need her help as much as I just needed my mom—the comfort of knowing I could cry in her arms or ask for a hug.

We sat in an office with a woman named Ronnie and looked through several albums of floral arrangements. Then she showed us into another area where pictures of caskets hung on a wall. I studied them without knowing what I was supposed to be looking for. As Ronnie described the pillows featured in several of the caskets, I thought, Laci doesn't need a *pillow*. I didn't like anything. In reality, I simply didn't like being there. Once I realized I didn't like being there, I was able to get through it. In the end, I chose a beautiful white casket with gold trim.

I gave Ron a full account when I got home. He thanked me for being strong enough to do it on my own.

Finally I arranged for Father Joseph Illo of St. Joseph's Catholic Church of Modesto to lead the service. We couldn't set a date because we didn't know when Laci and Conner would be home. We had already been given a date for their return but that was changed when the defense didn't finish their examinations.

Finally, we got word that Laci and Conner were ready to make the trip home. On August 21, amid much secrecy and pleas to the media to respect our privacy, Laci and Conner arrived at the morgue in Modesto. That same day I received an e-mail from Jackie. She began by telling me that Scott was "brokenhearted over not being able to protect his family on that fateful day in December . . ." But the heart of the message was so presumptuous, it was hard to believe. Jackie wanted us to postpone Laci's funeral.

"We are writing with an appeal to your heart," she wrote. "Though by law you are granted the decision on how to handle the remains of all our loved ones, we ask that you postpone the service until such times Scott is exonerated and we can all join together as a family to mourn for your daughter, Scott's wife, ours and your grandson and Scott's son whom have been taken from all of us so cruelly."

As Scott's mother, Jackie was entitled to have blind faith in his in-nocence, I suppose. But for her to assume that Laci's family felt the same way was offensive, and I wasn't putting anything off until Scott was "exonerated." Everyone I showed the e-mail to agreed. The reac-tion was unanimous among Ron, Brent, Amy—everyone. Laci's fu-neral was going to be a private affair for family and friends, and we decided it would be inappropriate for the Petersons to attend. We had to consider the feelings of those who would be there. I had our attor-ney send a letter to Jackie saying we wanted to be left alone.

Before we buried Laci, I wanted my own personal time with her when I could say good-bye. The morgue where Laci and Conner had been brought in the middle of the night was almost directly across the street from our house. If I looked over our neighbor's back fence, I could see the small brick building.

I was disturbed when I heard they were there. The morgue was so institutional, impersonal, and cold. I wanted them moved to the fu-neral home, which seemed to me to be a nicer, more peaceful setting. I complained to Alex Loya, who said there wasn't any other choice, they had to be at the morgue.

I didn't understand until he told me, with much difficulty, that their bodies needed to be kept in a freezer, and the funeral home didn't have one.

So they stayed at the morgue, and every day I drove to the shopping center across the street, parked the car, and stared at the building where Laci rested. I sat there and cried, thinking about Laci and Conner inside, wishing I could be with my daughter one more time. I wanted one more time to see her and talk to her and tell her that I loved her.

I hit a low point on August 27. It was two days before the funeral, and I was at home alone and so depressed that I couldn't move. It was the reality of the moment—I was about to bury my little girl. I hadn't been with Laci for months. I was never going to see her again. I'd never pick up the phone and hear her say, "Hi, Mom." I'd never receive another Mother's Day or birthday card from her. I'd never meet her baby boy, my grandson, Conner.

I wanted to be with her more than I'd ever wanted to be with her. I *needed* to be alone with her to say good-bye.

And then I needed it to be *now*.

I went into the bedroom and picked up some of Laci's clothes, which I'd placed in a plastic bag to preserve her smell. I also grabbed a teddy bear that I'd bought for Conner. I sat in Laci's rocking chair, put the clothes up to my face, and breathed in my daughter's scent. I could smell her so clearly, and as I did, she came back to life in my mind. A different memory appeared with each breath. I could see her, hear her, almost touch her. I held everything close to my heart, doubled over, and cried.

It literally hurt me, that's how hard I cried. I cried from the inside out. I'd never felt this kind of pain.

I missed Laci so much.

I couldn't believe I was going to bury her.

I called Sandy, and through my sobs, I told her that I needed to be with Laci. She came over and sat with me for a while. Eventually, she called Kim, who arranged through the Sheriff's Department for Laci to be transferred to the funeral home late that night so I could visit with her the next day. Laci's body was put in the white and gold casket I'd picked out and placed in a private room. Conner was placed inside with her.

Ronnie knew I'd be coming to the funeral home and she greeted me politely, before taking me into a large room where I could be alone with Laci. The casket was in the middle of the room with a big, beautiful spray of flowers that covered the entire top. Ronnie pulled a chair beside it. I looked at it for a moment, then turned to her.

"Is Laci really in the casket?" I asked.

"Yes, she is," she said. "So is the baby. If you'd like, I can open it. They're in a sheet."

"No, thank you," I said.

"You can just put your hand in and feel her," Ronnie said.

"No, thanks," I said.

Ronnie excused herself, shut the door, and left me with Laci and Conner.

I stood still for a minute or two, unable to move. Eventually I sat down in the chair and stared at the casket. My hands stayed in my lap. I looked at the finish on the casket, the flowers, their leaves, and then the casket again. She was inside.

Laci. My baby. I tried to remember everything I could about her. My pregnancy. Her birth. Her first steps. Little girls' softball. Cheerleader tryouts. Her first kiss. Her first love. Her call to tell me that she was pregnant. . . . How do you replay an entire lifetime? I saw her smile brighten the room. I heard her laughter, her cries, and her voice on the telephone, "Hi, Mom. . . ."

I thought about how so much of life is made up of the little, seemingly uneventful moments that happen in between the big events. Everyday life. Morning cereal. Homework. Carpools. Getting in trouble for leaving the skating rink. Running into a room, breathlessly saying, "Guess what?" Or "Look at this!" Meeting for coffee. Saying goodnight. . . .

I relived as many of those moments with Laci as I could remember. Then, at some point, I stood up and walked around the casket.

Slowly, tentatively, I reached out and felt it. I touched the condensation with my open hand; I wanted to feel her, and I knew these cold spots were the places where Laci was. I kissed each one of them.

But I wanted to kiss *her* good-bye. I wanted to hold her hand, to tell her how much I loved her, how much I missed her. I wanted her to know how terribly sorry I was that this had happened to her, how sorry I was that I didn't save her life. . . .

I don't how long I was there when I finally felt it was okay to leave. I'd talked to Laci. I had said good-bye. And my eyes had run out of tears.

"Please, God," I added, softly, on the way out, "watch over Laci and Conner."

On August 29, we laid Laci to rest, giving her the peace and privacy she deserved. Attended by 250 people, Father Illo's service at St. Joseph's Catholic Church was a simple, poignant, spiritual one. Sandy read from Corinthians, Gwen and Rene Tomlinson gave the eulogies, and Father Illo said, "If any death was senseless, Laci's was. Why did she and Conner die? What insanity drove the killer to destroy such beauty and such life? For this there is no answer."

The service continued at the cemetery where my grandparents, my father, and other family members were also buried. With so many words having already been spoken, we wanted the scene to be mostly silent, with time for each person to contemplate Laci and Conner in their own way. We had two white doves released to symbolize Laci and Conner, followed by another twenty doves—angels to help them up to heaven.

Ironically, we were sitting under an awning when the doves were released and we were unable to see them. However, one lone bird fluttered under the canopy and buzzed Amy, leaving a little present in her hair, on her face and shoulder, and we burst out laughing.

"That's Laci," I said. "That's just so Laci."

It wasn't the last of Laci, either. After the funeral, all of us went to Patty's house for a reception. We told stories about Laci, and we laughed, smiled, and cried bittersweet tears. By early evening, most everyone had gone home. Only a handful of us remained. We were about to pack up when someone called us to the front. We looked out the window and saw a large swarm of dragonflies—Laci's favorite.

"I've never, ever seen that before," Patty said.

We knew.

"It makes so much sense," I said. "Laci's still here with us."

Part Four

Justice for Laci

"Divorce is always an option, not murder."

Sharon Rocha

Chapter Twenty-four

After Scott's arraignment in April, DA Rick Distaso had warned us there was a possibility we might not get to trial for five years. I didn't see how I could wait two years, even one year, let alone five. But by September, much to my relief, we seemed to be moving forward faster than expected. Step one, the preliminary hearing, a minitrial at which the judge would hear select evidence and decide if there was enough to hold Scott over for a trial, was scheduled after one delay and another, for October 29.

On October 7, Amy and I met separately with Distaso. Both of us had already been informed that we'd be testifying at the prelim. Knowing that testifying can be extremely stressful, Rick sought to ease potential nervousness by explaining the Q&A procedure of being on the witness stand. I liked his manner—direct, calm, thorough, real. He told me the procedure would be simple. He'd ask the questions, and I'd answer by telling the truth.

"I'm not nervous," I said.

"Good," Distaso said.

"Frankly," I said, "I'm looking forward to it."

Later, after one of the numerous hearings that took place prior to the prelim, Rick told us that he wasn't sure if we'd be able to attend the prelim or the actual trial because we were witnesses. I took a deep breath. I wasn't a lawyer and didn't know how trials worked. Up to that point, my experience with the judicial system was limited to taking

Brent to traffic court when he was in high school, a three-day stint of jury duty, and Scott's arraignment. But I knew this much: I *needed* to attend the prelim, the trial, and anything else that concerned Laci. I *needed* to know what happened to my daughter. I *needed* to be in that courtroom when detectives and investigators revealed their findings. I *needed* to be in that courtroom for Laci. Even if Scott never looked at me, he'd know by my presence that Laci wasn't forgotten.

I told Rick I had to be in that courtroom. I told him all the reasons why. I also told him that it was my right as a mother to represent my daughter. He said he understood, but he also explained the law. I found it hard to believe that the victim's family members could be denied access to the proceedings, and suddenly I understood the expression I'd already heard a few times: "Victim's NO Rights."

"We'll have to wait and see," he said.

On October 17, I met with DA Dave Harris. He'd once promised he'd tell me whatever he could about Laci, and I had a question: I wanted to know about the condition of Laci's body when she was found. We'd heard the rumors but we'd buried her without knowing anything for sure. Suddenly I wanted the information, or so I told myself.

Again, because I was a potential witness, he couldn't tell me anything.

"Actually, I don't really want to know," I said. "I just want to be prepared for what's coming up in court. If I don't want to be there on a certain day . . ."

"We will give you whatever warning we can," he said. "There will be difficult days, and we'll warn you ahead of time."

A week later, the ground shook beneath my feet. It was the roar of the nearly one thousand motorcyclists who turned out on October 25 for the first annual Laci and Conner Memorial Bike Run. Laci's cousin, Shawn Rocha, spent months organizing the day. He wanted to keep the focus on the human loss, on what happened to Laci and Conner, rather than on the drama whipped up by lawyers in the courtroom.

"For me, it came down to not allowing her to be lost in this horrific story," he told actor Mickey Jones and me at the event. "I wanted to do something positive. I thought if we could show support, it might boost not only the family, but everyone's spirits."

It did. And we got another boost when I learned that we could sit inside the courtroom during the hearing, as would the Petersons, who'd been in the same situation as us. October 29 came fast, and we found ourselves in Courtroom No. 2 at the Stanislaus County Courthouse. We avoided the media by coming in the back, and then going through a private security screening. The courtroom was old and small, with about eighty wooden chairs for viewers, plus room on the other side of a wood railing for the jury, clerks, attorneys, and the judge. Before I entered, I already knew where I wanted to sit—in whichever seat was closest to Scott.

As I've said, he'd not only see me, he'd feel my presence, and also Laci's.

The Petersons—usually Jackie, Lee, Susan, Joe, and Janey—sat in the front, while Ron, Amy, Brent, Rose, Dennis, Susie, Gil, Gwen, Nancy, Stacey, Lori, Kim, Rene T., and Rene G., and I sat across the aisle from them. Jackie spoke to me only when she thought a reporter might be watching; when it was just the two of us, she didn't even bother to smile. Joe always said hello, Susan was always cordial, Lee barely acknowledged me when I offered a hello as we passed each other going to and from the witness stand on October 31.

I didn't know how I'd react when I saw Scott come into the courtroom. I was sure I wouldn't cry the way I had at his arraignment when he'd entered in shackles and his orange prison jumpsuit. I'd come a long way from that first time in court. When he entered, he wore a nice suit and he was grinning. I felt anger rise in me. I dared him to look at me. *Just look at me. I want you to look at me.* But he just kept grinning, and didn't look me in the face.

The prelim included presentations of and debates over a strand of hair, the wire-tapped phone conversations, findings from the tracking dogs, DNA, and a host of other evidence. The prosecution called the witnesses, presented their evidence, and the defense attempted to pick holes in it or invalidate it altogether.

When I testified, it was the first time I had eye contact with Scott.

We looked straight at each other, and I didn't see anything in his eyes. I kept looking for the Scott I knew, but he wasn't there. I didn't recognize this Scott Peterson. Though he appeared to listen to my testimony, the expression on his face confirmed that there was no connection between the two of us. The Scott I knew and loved, the Scott who, once upon a time, loved Laci, no longer existed.

From the hearing's first day, the bailiffs arranged for the families to leave the courtroom one at a time. As one family exited, the other remained seated, and a bailiff was always present to assist each family. On one occasion, though, as we filed out, Jackie and Lee stepped into the aisle, cutting Brent off from the rest of us. When he caught up to us, he told me that Jackie abruptly turned around and said hello and asked how he was doing.

"Really?" I said suspiciously.

I knew Jackie didn't like Brent. She'd once told me as much, which made me wonder why she suddenly went out of her way to speak to him. Then of course I realized the courtroom had been full of reporters watching the two families. She was putting on a show for them.

Apparently a bailiff saw Jackie and Lee cut Brent off in the aisle, and when we returned to the courtroom, he asked if I wanted him to tell the Petersons not to speak to us anymore. I said I wasn't concerned about it. Perhaps the bailiff had his own concerns, though, because a moment later I heard a loud banging noise. I turned and saw Scott's sister-in-law, Janey, literally stomp out of the courtroom. I guess the bailiff said something she didn't like.

Mark Geragos, with all of his prehearing motions and posturing, was at the top of my list early on. He swaggered into the courtroom every day as if he owned it. Sometimes, as he entered, he paused in the doorway, leaned against the wall with his arms folded across his chest, and slowly surveyed the room. On one occasion, after nodding to some reporters, he zeroed in on me and our eyes locked. He stared, and I stared right back. He turned his eyes away first.

If that was an attempt to intimidate me or make me feel uncomfortable, it failed. Geragos's tricks and tactics didn't work on me. Maybe he didn't get it. I was in that courtroom because my daughter had been murdered, not because I wanted to be there. Nothing compared to that pain. At the same time, it gave me the strength and courage to fight.

As for the hearing itself, I took detailed notes on a yellow legal pad. Whereas I'd once written down Laci's first steps and words in a baby album, now, tragically, I was recording her death. There was so much information every day, afterward I had so many questions, and I needed my own reference material.

The first witness Distaso called was FBI forensic analyst Dr. Constance Fisher, who applied her expertise in mitochondrial DNA to identify the hair found in the pliers on Scott's boat. Based on her tests, she said the hair could've come from one in 112 people, including Laci, which was pretty much proof.

While that presentation tended to be dry and technical, I perked up when Laci's housekeeper, Margarita Nava, was called. From her testimony, I learned that Laci had grocery shopped at Trader Joe's on the morning of December 23. She carried the bags two at a time from the car to the door, where Margarita asked if she could help. The significance? Scott had originally told police that he moved the mop and bucket in and out of the house for Laci because it was too heavy for her to lift. Yet she's bringing in these groceries?

After Amy and I testified (we focused on the night Laci went missing), Lee Peterson took the stand. He reported that he'd spoken with Scott around 2 p.m. on Christmas Eve, which would've been the time when Scott was out on the bay. But Scott never mentioned anything about a boat or fishing to Lee. Why not? Why didn't he tell his father what he was doing?

On November 4, police officer John Evers was sworn in, and I realized he'd been the first officer dispatched to the park on December 24, the night Laci was reported missing. Until then, I hadn't thought about him. He was also the officer who went back to her house with me after I asked about her purse. In his testimony, he mentioned seeing the bucket and mop on the walkway in the front courtyard; I'd read about it but didn't know where it had been.

Evers's testimony was also the first I heard about a scrunched rug in front of the side door leading from the den out to the patio. He said that when the police questioned Scott about it on the night of the twenty-fourth, he'd casually straightened it out with his foot and blamed the pets for messing it up. But that didn't make sense to me. If Laci had really cleaned the floors in preparation for Christmas brunch, she wouldn't have let the pets back in. Furthermore, according to what Scott had told investigators, Laci was mopping the floor when he left to go fishing. Yet she hadn't started to bake. I think most women wouldn't mop until they'd finished cooking.

"Do you think the police think the rug was scrunched because Scott dragged her out of the house through that door?" I whispered to Ron.

"I think so," he said.

If you opened that door, you stepped onto the patio. Scott had backed his truck next to the gate on the patio on the twenty-fourth.

During the break, I reminded Ron that I'd noticed a large wooden pallet blocking the door when I'd fed McKenzie and the cats while Laci and Scott were in Carmel before Christmas. I'd moved it and put McKenzie's bed next to the door, hoping to give him a little more warmth from inside the house.

I told Ron that when Laci and I spoke on the nineteenth, she'd asked if I'd moved the pallet, and I'd said yes. She'd told me that Scott had put it against the door for a reason (what reason, I don't know) and he'd moved it back. Later, following her disappearance—December 28 or 29, I couldn't remember—I'd noticed it propped against the fence. I knew it wasn't proof enough for court, but to me it indicated he'd dragged Laci out of the house.

Evers said one more thing of note. On the night of the twenty-fourth, he'd asked Scott what he'd been fishing for, and Scott hadn't known.

On November 6, Al Brocchini took the stand for the first of three days of testimony. Most of the information in his testimony was new to me, and the rest clarified things I'd heard. Gwen's husband, Harvey, for instance, remembered seeing a tarp in the back of Scott's truck on December 24. Two days later, that tarp was found, bunched up, in the tool shed with fertilizer on it. Al said the detectives also discovered the boat cover in another shed beneath a weed blower that was leaking gas.

The Scott I knew would never allow gas to leak or fertilizer to spill on something.

They also found a handgun in his glove box. I was shocked to learn he had a gun.

Furthermore, Al said that Scott had purchased a two-day fishing license on December 20 but dated it the twenty-third and twenty-fourth. Why date it the twenty-third when he had no intention of fishing that day? Al also described Scott's purchase of the Mercedes he was driving when apprehended and told the "boy-named-Sue" story he gave the seller. Again, I asked myself why, why the lies?

Apparently the testimony hit a nerve with Jackie. During a break, she approached the two detectives, Craig and Al, in the hallway, shook her finger at them, and said, "Shame on you." When Al was cross-examined about the phone conversations Brent and I had taped with Scott, she shot a glare across the aisle at me, as if I were the bad guy. And when Al brought up Laci and Scott's life insurance polices, she jabbed her finger in a notebook in her lap, making a point that I didn't understand.

Even in abbreviated form, I thought the evidence was damning of Scott. Amy Krigbaum, the first neighbor Scott spoke to on the twenty-fourth, recalled him saying that he'd spent the day playing golf. Det. Dodge Hendee described the crowded conditions of Scott's warehouse, his boat, and the traces of cement he'd found. When we'd had dinner on December 15, Laci had remarked that Scott's warehouse was so full he had to climb over things to get through it. It was, I now realized, another piece of the setup. Scott and Laci had stopped by the warehouse on the twentieth and she had gone next door to use the bathroom. It appeared to me that Scott had two objectives: (1) he wanted her to be seen there; and (2) he didn't want her to see the boat parked in the warehouse.

The most upsetting evidence came when the coroner presented the autopsy findings and described the condition of Laci and Conner when they were found. As promised, the DAs warned us about the testimony, and Ron, Brent, Amy, and I stayed out those days. Scott didn't attend either, one more example of him avoiding responsibility. I thought he should've had to sit there and listen to the grisly details.

On November 18, the final day of the prelim, DA investigator Steve Jacobson discussed Scott's affair with Amber. I was spellbound as the investigator described how Scott met Amber Frey's friend Shawn Sibley at the convention in Anaheim on October 23, 2002. I recalled that Laci had wanted to give Scott a thirtieth birthday party on the twenty-fourth, his actual birthday, but he wouldn't tell her when he was going to be home.

Suddenly I knew why: he was partying with Shawn. He'd asked her if she had any single friends he could meet and joked that he might have more luck with women if he added the words "Horny Bastard" to his name tag. Apparently he fit her definition as a nice, eligible single guy and fixed him up with Amber the next month.

Jacobson's testimony was also the first time I heard about the staggering number of phone calls between Scott and Amber. Between November 22, 2002, and February 19, 2003, 241 calls were made, including 16 on December 26, 2002—less than forty-eight hours after Scott told me his wife was missing. (During the trial, we'd learn about even more calls, some made from phones other than the three discussed during the prelim.) Jacobson also revealed all the trips Scott made to the Berkeley Marina during the investigation. This was more confirmation that we didn't know Scott Peterson. We had no idea.

Following Jacobson's testimony, the prosecution wrapped their presentation. After lunch, Judge Girolami delivered his ruling—the evidence was sufficient to keep Scott in jail for trial. Though we had expected the case to move ahead, we were still relieved. I remember telling Kim afterward that I felt a letdown, not quite a depression but close to it. I'd expected to learn more than I did from the hearing. I'd hoped to fill in the blanks between my last conversation with Laci at eight thirty on December 23 and whatever happened to her on the twenty-fourth. As it turned out, I knew a little more than I did before but not enough, not nearly as much as I'd wanted. I still didn't know *what happened* to Laci. And I didn't know *why* Scott did it. I wondered if I ever would.

Chapter Twenty-five

For three days in late December, I felt almost like my old self. I'd been busy helping to organize the First Annual Laci and Conner Blood Drive benefiting the Delta Blood Bank, and it made me feel good at a time when I rarely felt that way. People saw me smile, something else that had been in short supply over the past year. But I had reason: The three-day drive brought in record donations when it was in short supply, and as it was explained to me, we actually saved lives.

Otherwise the Christmas season, as you'd expect with the first anniversary of Laci's disappearance, was extremely tough. I cried regularly. Ordinarily we had big family dinners on Christmas Eve and Laci was typically at the center of every celebration, but this year was bleak, sad, and depressing. With the trial looming ahead, there was simply no bright side to look forward to.

One day Kim asked me to speak to Cydney Carpenter, a mother like myself whose daughter, Heather, a beautiful twenty-two-year-old from Redding, California, hadn't been seen since she left a party with a seventeen-year-old boy in early August. According to Kim, Cydney and her husband were having a very hard time, which plainly I understood, and Kim thought hearing from me might provide some much-needed support to the Carpenters.

A few months earlier I'd done the same thing, calling a woman named Boni Driskill, whose daughter, Lacy Ferguson, had been mur-

dered when she left a Modesto convenience store after buying cigarettes and stepped into gunfire between two gang members. She had
even picked up flyers at the volunteer center for my Laci.

I felt like I had helped Boni. I knew talking couldn't ease any of the
pain, but I also knew it helped to talk to someone who understood the
depth of the hurt, and only someone who's had a loved one murdered
knows it.

I felt that way when Carole Carrington of the Sund/Carrington
Foundation called me four days after Laci disappeared.

I planned to call the Carpenters one evening, but that afternoon
Kim called to say that Heather had just been found.

"Alive?" I asked hopefully.

"No," Kim replied. "It's a homicide."

I waited for Kim's okay, then called the Carpenters. I spoke to Ed
first, and then he handed me over to Cydney, with whom I had a long,
intense, tearful conversation. It's amazing how that happens, but we
simply knew what to say to each other as we were unfortunately familiar with the tragically sad emotions of having a daughter murdered. I
felt as if we'd known each other forever. I told her the truth: it's
unimaginably hard, there's no pill to take, no easy antidote, and no
predictable course.

"I can't tell you how many millions of times I've closed my eyes and
wished I could wake up from this nightmare and find everything back
to the way it used to be," I said. "But that's not the way it works."

I was sympathetic, of course, but wanted to be honest about what
to expect. I warned them that life would change, and everything would
seem different. I described how you feel disconnected from your old
life, and you lose the hope and anticipation of the future. I told them
about the sadness, anger, and unending grief.

Indeed, as I thought about what I went through, I realized how
everything in my life was recalculated from the date Laci disappeared.
Then came new milestones—instead of Laci's baby shower and Conner's birthday, I added the dates they were found, her memorial, their
funeral, the date I testified at the prelim, the start of the trial. . . .

The Carpenters asked lots of questions. I told them that I got comfort from visiting Laci's grave frequently, and I got strength from family and friends. While some let stressful situations pull them away from relationships and while marriages often crumbled, I was drawn closer to Ron, Brent, and Amy, along with so many other family members and friends. I realized how I needed even my own mother's comfort when I was picking out Laci's casket. And my friends were indispensable.

Most of all, I urged the Carpenters not to let anyone tell them when it was time to stop grieving. From my experience, I knew that everyone does it differently, and everyone finds their own way. Whatever that is, I said, you're entitled to grieve for your daughter. Sometimes people look at you like, Enough already. Sometimes you look at yourself and wonder if it will ever end. I didn't have the answer. I only knew there was no timetable.

In mid-December, the defense requested a change of venue, arguing that the pretrial coverage—I think Geragos claimed almost ten thousand articles and countless hours of television—prevented Scott from getting a fair trial in Modesto. Geragos's preference was Los Angeles, his hometown. On January 8, Judge Girolami moved the trial to Redwood City, a midsized city halfway between San Francisco and San Jose.

I was disappointed. Even without traffic, Redwood City was more than a ninety-minute drive from Modesto—up to three hours on a weekday—which meant we'd have to relocate for the trial, and I didn't look forward to being out of town for the four to six months it was expected to last. Distaso, Harris, and the whole prosecution team felt the same way, since the change of venue required them to move their offices, including all the evidence, to bring witnesses, and to live away from their families.

I thought Scott could've received a fair trial in Modesto, and I still do. But for the sake of eliminating one possible reason for an appeal, I was willing to make the sacrifice and head to Redwood City.

It was scheduled to begin on January 26, 2004; the interim was filled with motions and hearings. Most struck me as a waste of time;

some were beyond me. On January 8, Geragos's motion to dismiss was rejected. A week later, a new judge listened to a recap of evidence at a hearing to determine whether Girolami had been right to bind Scott over for trial. The original decision was upheld. Two weeks later, Girolami said he didn't want to move to Redwood City and was replaced by retired Contra Costa County Superior Court Judge Richard Arnason. Then Arnason was removed from the case and retired Alameda County Judge Alfred Delucchi was appointed. Delucchi had been retired since 1998, but he was described as someone who ran a disciplined and fair courtroom. He sounded good to me.

Ron and I were concerned about how we were going to move to Redwood City for six months. There were many issues, including, and not least, the cost of upending our lives for that long. But two angels came to our rescue from out of the blue. A retired couple with a second home in Redwood City contacted the Stanislaus County DA's office to offer us the use of their house. On February 4, we met them and accepted their generous offer. They'd followed the case and were sorry we'd lost a daughter. They, too, had lost a daughter, though not to murder. They were lovely, caring people. On several occasions after the trial started, we'd return to the house and find a freshly baked cake on the counter and a note with our name on it. Often there were two, three, or four cakes—each one with a note to a different person.

On February 11, Judge Delucchi began the *in limine* hearings, or the lemonade hearings, as my friend Patty dubbed them. These hearings were about specific legal points, basically opportunities Geragos took to argue that numerous pieces of evidence should be eliminated. Among the issues debated were the wire taps, Scott's TV interviews, and findings from the dog handlers. But loss was on our minds as Ron pointed out that we should've been celebrating Conner's first birthday rather than listening to Geragos argue about the accuracy of GPS tracking.

If matters weren't already stressful enough, a TV network was about to air the made-for-TV movie *The Perfect Husband: The Laci Peterson Story*. I thought the timing was inappropriate considering that jury selection was about to start. I complained to Rick Distaso, who said they couldn't do anything to prevent it from airing. In that case, I watched an advance copy I'd received, curious to see their take on things. As it turned out, I thought the depiction was inaccurate, exploitative, insensitive, and unnecessary. It may have entertained the public, but it added more pain to our lives.

In March 2004, the two-month jury selection began. Prosecutors had told us it was likely to be a long, boring process, so we didn't attend. There was only one day I wanted to be there, April 14—the anniversary of the day Laci was found. Dates mean something to me, and I wanted to remind Scott that I knew what day it was, and I wanted him to know, too.

I knew that Scott was living in a tiny cell at Maguire Correctional Facility, a far cry from the wide-open fairways of Del Rio Country Club, but I didn't think that was enough punishment. I called Rick and told him about the upcoming anniversary and my interest in attending court that day as a reminder.

Rick said he had to look into it. When he called back, he explained that when we said we didn't plan to attend jury selection, the prosecutors and the defense made an agreement that neither family would be allowed to attend. I wasn't aware of that agreement till he told me about it, but since it was already in place, I couldn't do anything about it.

I was really disappointed but, grudgingly, I told him that I understood. Then Jackie and Janey showed up the morning of the fourteenth. Coincidental? I don't know. As soon as Rick saw them, he approached Judge Delucchi and reminded him of the agreement. As a result, Jackie and Janey were asked to leave.

Rick called to tell me what happened, knowing I wouldn't be a happy camper if I heard anything on the news about Jackie and Janey being in the courtroom after he'd told me I couldn't attend. He was beginning to know me, and he was 100 percent right.

In the midst of jury selection, I participated in the Sund/Carrington Foundation's annual Vigil of Hope, a march through downtown Modesto for families of murder victims. For me, it was a chance to continue giving back and perhaps find some purpose in all this pain. The event began on March 12, with a reception for participating families. I met Ed and Cydney Carpenter, recognizing them the instant they walked through the door. We picked up our conversation like old friends.

There was also a twenty-something woman who'd traveled all the way from Georgia for the vigil. Her name was Geneva, and she was staying with her aunt in Oakland. She said that she'd called me at home a few times recently but I'd hung up each time before she could get out three words. To my embarrassment, I remembered, and told her that strangers called me every day wanting to give their input about what happened to Laci and told her I'd reached a point where it was just too painful to hear.

After I had apologized, we sat down by ourselves and she told me the story that brought her to the vigil, that her sister, the mother of two precious little boys, had been murdered in Las Vegas. She'd taken over raising the boys, whom I also met that day and who obviously loved her very much. She impressed me as a sweet, caring, thoughtful woman. When I asked why she'd called, she said that she just wanted to connect with someone who'd been through the same thing.

I understood immediately.

We talked in some detail about her life, both before and after her sister's murder. I thought back to my very first conversation with Carole Carrington and the things she'd told me: she couldn't focus; she was easily and quickly distracted; she couldn't sleep. I'd experienced the same and I felt better knowing it was normal, and I said the same to Geneva, who e-mailed me in November 2004 with good news: after more than a year of trying, she'd legally adopted her nephews.

On March 13, the day after the reception, more than two hundred people gathered in downtown Modesto for the Vigil of Hope march. It began at the courthouse and finished at Graceada Park. I didn't fully anticipate the intensity of the event, but every person there was just like me—someone with a family member who'd been murdered or was missing.

The connection among us was extraordinary. You could feel the

264 ✹ *Sharon Rocha*

pain, hurt, grief, and even the hope. To me, the saddest thing was looking out and seeing people who didn't know where their loved ones were. At least we had found Laci and Conner. I met some people with brothers, sisters, children, or parents who'd been missing for years. They didn't have a clue what had happened. Every day they woke up wondering if he or she would turn up that day.

Given the audience, I wanted my speech that day to be extra-special. I worked hard at crafting my thoughts, starting with an extended thank-you to Carole and Francis Carrington for starting the Carole Sund/Carrington Memorial Reward Foundation. Then I acknowledged the common thread among all of us, and I saw many heads nod when I said "my world came to a screeching halt" the day Laci disappeared.

"Nothing seemed right. Everything appeared out of place. I know what the problem is. I'm having a nightmare. Wake up! Somebody, please wake me up! I can't stand this nightmare. Dear God, let me wake up!

"Then comes the horrible realization. I am awake. I have been awake the entire time. I am not asleep and having a nightmare. I am awake and I am living a nightmare!

"It has been about fifteen months since we lost Laci. However, I still hurt as much today as I did then. I heard the expression 'Grief is the price we pay for love.' I still cry every day.

"I like to believe that I can cry as loud and as much as I want while I'm taking a shower because the sound of the water drowns out the sound of my crying. I like to believe the same while I'm blow-drying my hair.

"Of course, that's only my fantasy because I'm sure the entire neighborhood can actually hear me.

"One other time that seems exceptionally difficult for me is when I am alone driving my car. I find that at times I just burst into tears. I'm not sure why that happens when I drive. Maybe it's because I'm alone or maybe I saw or smelled something that I'm not even aware of but subconsciously it makes me think of Laci.

"I can only hope that those of you who are suffering through your own tragedy have the support you so desperately need. Surround yourself with your friends and family. Talk to them. Tell them how you are feeling. Cry as much and as often as you feel you need.

"And to those friends and family members of the victim's family, be there for them. Don't allow them to go through this alone. Listen to them when they want to talk. Let them cry and express their emotions when they feel the need. Give your strength to them. They may not ask for your help or tell you they need help. However, they do need you—more than you will ever know."

I closed with a message to family members about their right to grieve. "Don't allow anyone to tell you when it's time to stop crying, when it's time to move on or when it's time to get over it. Only you can know when that time is right.

"We will never stop crying for the loss of our child; we may only not cry as often. We will never be able to completely move on, because a part of us has died and been left behind.

"And lastly, we will never, ever get over it, period!"

Afterward, I was approached by a young, slight woman from New York. She said she'd come to the vigil because her sister had been murdered, and she'd been moved by my confessions. Wiping her tears, she said that I had expressed all the things she'd felt but hadn't been able to articulate, and it helped her. We were there to help each other, I said. We hugged and I cried with her.

I found the best therapy for me was helping other people. If that meant sharing our tragedy or bringing attention to the profound effect of loss from violent crimes on families in general, I was willing to risk opening my heart. Between the Unborn Victims of Violence Act, which had been passed in the House, and the speech that day in Modesto, I felt like I was making a positive difference, and that gave me strength.

On March 22, I once again went to Washington, D.C., and this time joined the families of several other murder victims in lobbying senators to pass the Unborn Victims of Violence Act, which they did three days later. Unfortunately, I missed the press conference because I had gotten sick again, but Ron attended, then we went home the next day, after being told that the president probably wouldn't sign the bill for two to three weeks.

Four days later we were notified that the bill signing would actually be on April 1. Even though I was still sick when we flew back east again, I wasn't going to miss this special date with history. This bill was important to me. I wanted to be standing alongside the president of the United States as he signed the Laci and Conner Bill into federal law.

We met President Bush in the White House's Green Room prior to the signing ceremony. There were a number of us—families of victims—there supporting the bill, and we lined up when the president came in. He moved down the line, introducing himself. I noticed the other families held pictures of their murdered children; I didn't. It had never occurred to me to bring one.

"I'm George Dubya," he said to me.

It wasn't President Bush. Or George Bush. It was George Dubya. With that introduction, I felt completely at ease.

"I'm Sharon Rocha," I said.

He smiled. "I know who you are."

I laughed and said something about how much the bill meant to me. I added a bit about Laci and Conner.

"Now don't make me cry," he said genuinely.

"Don't make me cry," I replied.

"No, you don't understand," he said. "I cry very easily. I was in Iraq and I started talking to an Iraqi lady, and I just started bawling like a little baby."

"Well, don't worry," I said. "I brought extra tissues just in case."

Before signing the bill in the East Room, the president made a few remarks, which included a mention of Laci and Conner, and again, I could hear Laci saying, "Nah-ah, Mom." He signed the bill as we watched approvingly, and afterward we spoke to some of the senators and congressmen and -women on the stage. After a minute or two, the president looked at us and said, "Are you ready to go? I'm the quickest way out of here if you're ready."

Then he offered me his arm and I looped mine through his, and we walked out.

I heard Ron, a step or two behind, say, "Uh, Mr. President, she's with me."

Chapter Twenty-six

I was told that during a trial the defense has the right to keep witnesses from entering the courtroom except when they testify. I think the law is cruel, wrong, and should be revised. But it was the situation we faced in the last days of May. The first day of the trial was to be June 1. I called Rick every day and asked if there was any word on whether we'd be let in the court, and when there wasn't, I told him I didn't want to be a witness if it meant I couldn't be in the courtroom for the trial. He told me he'd given that some thought but felt I was an important witness.

We packed our bags and headed to Redwood City anyway. I planned to go to court regardless. I couldn't imagine not being inside the courtroom, and Ron, Brent, Amy, and Dennis were right beside me. If the defense wasn't going to give us permission, then authorities were going to have to throw me out.

We were up there the day before the trial and the prosecutors still hadn't received an answer from the defense on the issue of our attendance. Finally, at the last possible minute, we got the word—we could be inside.

We'd waited a long time and now, as a family, we were primed for the trial. Ron took off from work, Brent's co-workers donated their vacation time to him, and Amy took a short break from the salon. The trial ran Monday through Thursday, allowing us to spend Friday and the weekends in Modesto.

The Redwood City courtroom was double the size of the old one in Modesto, but it didn't seem big enough for the two families. From the first day, it seemed to me that the Petersons blamed us for Scott being on trial. During a break, as I stepped into the aisle, I said hello to Lee. He glanced at me, then looked away, and I heard him snort. I thought, Okay, I won't put myself in that situation again. A few days later, though, I was behind Lee as he opened the door to walk into the courtroom, and he let it slam in my face.

As for the trial itself, we were warned it would probably last four to six months. We didn't know what to expect, just that it would be long and contentious. I came in on the first day focused, nervous, and ready to follow every detail. I had my legal pad, took copious notes, then reviewed them at night. That became my routine throughout the trial: in court Monday through Thursday, never to bed before midnight, then awake another hour or two, thinking, my mind too busy to shut down. By the time we returned to Modesto on Thursday night, I was so tired I'd spend all of Friday in bed, recuperating.

In his opening statement, Rick Distaso described Scott as a deliberate, calculating liar who plotted his wife's murder. In his summary of their case, he mentioned that Scott changed his alibi from golfing to fishing; he'd lied about his affair with Amber Frey; he was unable to recall for anyone what fish he was fishing for, then remembered he'd been after sturgeon; and when the police checked his truck, they found a bag of unopened fishing gear behind the front seat.

Facing the jury, Rick said that Scott's biggest lie was denying he'd murdered Laci. Scott did it and pretended he didn't know a thing the whole time hundreds of people searched for Laci. He kept up the act while Laci's family, us, pleaded for her safe return. Laci and Conner, Rick pointed out, were found in the same bay where Scott said he'd gone fishing. Was that a coincidence? No, he said, not at all.

Rick seemed to score a big point when he brought up Scott's assertion that he and Laci had watched Martha Stewart make meringue cookies before he left the house around 9:30 a.m. on December 24. That meant Laci mopped the floor, changed clothes, and walked

McKenzie before disappearing by 10:18—the time neighbor Karen Servas had found McKenzie. Not only did Rick make that seem implausible, he said that a review of the Martha Stewart show didn't mention meringue at all.

You could feel the impact in the courtroom. But Geragos turned it into the trial's first controversy the next day when he delivered his opening statement. Drawing jurors' attention to the large TV screen that had been set up in the courtroom, he played a videotape of the Martha Stewart show that aired on the twenty-fourth and grinned broadly, as did Scott, when Martha made meringue. He stressed it by playing the video a second time.

I knew it was early in the case, but suddenly I had pangs of Scott walking free, and it made me sick. But the whole Martha Stewart issue ended up biting the defense when prosecutors figured out that the meringue demonstration came forty-eight minutes into the show, which showed that Scott couldn't have left the house at nine thirty as he claimed. Furthermore, it gave Laci an impossibly small window to mop the floor, curl her hair, change clothes, and so on, before McKenzie was found at 10:18.

But Geragos's opening statement was an indication of the leeway he had to say anything he wanted. Though he called Scott a "cad," it was only to acknowledge what was indisputable, and then to dismiss it by telling the jury that Scott was "not charged with having an affair." Summing up the case against his client, he maintained that investigators got "zip, nada" and promised to show that Scott was "stone-cold innocent."

I was enraged by the way he was able to twist reality. He said the baby's room was decorated in a fishing theme because Scott was a fisherman. (Later, when I testified, I made a point of saying that the baby's room had a *nautical* theme. It had *nothing* to do with fishing.) He stated that Laci needed to walk because her ankles were swollen. (What? That was ridiculous.) He said Scott built the nursery. (He put together the crib and hung a couple shelves, but it had been painted months before Laci was pregnant and there was nothing to build.) He claimed that they bought a large amount of furniture before Christmas. (If they did, I never saw it or heard about it.) Finally, in what I assumed was an attempt to show Scott intended for them to have a long and happy future, he said they'd recently purchased a membership at the Del Rio Country Club. (But Scott's parents gave him the money, and rather than name his wife the beneficiary of his membership, as was the practice, he chose Lee and Jackie. Was that another signal he knew Laci wouldn't be alive?)

Throughout those first two days, and every day thereafter, I studied the jury for their reactions. From my vantage point, I couldn't see all twelve of them, but I saw enough to know they were impossible to read. Their expressions were interested, but not emotional, and they never changed. I didn't have any idea how the opening statements impacted them.

At the end of day one, I assumed they felt like me—simply eager to get on with it.

As in the prelim, the trial began with housekeeper Margarita Nava, followed by Fred Eachus from Trader Joe's, who'd helped Laci shop on the twenty-third, and then two women from Sweet Serenity Day Spa, where Laci had gone for a facial. Next came the owner and manager from Amy's salon.

It was small, inconsequential stuff, and it seemed the case was beginning in slow motion. Impatient, I wanted to leapfrog straight to the night of December 24 and the details of what *really* happened. I didn't understand how a trial unfolds, the strategies, and the bases that need to be covered. The media also hungered for meatier stuff and criticized the prosecutors as boring and tedious.

But Ron calmed me by comparing the trial to building shopping centers, his profession, explaining that before putting up any sort of large structure, it was crucial to lay a strong foundation, and that's what the prosecution was doing.

"You have to take the time to do it right," he said.

Amy was next. She was the last one in the family to see Laci alive, and I saw the stress on her face as she testified about that final night they spent together at the salon. She described the clothes Laci had worn and her demeanor (quiet and tired). She also recounted assisting the detectives in their February 18, 2003, search of Laci and Scott's home and discovering the maternity blouse Laci had worn to the salon wadded up in a dresser drawer—something Laci *never* would've done.

Amy also recalled that on the twenty-third, while doing his hair at the salon, Scott had invited her back to the house for pizza. She'd declined, saying she had a friend in from out of town. I'd heard this story before, but hearing it again made me realize once more about how calculating he'd been, how he'd wanted everything to seem normal before killing her, how . . .

As was the case after almost every session, I left the courtroom with numerous questions, and this day it was, How could we have not known? How could Scott have carried out this horrible act right in front of us? How could we have not had a clue? The answer? Carefully. The whole time they lived in Modesto, we got together as a family on average once a month, never in any set schedule. It was only around October 2002 that we saw each other once a week, usually for Sunday dinner at our house, and as Ron pointed out, Scott was the one who promoted the increased family time, not Laci.

Ron thought that was part of Scott's plan—setting us up to believe that he and Laci were happier than ever, especially with a baby on the way. In the meantime, Scott was seeing Amber, ordering phony diplomas, and scheming to kill Laci.

If only I'd been able to inject such speculation when I took the stand on June 7, but that wasn't allowed. Nor was it brought up. It was the fourth day of the trial when I was sworn in, and I was already exhausted. My testimony focused on Scott's phone calls to me on December 24, 2002, and what transpired that evening. I also described Scott's unusual behavior and apparent lack of concern for Laci as we searched for her in the hours and days after she went missing on Christmas Eve.

Rick also played a tape recording of the conversation I had with Scott on February 13, 2003, when I pressed him to tell me exactly what had happened. As I entered the courtroom that day after a break, I saw Rick and Geragos talking at the podium. I realized they were playing the tape softly before court resumed. Geragos waved me over and asked, "Is that you?"

"Yes," I said.

"It sounds awfully speedy," Geragos said.

The tape was playing a little too fast but I said, "Well, yes," and, recalling the conversation and the way I got madder and more upset at Scott by the second, I added, "and it's about to get a lot speedier."

My turn on the stand was straightforward and without drama. I spoke directly to Rick, answering his questions as if we were having a conversation. I avoided eye contact with the jury; I didn't want to feel like I was performing.

That said, I left the stand frustrated. I felt like I didn't get the chance to talk about so many things. Amy felt the same way. Many of us left the stand wishing we'd been able to say more, but we hadn't been allowed or we weren't asked the right questions or the defense objected. I didn't want to give Laci's life history, but I wanted the jury to know her as a real person.

If allowed, I also would've told the jury about the last night Ron and I spent with Laci and Scott, December 15, which I thought revealed how distant and detached Scott had become from Laci and her pregnancy. I'd placed my hand on her pregnant belly, hoping to feel the baby move, and after getting nothing, I put my head on her tummy and said, "Hello, little Conner. This is your nana speaking. I love you and I can't wait to meet you."

I wish I could've told the jury how Scott didn't say a word that night, how it hurt Laci, and how disappointed she sounded as she said, "Scott doesn't leave his hand there long enough to feel the baby move."

I wish I could've asked, "What kind of husband is that?"

But I wasn't allowed. When I tried, Geragos objected to it as hearsay, and the judge agreed.

Still, I thought the jury was getting a disturbing picture of Scott Peterson. According to Brent's testimony, Scott had job troubles. Rose recalled Scott telling her that he was "kind of hoping for infertility" when Laci was having problems getting pregnant. Sandy showed how Scott had showed her his hands and said, "I wouldn't be surprised if they [the police] find blood on my truck because I cut my hands all the time." And Ron recalled his surprise when Scott told him on the night of December 24 that he'd gone fishing that morning, and how when Scott said he'd left the house at nine thirty, Ron had joked that's when real fishermen came back. Scott didn't provide more details about his fishing trip, and Ron pointed out that was the last time they'd spoken.

During his cross-examination of Ron, Geragos diverted attention from the real issue—that Scott was not a regular fisherman—by getting Ron to admit that he'd also gone fishing that morning, his implication being that going fishing was a perfectly normal thing for Scott to do. Geragos didn't mention that Ron had told detectives he'd fished that day, or that his favorite fishing spot was only twenty minutes away from home, or that he went fishing all the time, often stopping for a few minutes after work just to unwind. In other words, it wasn't out of character for *him*.

Ron expected Rick to bring up all of this on redirect, and when it didn't happen, he was devastated. He felt foolish, like he'd let down Laci. Our biggest fear was failing Laci.

But Gwen added to the unflattering portrait of Scott, and then her husband, Harvey, provided more devastating blows. First, he said that, from what he'd observed, Scott had been more upset after burning chicken at a July 4 barbecue than over Laci's disappearance. He also revealed that Scott had told him that he'd spent the day of the twenty-fourth playing golf, not fishing.

Harvey also described following Scott to a mall, the opposite direction from where he'd said he was going to hang flyers. But rather than do so, Scott sat in his truck for forty-five minutes. Harvey also trailed Scott to Del Rio Country Club, where Scott played golf. Given the circumstances, Harvey called such behavior strange. When defense attorney Pat Harris asked if Harvey thought it was strange for a grown man to spy on someone, without missing a beat, he said, "Yup," and everyone cracked up.

Gwen provided some unintentional humor, too. Her first day on the stand began late, just before court adjourned for the day, and as it concluded, Judge Delucchi instructed her to stay seated in the witness chair until the jury left the courtroom and he dismissed her. Apparently, Delucchi forgot to dismiss her or she expected him to speak to her directly, because she was still seated, wearing an expression that reminded me of a first-grader waiting to be excused from class.

As Delucchi was leaving the courtroom, he turned and saw her. "You can go home now," he said.

"Oh? Okay," Gwen said, finally getting up. "Thank you."

Later I told her I was expecting to find her still seated there the next day when I walked into the courtroom. It was a rare moment of lightness. We were barely two weeks into the trial, but it already seemed like two years.

Chapter Twenty-seven

Perhaps the hardest thing about the trial was seeing Scott Peterson every day in court, knowing he was there and Laci wasn't. He was apparently unfazed by the serious charges he faced, confident of beating them, continually wearing that placid grin, which drove me crazy. I felt like he didn't get it. While we were riddled by anger, tension, and anxiety, he made notes, traded comments, and occasionally laughed with his attorneys, Pat Harris and Mark Geragos.

One day, before the morning break, Gwen was in the hall with two other witnesses when Lee exited the courtroom. According to Gwen, he walked over to them, flashed a big grin, pumped his fist, and exclaimed, "YES!" Gwen was livid and that was enough of Lee Peterson for her.

At the next day's first break, as Lee exited the courtroom, Gwen asked what was so funny. Without answering her directly, he turned toward some reporters and, feigning puzzlement, said she was telling him that he's not allowed to laugh. Later, after my friend Patty's sister testified, Jackie approached her in the hallway and shook her finger in her face and told her, "Shame, shame on you!"

Their remarks were constant, and I thought misdirected. They should've been angry at Scott, not us.

The facts continued to tell the real story. Neighbor Karen Servas's testimony put a timeline on the case when she said she found McKenzie wandering on his leash at 10:18 a.m. Another neighbor,

Amy Krigbaum, said Scott also told her that he'd spent the twenty-fourth playing golf, not fishing. My sister, Susie, recalled being at Scott and Laci's house on Christmas Day and overhearing a couple of police officers tell Scott that two witnesses thought they'd seen Laci the day before crossing the footbridge in the park. She said to him, "That's great news!" But Scott dismissed the tip, saying Laci didn't walk over there. Susie was startled by his response. Maybe Laci didn't usually walk over there, but for damn sure she'd never gone missing before, either. What kind of husband wasn't even going to consider the possibility that it could've been her?

Modesto police officer Matt Spurlock, among the first officers at the scene on December 24, recalled finishing his walk-through of the house that night and seeing Scott step out the front door, throw down his flashlight, and say, "Fuck!"

At that, Geragos leaped up from his chair and complained that that statement by Spurlock hadn't been provided in the discovery and he wanted it struck. When the judge refused, Geragos asked for a mistrial, prompting laughter from some in the courtroom. Geragos whipped around and started to point at *us* as he spouted he didn't need to hear (laughter) from the peanut gallery. I think he thought we were the source of the laughter, but it didn't come from us. Not one of us had even smiled. Then, as far as I was concerned, Geragos did something that should've gotten him censured. Phillip Williams of Motherhood Maternity was on the stand and confirmed the make of pants on Laci when she was found. As Rick questioned him, a photograph of the pants was put on the large screen in the courtroom, and it was still up there as Geragos stepped forward to begin his cross-examination. Glancing at the screen, then at Williams, Geragos said, "This isn't going to be about burnt chicken, is it?" It was a reference to Harvey Kemple's earlier testimony, which seemed to have struck a chord with the jury, and laughter rippled softly through the courtroom. I thought his remark was disrespectful, unnecessary, crude, and insensitive. I was disappointed in the judge for allowing him to get away with such a remark, and at reporters for not going after the attorney for being so grossly offensive.

Geragos seemed immune to criticism. The media treated him like a celebrity. At times I couldn't help but wonder if people thought of this as an HBO series, not a murder trial. The next day, before entering the courthouse, as happened every morning, reporters asked how we thought the trial was going.

"I think that Mr. Geragos needs to stop joking so much," I told them. "There's nothing humorous about the fact that my daughter was murdered."

If it wasn't one thing, it was another. As Brent went through the security check on June 17, he happened to find himself next to Juror 5, a young man named Justin Falconer, who said something to Brent as he picked up his keys. A TV camera positioned to take video of our daily arrivals and departures captured the moment. There was no sound, but reporters trying to read their lips reported the juror said something along the lines of "You're going to lose today."

In reality, the juror, noting the ubiquitous TV camera, jokingly said, "I'm getting in the way of you being on the news tonight." Inside the courtroom, Brent told me what had transpired, and he told Rick and Dave right away. Judge Delucchi met with attorneys, investigated, and concluded "there had been no misconduct." But two days later, after Laci's girlfriends and yoga instructor testified that Laci was too fatigued to have walked McKenzie, Juror 5 was abruptly dismissed from the case, taking us all by surprise.

Then my surprise turned to dismay as Justin Falconer talked to reporters outside the courthouse and trashed the case against Scott. He said he wasn't convinced Scott was guilty and would've voted to acquit. He said, "Pregnant women are crazy." He said more, and the press ate up every word, as he was their window into the jury.

We were less than three weeks into the trial. What happened to listening to all the evidence? I'd be lying if I said his comments were anything but troubling, not just for their offensiveness toward women but also for his predetermined bias. As he was passing himself off as reflective of the entire jury, he really tested my faith in the system. But I got through this difficult time by weighing Falconer against Rick and Dave, who I thought were doing a terrific job. I had to believe in someone, and I chose the DAs. I'd gotten to know them personally and professionally, and they were top notch. So I let go of my fears and let them do their job.

It seemed to me that Geragos tried to take advantage of the situation with Juror 5 by immediately asking for a mistrial, blaming the media for interfering with the jury. But Delucchi, who appointed an alternate juror and warned the remaining jurors to avoid news accounts of the trial, dismissed Geragos's motion, explaining, "We have to live with the media." A few weeks later, Delucchi was inspired by a comment from an officer with the Modesto P.D. to remind everyone to adhere to the gag order—or else. He seemed to mean it.

But that same day I learned the Petersons had recently taped an interview with Barbara Walters for airing on July 9, a clear violation of the gag order. In addition, they'd already given an interview for a three-page story in the *San Francisco Chronicle*, and Delucchi, despite his warnings, didn't do a thing to them. Incensed, I asked Craig Grogan if Delucchi was going to prevent them from airing the *20/20* interview. He said probably not, and that made me even madder since the Petersons and everyone else had known about the gag order for more than a year.

Tired of them getting away with these infractions, I did something I shouldn't have. At the next break, I stormed out of the courtroom and went to the downstairs cafeteria, where I knew the Petersons spent the breaks. Lee was there by himself. I walked up to him.

Mindful of Delucchi's warning, I told Lee, "Now you know what the gag order is all about."

Then I looked for Jackie. First, I checked the ladies room, but she wasn't there. I found her walking down the stairs with a friend. I started up the stairs and said the same thing I had to Lee: "Now you know what the gag order is all about!"

I had a similar encounter with Janey. Then, before they had an opportunity to twist these encounters into something more than they were, I told Craig what I'd done. I'm glad I did, too. After lunch, a bailiff called me aside and said that Lee had complained that I'd accosted him. I laughed, said he'd exaggerated, described what I'd done, and then said, "If that's considered accosting him, then I guess I did. However, let me tell you what he's been doing."

The bailiff had the same reaction as the judge; he didn't want to deal with it.

"You don't want the judge to know about this," he warned.

"Why?" I asked.

"You don't want to make him mad," he said.

I knew he was right. Judge Delucchi was doing an excellent job of managing a case that had threatened on several occasions in less than a month to boil out of control. We still had another four or five months to go. The Petersons, the media, and Geragos were going to be in the court every day whether or not I liked it. I couldn't let them annoy me. My job was to pay attention to the facts.

I remember taking a long walk that night and reading through my notes from court. I didn't sleep well. That was the last time I spoke to the Petersons.

Brocchini, too, was having a tough time on the stand. During his testimony, which ran from June 22 through June 29, he admitted that while reviewing a tape of the Martha Stewart show that aired on the twenty-fourth, he'd missed her demonstration about meringue. Geragos used that error as the basis for claiming the entire police investigation was full of mistakes. Geragos also attacked Brocchini for ignoring some of the thousands of tips that came into police and he tried to whip up a conspiracy theory by accusing Al of intentionally omitting notes from an interview with a woman who'd seen Laci outside Scott's warehouse on the twentieth.

The press, eating up Geragos's slick lawyering theatrics, came down hard on Al, and I saw the strain on his face. But during Rick's redirect, Brocchini acknowledged the Martha Stewart oversight. As for ignoring tips, he said that the police had received thousands and couldn't look into each one. And he brushed off the ridiculous conspiracy theory, saying another officer submitted the interview with the woman from the neighboring warehouse. He'd turned over his own notes to the DA, too. Everything he said was credible.

I think Al's integrity, even when he erred, not only saved him but hurt the defense. Asked by Rick about some tip he didn't investigate, Al recalled speaking to a college friend of Scott's who remembered him describing the perfect way to dispose of a body. According to Al, Scott, for whatever reason, told his friend that he'd "tie a bag around the neck with duct tape, put weights on the hands, and throw it into the sea."

You can imagine the sickening effect that had on me. All of a sudden I had a graphic image of what he did to Laci. I wanted to throw up. I barely heard Geragos go after Al, who, under questioning, admitted the original account didn't include mention of duct tape. But on Rick's redirect, he explained that he hadn't reviewed the material for months. It was, he said, an honest mistake, and to top it off Al also disclosed that they had never given credence to this person because he wasn't even credible. I think the jury believed him. Whatever Al's misgivings were about his testimony, I thought he did an excellent job.

The jury also saw a videotape of Al interviewing Scott at the police station on the twenty-fifth. It showed why Al said he suspected him from the start. On the tape, Scott didn't once appear distraught, frantic, scared, nervous—anything you'd expect from a man whose pregnant wife had just disappeared. He was perfectly calm and casual as he answered questions as if nothing out of the ordinary had happened.

I tried to imagine what I would've thought if I'd seen this tape after it was shot. It explained why I had felt such conflict about Scott early on. I was sure it had a similar effect on the jury. But there was to be more damning testimony. Before Al left the stand, Rick had another question. Holding a list of calls between Scott and Amber, Rick cited one from December 25 during which Scott said that he was spending Christmas with his family in Maine. After a pause, he asked Al where Scott really was on Christmas Day.

"In the police station," Al said.

You could feel the chill in the courtroom.

Chapter Twenty-eight

If I had any feelings left at all for Scott Peterson, they disappeared once Shawn Sibley testified. Shawn was Amber's friend, the one who'd introduced her and Scott, and as such, she was a key witness. I'd been eager to see her, and I liked the confident way she walked to the stand. I was even more impressed when she spoke.

Strong and credible, she talked about a Scott Peterson that I didn't know, and I'm positive Laci didn't know him, either. She described meeting Scott at a business conference in Anaheim on October 23, the details of which we'd heard during the prelim, but it was still equally maddening to hear her recount how Scott had asked what he could write on his name tag to help him get women. He suggested "Horny Bastard." She said that she took his name tag and on the back wrote, "I'm Rich." She also recalled when she found out he was married and confronted him on December 6, which was when he gave her a tearful account of losing his wife.

I knew most of this and hearing it from Shawn was profoundly upsetting to me. The picture really started to come together. *He'd lost his wife?* He'd used the word *lost* weeks before murdering her. I could only imagine the jury's reaction. I hoped they saw what I did. On December 7, he began looking for a boat. The next day he researched currents in the San Francisco Bay, where he happened to be "fishing" on the day Laci disappeared, the day he *lost* her. Looking at it that way, it was pretty clear to me that Scott had revealed his intention when he told Shawn that he'd lost his wife. In fact, in his mind, he'd already killed her.

I stared at Scott throughout Shawn's testimony and I continued to watch him carefully as others added to the guilty picture. I kept looking for glimpses of the Scott I'd known, and when that failed, I watched for glimpses of a human being. I wanted to see if I could spot normal emotions, like sadness or regret, anything for that matter, but I saw nothing. It was more confirmation that I didn't know this Scott Peterson, this person who murdered my daughter.

There were times when he didn't even seem present or engaged. Or so it appeared to me. For instance, the day Judge Delucchi played tapes of the interviews that Scott had given to local TV reporter Gloria Gomez and ABC's Diane Sawyer. Delucchi was determining how much of each he was going to let in before he let the jury see them. As they played on the large screen in the courtroom, I kept one eye on Scott. He glanced up once during the Gomez piece and seemed equally uninterested in the Sawyer interview, otherwise shuffling through papers and laughing with one of his attorneys, Pat Harris. For whatever reason, during the Sawyer tape, Geragos left the courtroom altogether.

On August 10, Amber Frey took the stand. She was the trial's most anticipated witness thus far, and she received attention commensurate with that distinction. Everything was noted, from when she arrived in town, who she brought with her, and what she wore to court. Her attorney, Gloria Allred, stuck to her side. Amber was escorted into the courthouse through an underground tunnel. When I finally saw her in person, she appeared to be nervous. But she calmed down as she identified Scott in response to the first question and then went on to recount the details of their relationship.

To be perfectly honest, I thought Amber's actual appearance was blown out of proportion. This may be splitting hairs, but it was all about those tapes Amber made of her phone conversations with Scott. They made the case. They were absolutely crucial, revealing Scott for the cold, calculating liar he was. They stunned me. You didn't just listen to the two of them speak. You felt the conversations. I had a visceral reaction as I listened to Scott lie. I also saw their effect on the jury, which until then had shown no emotion or opinion. But as the tapes played, I saw Juror 8, a man who ordinarily sat with his arms crossed, impassive, gradually lean farther back in his chair and listen intently with an expression that revealed disbelief at the things he heard Scott say to Amber. Other jurors did the same.

To me, there were two key conversations, both on New Year's Eve. The first was when he told Amber that he was at the Eiffel Tower in Paris when in reality, as everyone in the courtroom knew, he was at the candlelight vigil in East La Loma Park. Then he called a second time and said he'd ducked into an alley.

"It's a lot quieter now," he said. "They were playing American music that was really neat."

Neat? I was nauseated by what I heard on those tapes. They were shocking. I couldn't believe what I heard from this young man who had always referred to me as "Mom." It didn't make sense unless of course . . .

Well, I knew he did it, but I wasn't one of the twelve who needed to be convinced. I listened in a stunned, paralyzing silence, crying, holding on to Ron's and Brent's hands. I remember one conversation Amber and Scott had at midnight on New Year's Eve where his voice sounded scary, like a desperate growl. It was a raspy, eerie monotone that I'd never heard before. Ron, Brent, and I looked at each other in disbelief. For several days, as the tapes were played, Amber moved back and forth from the stand to the gallery, where she and Gloria sat behind us. She said she had a very difficult time answering questions, listening to the tapes, and being in the spotlight, but these were also some of my hardest days of the trial. I felt nothing but revulsion listening to Scott lie and flirt without an iota of conscience.

"Was Laci aware of the situation about me?" Amber asked.

"Yes," he said.

"She was?"

"Yeah."

"How'd she respond?"

"Fine."

I couldn't let go of the reaction those tapes provoked in me. The conversations haunted me. I took the transcripts home and reread them at night, analyzing them, searching for meaning between the lines. I think they came as close to a confession from Scott as we got during the trial. I'll never know if my theories were right or wrong, but here are the notes I made about some calls:

January 1, 2003—Scott talks about having a mid-life crisis. On June 9, 2002, the day Laci discovered she was pregnant; she and Scott were at our home. Laci looked at Scott and said he's having a mid-life crisis because he's turning 30 and becoming a father all in the same year. I looked over at Scott and joking said, "Get over it. 30 isn't mid-life and becoming a father is supposed to be a wonderful thing." (He's beginning to feel trapped and his life is slipping away from him.)

Scott tells Amber about a book he is reading. He says it's about a man hitchhiking across country. "It's mentally interesting to me because I never had a prolonged period of freedom like that from responsibility." (He wants to be free.)

Scott says, "The fucking dogs keep barking. I want to kill it." (Scott is supposed to be in Europe but the barking dog is really McKenzie in his backyard in Modesto. Laci gave McKenzie to Scott for their first Christmas together. He wanted to distance himself from all things that reminded him of Laci.)

January 4, 2003—Scott tells Amber he needs more experience with words to be able to explain what he is trying to say. "You hire a painter that can do a portrait of people to try to represent them? And he can really do it . . . and you never know what's gonna be behind it. And if you look at the portrait you would know who the person is." (He wants to reveal to Amber what he has done to Laci and who the real Scott is.)

He said his favorite movie is 'The Shining'. (About a man who tries to murder his wife and son.)

Scott's explaining to Amber that he thinks he is an intelligent film fanatic. "Like here's a good one. Have you ever seen the movie 'The Last Supper'? . . . And if they could change their point of view to a more liberal point of view, they wouldn't kill them. But they would kill them if they remained conservative and hateful. I like how the supper that they start out with has an amazing feast for the guy and then they slowly just uh . . . they go down hill to pizza." (Laci's "last supper" was pizza. Did he consider her to be conservative and hateful?)

Scott tells Amber ". . . another thing you would have to say is that love doesn't mean that people can be together forever." (Self-explanatory.)

Amber asks Scott how he's doing this New Year (he had told her this would be his first holidays without his wife) and Scott's answer was happy at times, sad at others. Amber says she knew this was going to be a hard holiday for him. He said, "Well, I don't think about it. Amber you go to sleep now, I miss you." (He doesn't want to discuss this because he really doesn't think about Laci and what he did to her and immediately dismisses Amber.)

January 6, 2003—Scott interprets a poem for Amber and says "my hands around your waist . . . you know like anchors for people." (When I heard Scott say the word anchor, I literally couldn't breathe. I looked at Ron and said, "I think I'm going to have to leave. I feel sick to my stomach." Instead, I sat still, took several deep breaths and stayed in the courtroom. I thought Scott was telling Amber he put anchors around Laci.)

Scott said, "Across from the house where she disappeared there was a robbery." (He's telling Amber Laci disappeared from the house, NOT the park as he led everyone to believe.)

When Scott admits to Amber that he's married and Laci is missing she confronts him about him telling her in December he lost his wife. Scott's response about Laci now missing was, "She's alive. In Modesto." (I can't believe nobody ever picked up on this. But, how did he know whether she was alive or not? WHY did he say this? Just to buy some time with Amber?) Between two phone calls less than thirty minutes apart he goes from "She's alive" to "God, I hope she's found alive" to "I've been losing hope . . . for the last couple of days."

January 7, 2003—Amber asks if they found anything after search-ing the house and the warehouse. Scott answered, "No. Otherwise I wouldn't be, you know, free." (I would think an innocent man would have said, "I wish they did so I would know where my wife and baby are," instead of "I wouldn't be free.")

February 8, 2003—Scott tells Amber, "You know all the answers to the things you want to know. About them all." She said, "I do?" He said, "Yes. I wish I could tell you, but you've guessed the answers to all of them. . . . you don't have the answers, but you've guessed at them and you know them and it's gonna take time . . . for me to be able to tell you." (As far as I'm concerned, Scott just confessed that he murdered Laci. Amber has been asking him for weeks if he did, and now he admits she guessed and knows the answers to her questions.)

The last couple of phone calls played in the courtroom had been made in mid-February, after Amber told Scott that she no longer wanted to see him, and their tone was different. Scott sounded desperate, and of course he was. He didn't want to lose Amber, which, I think, was the reason he'd practically confessed to her. I don't think he loved her. I think he wanted her around. Other than his family, he didn't have anyone else.

Yes, it was pretty clear he was desperate. He'd murdered his wife and baby. He'd lied to his girlfriend. He'd lied to everyone who crossed his path. I don't think even Scott knew the truth anymore. Actually, I think he did, but he couldn't face it. It was easier to keep telling lies. Except they got more complicated, harder to keep straight, and even-tually he realized the walls were closing in and it was just a matter of time until he was arrested.

In the end, he didn't even get the girl—or his freedom. He had nothing.

Amber finished testifying on August 24. Just as I had after her press conference, I thanked her for being so courageous, and I meant it. Those tapes made a powerful impression on the jury. She'd done a good job. As she left with her baby and her lawyer, I sensed she was heading into a new life as a celebrity, and while I might not have approved of the way she cashed in so quickly, I hoped the future would be good for her and her children.

Meanwhile, the trial continued, now more focused on the crime than on the individual. DA investigator Steve Jacobson, presenting information gleaned from tracking Scott's cell phone calls, narrowed the window of his alibi even further. While Scott claimed to have left for the bay on December 24 around 9:30 a.m., Jacobson said he made a call from near home at 10:08. Karen Servas found McKenzie at 10:18. His story didn't add up.

At three months into the trial, the prosecution was hitting its stride. The criticism was behind them, and Rick, Dave, and Birgit Fladager were rolling out their case methodically and to maximum effect. It wasn't just that Scott's story wasn't holding up; he was being exposed as a liar and a murderer.

It didn't seem to play well with his family, I can tell you that, and the tension it created spilled into the hallway. On September 2, as Brent and I left the courtroom, Lee Peterson was positioned in the hallway so that we had to walk by him. I bumped Brent's shoulder, a kind of gentle warning to not engage, and we kept our eyes straight ahead. But as we passed, Lee muttered, "Looks like Scott was looking all over for her." We didn't even acknowledge him.

When we returned to court after Labor Day, Lee Peterson instigated another situation. I was taking the escalator down, standing between Ron and Alex Loya of the DA's office, and as I turned to say something to Alex, I overheard something, or rather someone, say something. I looked around and spotted Lee and Jackie by the rail on the floor above us, near the top of the Up escalator, and what Lee had shouted in our direction was something like, "It sounds to me like your people don't have any evidence."

He obviously meant it for us, and Ron couldn't resist the bait.

"They have plenty of evidence, Lee," he responded.

Glaring at Ron, Lee shouted, "You idiot!"

Then it was Jackie's turn.

"Scott went fishing just like you did," she said.

Needless to say, this wasn't a high point of civility. It was, of course, what happens when people reach their breaking point. As their voices echoed through the hallway, I was absolutely shocked at their behavior and verbal attack on us. I could understand their frustration and concern for their son, but we didn't put him in the defendant's chair. Scott did that all by himself. Their anger was misdirected. Laci was dead, murdered, and they showed no compassion for us, only bitterness and hatefulness. After that incident, I worried about Lee and Jackie losing control, especially Lee, who I feared had the potential of getting physical. I wanted nothing to do with them. I told the prosecutors about my fears and warned them about Lee's behavior, how he lingered in the courtroom and made snide comments under his breath, and that it happened more and more frequently. In fact, it happened again right after that. On September 9, Brent came into the courtroom and said he had had a run-in with Lee as they came through the metal detector. Apparently Brent, in reference to the incident the day before, had said, "I heard you've been shooting your mouth off."

"You have a problem with that?" Lee asked.

"Yes, I do," Brent said.

"Well, I have a problem with your face," Lee snapped, and then he picked up Jackie's oxygen tank from security and gave Brent a stern look.

I didn't know quite how to handle this latest altercation. Lee, for his part, complained about Brent to Geragos, who went to Judge Delucchi and said God only knows what. After court, Birgit and Rick took us into a small side room and said the judge had lost his temper and banished both families to the back of the courtroom from our front-row seats.

I felt that Geragos would have liked to have had both families out of the courtroom and complained to the judge at every opportunity he got. I think he wanted the judge to ban us so he didn't have to do it and look like the bad guy. Part of what bothered me so much about all of this was that we didn't even know (and still don't know) what the accusations were. We were never told nor were we allowed to say whether they were true or not. For all I know, they could have been complete lies.

Birgit said the judge said that they could only tell us that we were being moved to the back of the courtroom.

"No, no, no, no!" I said. "There's no way I'm going to sit in the back!"

And I wasn't. To me, it was a slap in the face. In my opinion the judge was too lenient on the Petersons. If he'd clamped down on them early on for violating the gag order, we wouldn't have gotten to this place. Rick and Birgit bore the brunt of my rant and rage; I'm sure they were shocked by the way I carried on and thought I'd calm down if they waited. But I didn't.

And it wasn't only me. Ron was angry too, just not as vocal, and Brent felt terrible. He apologized repeatedly, kept his head down, and punished himself for causing the problem. I wouldn't allow that, though. I told him it wasn't his fault and he had "nothing to be sorry about."

"I'm glad you said something," I said. "I'm tired of those people bullying us."

Birgit suggested that I write a letter to the judge apologizing for the trouble. While I appreciated the counsel, I said I didn't see what I or any of us in the family had to apologize for. We hadn't done anything. We took advantage of court being dark the next day, a Friday, and discussed this latest situation with people from the DA's victim's advocate group. They had a few ideas that didn't involve an apology, and I left feeling better. But they called that afternoon to say they had no luck changing the court's mind.

I was ready to explode that evening when I called Birgit and told her that I'd try to write a letter to the judge. I was only doing it, I said, because I didn't appear to have any other options. I spent all of Saturday thinking about what I could say as opposed to what I wanted to say, and on Sunday morning I sat down at the computer. That night I called Birgit in tears.

"I've tried all weekend to write a letter of apology to the judge," I said. "But I can't do it. I don't know what I'm supposed to apologize for. We're being punished, yet we can't be told why? This is outrageous."

"Did you write *anything*?" she asked.

In fact, I had written a letter, but as I told Birgit, it wasn't an apology. I couldn't do that. Instead, I'd written my thoughts on why the judge was wrong to have moved us from our seats, including a list of grievances that supported my claim. It amounted to an argument as to why we needed to be in that courtroom, in our seats, as if it was a right, not a privilege.

I read it to Birgit.

> *We came to Redwood City with the intention of attending this trial to hear the evidence against Scott Peterson. Laci was murdered and we NEED to know what happened. We NEED to know why she was murdered. We NEED to be in the courtroom to hear the testimony.*
>
> *We cannot depend on hearing the facts as reported from the media. We NEED to be in the courtroom for Laci, to be her eyes and her ears and her voice.*
>
> *We want justice for Laci and Conner. We want a fair trial. We want to make sure there are no grounds for appeal. We do NOT want a mistrial.*
>
> *We SHOULD be entitled to focus our complete attention on the trial. Instead, the circus-like atmosphere that surrounds this trial and courthouse is a constant diversion.*
>
> *When this trial is over the circus will move on. All the distractions, diversions, interruptions, etc, that transpired during the trial will be forgotten by most. However, all of this will have a lasting affect on our lives.*

The decisions that are made in this courtroom will affect our lives forever. This is our past, our present, and our future. The reality is, no matter the outcome of this trial, I will NEVER have Laci back and I will NEVER see my grandson.

We have already been through so much prior to coming to Redwood City. The following is a list of obstacles we have to endure in order to attend the trial of the man accused of murdering our daughter and sister.

1. *We know we are in the courtroom only because the defense has agreed to allow this. We also know, and it constantly hangs over our heads, that they can rescind that stipulation anytime they want. I requested that I not be a witness so I can attend the trial without restrictions, however, that was declined.*

2. *The Petersons have been allowed to violate the gag order over and over. There was a 3-page article in the* San Francisco Chronicle, *an interview with* People *magazine, an interview with the* Modesto Bee, *AND, in the middle of the trial they did a television interview with Barbara Walters that aired on July 9, 2004.*

3. *June 28, 2004 the judge reprimanded the MPD for violating the gag order and said EVERYONE who is a witness is under the gag order. I asked if the Petersons would be held accountable for violating the gag order if the Barbara Walters interview is aired. I was told they would not because the interview was recorded BEFORE this date. I know, and so do the Petersons, this gag order has been in place for over a year. So once again, they are getting away with this violation. I was very upset about this. Out of sheer frustration I went to Lee, Jackie and Janey Peterson and said to each one of them, "Now you know what the gag order is about." I know I should not have done this, but I did. I have never spoken a word to them since that day. I have tried to stay as far away as possible from them.*

4. *We have to constantly look over our shoulders to make sure there is no media around us when we speak for fear our conversation will be aired on the 5:00 news. And worse yet, it won't be reported correctly.*

5. *We have to constantly watch out for jurors, in the hallways, restrooms, cafeteria, for fear we might come face to face with one and be accused of doing something inappropriate.*

With my voice rising, I read her seven more points, including the last one, my account of the escalator incident that instigated this whole situation. She said it was strong and asked me to send it to her so she could give it to the judge on Monday.

I don't know for sure if Judge Delucchi read it, but at least Birgit gave me the opportunity to vent my frustrations. When the trial got under way again on Monday, the Petersons took seats in the middle row instead of the front. A few minutes later they were told they could return to the front row. We would've been in our usual front-row seats, too, but that week's testimony focused on forensics and pathology, so we stayed home. None of us wanted to hear any of those horrible details.

Our first day back in court was September 20, the start of what I considered the most crucial part of the trial, and I was full of anticipation. It was Craig Grogan's turn to testify, and as the lead detective, his job on the stand was to put the entire case together for the jury. We'd talked countless times since Laci disappeared, often because I wanted to ask him a question.

One day after listening to a phone conversation between Craig and Scott played in the courtroom, I asked Craig why he spoke so quickly whenever he talked to Scott but then spoke markedly slower every time he spoke to me.

"Well, that's because I ask you *one* question and then you ask me *five*."

"Touché," I said, laughing.

We had a good relationship, but he hadn't for the most part been able to give me the answers. Once the trial started, we rarely talked, a pretty drastic change from the way it had been. In fact, one day, I called him up. At first, I asked a question, then I gave up any pretense and admitted, "I just missed talking to you."

"That's okay," he laughed. "I haven't been interrogated for a long time."

That, as we knew, was about to change.

Chapter Twenty-nine

Rumors of trouble in the prosecution's camp flew around the courthouse when Craig Grogan took the stand because it was Birgit Fladager, not Dave Harris, who questioned him. But the switch wasn't a shake-up, as some speculated. Dave simply got extremely sick with the flu, the poor guy, and Birgit, who'd been prepping Craig, stepped in at the last minute. As it turned out, she did a spectacular job of lawyering in a high-pressure situation. Craig opened with a summary of the case's magnitude. He said the investigation produced more than 42,000 pages of discovery; over 10,000 tips; 115 audiotapes; and 193 sightings of Laci in 26 states, Canada, France, Italy, and even the Virgin Islands. Some 300 officers had been involved as well as 90 separate law enforcement agencies. Craig himself had interviewed or mentioned more than 300 people in his reports.

My own attempt to keep a record of the case gave me a pretty good idea of its enormous size and scope. I'd filled several boxes with all the newspaper and magazine stories I saw, and of course I documented everything I could, including my notes from the prelim and the trial. One time, I called Craig to ask a question and our conversation turned to the enormity of the case.

"We've got 29,000 pages," he said.

I thought to myself, I'm probably only 1,000 pages behind you.

I've heard over and over that Amber Frey was the star witness in the case. I disagree. The star witness was Craig Grogan.

On the stand, Craig had no difficulty articulating the reasons why the police made Scott their top and only suspect.

- He'd reported Laci missing (to me), but he didn't call the police.
- He was the last person to see her alive.
- His alibi changed and didn't make sense.
- He'd said he went fishing in the bay, but his fishing tackle was mostly for fresh water.
- The bodies turned up near where he'd been fishing.

Craig confirmed what others before him had said—that Scott didn't behave like a normal husband whose wife had disappeared, then turned up dead. He never seemed upset. Actually, he never showed any reaction at all. He never asked for the results of any of the searches—of his house, his warehouse, or the bay. Craig recalled Scott, in an early interview, suggesting that Laci was abducted for her baby. Then, bizarrely, Scott had asked, "After Laci has the baby, do you think I'll get half my family back?"

What? I wondered if I heard that right. What did he mean by *half my family*? He was so obviously suspicious in the beginning, and of course by the time Craig testified, I knew he was so obviously guilty. As far as I was concerned, if anyone still had doubt about Scott's guilt, Craig erased it when he said that after Laci and Conner were found, Scott never contacted law enforcement to ask if the bodies were theirs. I thought that was perhaps the most crucial observation.

What kind of normal husband wouldn't be curious enough to ask? Scott didn't have to ask, because he knew the answer. Besides, at the time the bodies were found, he was on the run in San Diego.

The prosecution played a tape of Scott two weeks after Laci disappeared talking with Realtor Brian Argain. The jury heard Scott telling the Realtor that Laci wouldn't want to stay there if she came back and he wanted to sell their house furnished. Birgit followed this by asking Craig to read an e-mail Scott had sent me back when I wanted to get in the house, explaining that he wanted to keep the Tiffany lamps that Laci loved so they'd be there when she came home.

If he knew that she loved the lamps, why did he want to sell the house furnished?

Listening to Craig's testimony caused me to wonder, as I had many times previously, if Laci would still be alive if she had never gotten pregnant. I thought she would've been. Something else I thought about: The week after Scott met Shawn was the week Laci got sick while walking in the park. Other than morning sickness, she hadn't felt ill during her entire pregnancy. I wondered if Scott could've been trying to poison her to cause a miscarriage, and when that didn't happen, maybe he decided the only choice he had was to murder her.

I'll never get answers to these questions or know if my theories are true. I don't know how Laci died.

One of the trial's most powerful moments occurred when Craig provided a list of forty-one reasons why he thought that investigators should search for Laci's body in the San Francisco Bay. I have a copy of the list, which I've read dozens of times—each entry, written in bold, confident capital letters, striking me as a piece of the puzzle showing how Scott plotted Laci's murder:

1) Ticket; 2) Gas; 3) Cell Sites; 4) Dog Track; 5) Tarp; 6) Claim/ Statement; 7) Boat; 8) Fishing Lic; 9) Fishing Tackle; 10) Anchor; 11) Whistle; 12) 3 Visits Rental Cars (Craig was referring to Scott's repeated visits to the Berkeley Marina); 13) Golfing Switch; 14) Golfing Statement Prior; 15) No One Knows Abt Boat; 16) Umbrellas In AM; 17) Body Not Found in Lakes; 18) Salt Water; 19) Deep Water Currents; 20) Current Chart + Bay (Internet); 21) Didn't Clean Up Shop; 22) Didn't Want News Spread Abt Boat "Not Going To Tell Boss"? 23) Paid Cash For Boat; 24) Boat Not Registered; 25) Boat Cover . . . Why? . . . Cover Body?; 26) Nervous Erratic Driving Bakersfield; 27) [missing] 28) X Mas Eve Low Risk Of Others At Dock; 29) Researched Other Boat Launch Areas; 30) Financial Probs/$1,400 Boat; 31) Media Coverage Abt Russian Bodys; 32) Gun In Glove Box; 33) Wet Clothes; 34) Scuffed Knuckle; 35) No Reason To Go Fishing Instead Of Golfing If He Didn't Have To Change Story

Because of Wits [witnesses]; 36) Quote Just Wanted Get Boat In Water; 37) Fishing Tackle Not For Salt Water; 38) Doesn't Know What Fishing 4; 39) Describes Island; 40) Test Boat Never Used Ocean; 41) Weather Conditions Bay.

Birgit led Craig through each point, then she had him address Scott's character and lack of credibility. Earlier, jurors had watched Scott's interview with Diane Sawyer and heard him tell her that he'd told police about his affair with Amber. Asked if that was true, Craig said it wasn't. Furthermore, Craig said Scott denied having an affair with Amber even after being shown a photo of them together at a Christmas party.

I watched the jury carefully the whole time Craig was on the stand, studying them for their reactions. During those eight long days Craig testified, there was no mistaking his effectiveness. For the first time since the trial began I had eye contact with every single juror except for one who was out of range. While none of them smiled, nodded, or gave any overt indication of their opinion, their willingness to look at me was a good sign. It told me they got it. Even the media reported that the prosecution's case had come together at last, and it had. On October 5, Rick called Det. John Buehler, the prosecution's hundred and seventy-fourth witness, and when he was done, the prosecution rested.

I felt confident when we left the courthouse that there wasn't going to be an acquittal. At worst, we'd get a hung jury. But Scott wasn't walking out of there, I knew that much. You couldn't sit in that courtroom, hear all the testimony, and think Scott was anything other than guilty. Nothing else made sense.

Now it was the defense's turn. I had no sense of Geragos's case, or if he even had one.

Not many people saw this, but one day in October, just after entering the courtroom, Lee Peterson approached Dave Harris and said, "Liar! Liar! Liar!" I thought that should've gotten him kicked out of court, if for no other reason but for the safety of the prosecutors. It seemed to me that he was becoming completely out of control. Geragos's defense, which ran a mere six days, included just thirteen witnesses. He did a good job of trying to destroy the prosecution's case but he never did deliver on his opening-statement promise to show Scott was "stone-cold innocent." Nor did he bring in any of the five key witnesses he'd mentioned as having seen Laci walking McKenzie on the morning of December 24. Geragos's best hope was Dr. Charles March, a fertility expert who theorized that Conner had survived until December 29, which, if correct, would have blown the prosecution's entire case. But under cross-examination by Dave Harris, March and his theory quickly crumbled. The jury actually laughed at him, and he pleaded with Harris to "cut me some slack."

After that fiasco, Geragos called Lee and Jackie Peterson. Jackie attempted to explain why she'd given Scott the $15,000 in cash he carried when he was arrested, but I didn't think she made much sense. Geragos was all bluster. Don't get me wrong, he did a great job defending Scott, but the prosecutors did an even better job. Ironically, in the end it was his own description of the prosecution's case at the trial's opening that best captured his own—"zip, nada."

On October 30, the Saturday before closing arguments were scheduled to begin, I was running errands in Gottschalks department store when I was approached by four women, each of whom offered condolences and said they hoped justice was served for my daughter and her baby. Later, at a jewelry store where I'd dropped off my rings for repair, a gray-haired man, probably in his seventies, asked politely if he could say something to me.

First he put his hand on my shoulder as if to steady both of us. I saw tears in his eyes.

"I want you to know that my church prays for Laci and Conner all the time," he said.

"Thank you," I said.

"*He* [meaning Scott] had better never show his face in this town again," he continued.

"I don't think that's going to happen," I said. "I feel pretty sure."

Another day I was doing my banking and about to get into my car when I noticed a young woman in the car parked next to mine staring at me. She said, "Excuse me. Aren't you Laci's mom?" I said, "Yes." It turned out that my Laci had taught her daughter, who was also named Laci. She told me that one day in school my Laci had given her daughter a pencil with her name on it.

"I want you to have this," she said. "You'll probably never find another one with the name spelled the right way."

She added that her Laci cherished that pencil, and she wanted me to know how kind she thought my Laci had been.

It was moments like this that got me through the worst times. Each time I encountered someone like that elderly man or this woman, their kind words became a tiny patch on my heart. I hoped that someday there would be enough to close the wound.

On November 1, my birthday, Rick Distaso delivered the closing statement, boiling down hundreds of hours of testimony into a single, searing image: "The defendant strangled or smothered Laci Peterson the night of December 23 or in the morning while she was getting dressed on the twenty-fourth." After explaining that strangulation didn't leave much evidence, he said Scott backed his truck up to the gate and placed Laci in the back.

Rick also showed jurors a photograph of Laci sitting alone at a Christmas party and reminded them that on the night that picture was taken, Scott was partying with Amber. "She had no idea what was coming," he said. He said that Laci probably trusted Scott more than anybody else in the world, but he didn't want to be tied to a kid for the rest of his life, he didn't want to be married anymore, he wanted his freedom, and so he killed her. Rick argued that Scott had premeditated Laci's murder. He cited Scott's purchase of a fishing license prior to his Christmas Eve fishing trip, the bag of cement he'd used to make anchors for the boat he hadn't told anyone about, and most obviously telling his girlfriend, Amber Frey, that he'd lost his wife.

"She [Laci] was dead to him a long time before he killed her," Rick said.

Even though the evidence was largely circumstantial, Rick told the jury that was more than enough, that Scott's prints were apparent all over the crime. "It's a simple case where a man murdered his wife," he said. "The only person we know who was there at the exact location where Laci's and Conner's bodies washed ashore at the exact time when they went missing is sitting right there," he said.

Then he pointed to Scott Peterson.

"That alone is proof beyond a reasonable doubt," he said. "You can take that to the bank, and you can convict this man of murder."

From what I observed, Rick seemed like he connected with the jurors, who took notes, nodded occasionally, and refrained from laughing when the DA mentioned Dr. March. The judge kept his eyes on us. I mostly watched Scott, who became an interesting read. He turned away when Rick displayed photos of him with Amber, and tried to look sad when Rick brought up Conner's condition at the time he was recovered.

On November 2, Geragos began his closing remarks by having Scott face the jury and then asking, "Do you all hate him?"

It was a rhetorical question, but still Scott looked as if the jury might answer and he probably wouldn't like their response. He looked, to me, to be concerned, even a little scared for a change. He paid close attention to Geragos as he argued that the prosecution's case was based on the hope that the jury would convict Scott simply because he was "the biggest jerk that ever walked the face of the earth." But he said that just wasn't enough. Proof of his client's innocence, he said, included Scott's invitation to Amy to join them for pizza dinner on the twenty-third and the lack of forensic evidence. As for Amber, he said that while Scott literally got caught with his pants down, he treated Laci with a great deal of respect.

The next morning, once Geragos was finished, Rick offered a brief rebuttal to some of the points Geragos had made. Then I saw something that really surprised me. Rick pointed out that Scott did indeed have a cut on his hand, confirming there were marks that were consistent with him strangling or smothering Laci. Scott began to physically shake. Rick put his hands up to his throat and said Laci could have scratched Scott when he was strangling her. Scott scowled at Rick.

Judge Delucchi read the jury their instructions and sent them away to deliberate. He said he'd give us two hours' advance notice when they reached a verdict.

And that was it.

I couldn't move. I sat in my chair, overwhelmed by sadness. I hurt. I didn't want to be there; we shouldn't have been there, and I felt that more than ever. Laci should be alive, enjoying her life with Conner and Scott. This was all so wrong, a terrible mistake. Laci was gone and never coming back. If Scott was convicted, he was headed to jail for life or a death sentence. Either way, the future promised more pain for everyone, nothing else.

As for the possibility of a hung jury, I didn't think about it. I couldn't imagine going through another trial.

I didn't feel a sense of completion. Tears poured out of me as the courtroom cleared. After everything we'd been through, everything we'd heard, I still didn't know exactly what he'd done to Laci, which was the one thing I'd hoped to learn.

What a waste of those beautiful lives—and for what?

I wanted to approach Jackie and Lee and say that I was terribly sorry about everything that had happened—sorry for them, for us, and I wished to God it had never happened. But several people talked me out of it.

We went upstairs to a room that had been set aside for our family and friends. I still was so upset as I glanced into the room and then remained in the hallway. I don't know how other people feel in that position, but I was too upset to talk to anyone. I was drained. At one point, Kim Petersen approached and asked if I was upset because the DA was asking for the death penalty.

"No," I said. "That's not why. I'm upset because of everything," I said, fighting back tears. "We shouldn't be waiting in a courthouse to find out whether Scott will get life or death. We should be getting ready for Thanksgiving with Laci, Conner, and Scott. We should be a family. We should be celebrating life, not consumed by all this death."

Chapter Thirty

"Listen to this," said Laci's friend, brushing some strands of blond hair from her face. She was one of several of Laci's girlfriends visiting her gravesite with me. It was a beautiful day, perfect for reminiscing about Laci, and at some point Stacey remembered what has since become known as "the ladybug story." Since it involved the prosecution, she was surprised I hadn't heard it, and proceeded to tell me.

Dave Harris was the first person to notice something. It was summer, and at the time he was going through Laci's photo albums, searching for images that might have an emotional impact in the courtroom. He realized from things he saw in various pictures that Laci had a fondness for ladybugs. She did, too—sunflowers, dragonflies, and ladybugs. A couple months later, as the prosecution was preparing for the closing statement, Dave began noticing ladybugs showing up on his sleeve, in his car, on the bushes where he walked, all around him. It happened too often to be a coincidence, he thought, but when he told his wife, she looked at him as if he'd lost his mind.

He continued to see them, though. One day he was in court, and things weren't going well. He was feeling a little down. But then he spotted a ladybug fluttering around the defense table. He watched it land on a book in front of Geragos. Dave was transfixed by it. As he later told me, they were in a courtroom with no windows, on the second floor of a building. The nearest door leading outside was on the opposite end of the building. The likelihood of this thing just flying in were slim to none.

He chuckled. Rick and Birgit looked at him the way his wife had, like he was insane. At the break, he told them about the ladybugs. While he thought they were a sign that Laci was watching over them, he kept that to himself and merely said they were good luck. Rick and Birgit dismissed his ladybug theory as nonsense. However, pretty soon they started to notice ladybugs, too, and then they sheepishly mentioned it to Dave. He still didn't tell them his Laci theory, but he reiterated that they had nothing to worry about as long as they were seeing ladybugs.

One day in mid-October, as Rick worked on his closing statement in his hotel room, he saw a ladybug on the outside of his window screen. At first he didn't pay attention to it, but the ladybug seemed to be watching him as he worked. So he stared back, smiling, as he remembered Dave's story. Later, he told Birgit and Dave about his sighting and they were amused.

I have it on good authority that there were no ladybug sightings during jury deliberations, which lasted just under seven full days, and from what I gathered, no one was thinking about ladybugs on Friday, November 12, the day the verdict came back. That was understandable. Rick, Dave, and Birgit all had plenty of important things on their minds that morning when they got a phone call summoning them to the courthouse. They thought they were needed to clarify questions from the jurors, something they'd been doing regularly. They didn't expect a verdict.

But then as Birgit finished getting dressed, she went over to her hotel room window and saw her new favorite red-and-black winged insect—on the inside. Actually, the ladybug was between the glass and the screen. It was a strange place to see one and almost impossible to imagine how it got there. Stranger still was the timing. For some reason, Craig Grogan knocked on her door and she showed him. I don't know how, but by this time Craig also knew about the ladybugs, and he took it as a very good sign. Right before leaving, she called Rick and Dave with the news, and afterward, she later told me, all of them knew it was going to be a good day.

As the jury deliberated, we stayed in Redwood City. We didn't want to be too far away with only a two-hour notice of a verdict. Every time the phone rang during those seven days, I jumped out of my skin, expecting it to be a verdict. Lt. Mark Smith of the criminal investigations division of the DA's office kept us posted. I finally told poor Mark not to call unless we had a verdict. Fortunately, he knew me better than that. If he didn't keep calling me with regular updates, even nonupdates, I would've called him every ten minutes.

There seemed to always be something to keep me on edge. For instance, Juror 7 was booted the first day, followed by the new Juror 5 asking to be released the next. Both times I was on the phone immediately, and both times Birgit assured me that everything was being handled by the book. "Just as long as it's not a mistrial," I said. "That's my fear. I don't want a mistrial or a hung jury."

On November 10, Geragos put a replica of Scott's boat on the corner of a downtown office building near the courthouse. I later learned he'd bought the building for more than $1 million. During the trial the judge had turned down his request to show the jurors a videotaped demonstration of how the boat would have tipped over if Scott had thrown Laci into the bay. He staged this bit of sidewalk theater after jurors had inspected Scott's boat in person, one of them even stepping inside and gently rocking it.

Brent was the one who called me into the living room to watch a live TV report about the boat. I watched for a minute, listening to the analysts call it a dangerous and dramatic last-ditch effort by the defense, but after a few seconds I wasn't able to stomach any more of it. Brent was disgusted, too. Inside the boat, there was a pair of stuffed overalls, minus the head, hands, and feet. Those parts were sealed off with duct tape. The defense intended it to represent Laci. There were other items in the boat, also supposed to represent the items in Scott's boat.

That demonstration was disgusting, cruel, heartless, and inhumane. I wondered how Geragos would have reacted if it had been his daughter and some lawyer had pulled that stunt.

We weren't the only ones who took offense. Later that day the decent people of Redwood City turned the boat into a colorful, flower-filled shrine to Laci and Conner. Local flower shops were inundated by orders, some coming from as far away as New Zealand, and the deliveries piled up until the boat was barely visible. One florist said they were receiving flower orders with a delivery address of "The Boat." Geragos's ploy had backfired.

I woke up on November 12 wondering if we'd go into the weekend without a verdict. I'd heard that juries in general didn't like to deliberate over the weekend, yet I'd also heard this jury had inquired about a chaplain, leading us to think they may have been planning to work through the weekend. I don't think anyone had a feeling whether they'd deliver a verdict that Friday. But then around eleven fifteen, just after I'd stepped out of the shower, my cell phone rang. It was Birgit. "I want to let you know we have a verdict—"

"Oh my God," I exclaimed.

". . . and be in the courtroom at one o'clock," she finished.

I hung up and began hyperventilating. I still had to get dressed but I couldn't move. I was paralyzed. All of a sudden the enormity of the moment and all the emotion hit me. This is it, I thought. This is it. We're finally at the end of this thing.

I didn't know what was supposed to happen next. No one had filled me in on the procedures.

Ron, betting against a verdict coming in, had gone to Modesto the night before. Kim Petersen, who'd come over to keep me company, located Ron at our attorney's office. Both of them left immediately for Redwood City. Brent, Susie, and Gil were already at the house. (Susie and Gil were with us every day during the trial.) Between all of them, they contacted everyone they could and told them to pass the word.

For some reason I couldn't catch my breath. All of a sudden I wondered if there was a hung jury and I started to panic. I stopped Kim in the hallway and asked if it was possible we were going to get a hung jury.

"Tell me exactly what Birgit told you," she said.

"She said the jury had reached a verdict," I replied.

"Okay, that means they've reached a verdict," she said. "It means they've made a decision. It's not hung."

I took a deep breath, a couple of them, in fact—until I was able to concentrate again on getting dressed. I felt more confident the jury was going to come back with a guilty verdict. Of course a verdict also meant the possibility of an acquittal, but I was 99.9 percent sure they weren't going to let Scott go as long as Juror 8 had a vote. That was my secret theory. Juror 8 was a large man who sat with his arms folded across his chest. Later I learned his name was John and he was a Teamster. I detected strong feelings as the trial wound down. Before leaving for court, I ran my theory past Kim. I told her that I thought Scott's only chance at acquittal was if the other jurors killed Juror 8. She agreed. But just when I started to feel comfortable with that, I started to wonder if Juror 8 had been acting that way just to throw everybody off.

By the time we were ready to go, I didn't know what to think.

Mark Smith drove me, Brent, and Amy to the courthouse and led us through the underground entry in order to avoid the media, which had amassed in the front. Ron drove up from Modesto with our attorney Adam Stewart, arrived at the house just after we left, and got a ride to the courthouse with Bill Grogan, a Stanislaus County DA investigator. As I took my seat in the courtroom, I still couldn't breathe. When Ron showed up, I told him I felt like I was going to fall off a cliff.

When we got word of the verdict, Brent had called his wife, Rose, and she'd raced into town from Sacramento, where she'd finished a test for her master's degree. Rose and Brent arranged to meet in the parking lot when she got to the courthouse. Just before the one o'clock start time, she called his cell phone to let him know she was there. He left the courtroom with a sheriff's escort to look for her, but somehow they missed each other and she walked in alone. Judge Delucchi kept sticking his head out, checking the courtroom. Everyone was there except Brent. I was in tears, praying that the judge wouldn't announce the verdict until Brent returned. I watched the clock and the door, alternating every second. The pressure was extraordinary. I felt sure this was the thing that would cause me to crack. I was barely hanging on.

I was having a difficult time seeing the door because there were people meandering all around. (Only after the verdict was read did I realize that both sides of the courtroom were lined with law enforcement who moved into the middle aisle in case there were any problems.)

"Brent, where are you?" I kept saying under my breath.

Finally, he walked through the door and took his seat, and I swear, not a second later, Delucchi sat down, too.

I was between Ron and Brent, and I held their hands tightly. I couldn't believe this moment had finally arrived. We had been through so much and suddenly, as I told myself, this was it. We were getting a decision.

I watched Scott Peterson enter the courtroom for what I would think must have been the biggest day of his life, but you never would've known from his expression. His face wore what by now was typical, a smile.

Then the jury entered, looking as they always did, walking in single file and filling their seats. Except something about their entrance this time was undeniably different. One juror, the woman who always had a warm smile, the kind of smile that made you want to get to know her, looked directly at me as she entered the courtroom, and that expression told me everything I wanted to know:

SCOTT WAS GUILTY.

I looked at Ron and Brent and said, "He's guilty!" I squeezed both their hands even tighter.

A few minutes later the clerk read the verdicts: "We, the jury, in the above-entitled cause, find the defendant, Scott Lee Peterson, guilty of the crime of murder of Laci Denise Peterson. We, the jury, further find the degree of the murder to be that of the first degree." I completely lost it and burst into uncontrollable tears. There was more: "We, the jury, in the above-entitled cause, find the defendant, Scott Lee Peterson, guilty of the crime of murder of Baby Conner Peterson." It broke my heart to hear her say *murder of Baby Conner Peterson*. He didn't have a chance. "The degree of murder to be that of the second degree."

I looked at Scott when both verdicts were announced. I couldn't understand why, but he was grinning as the clerk read the guilty verdict for murdering Laci. Only when the clerk read the guilty verdict for murdering Conner did that smile vanish. What was so funny about being found guilty of first- and second-degree murder?

For whatever reason, Lee Peterson was in San Diego and hadn't been able to make it. Geragos, too, was a no-show, claiming he hadn't been able to get out of another trial in Los Angeles. But Pat Harris was there and he looked genuinely sad. I didn't hear or see a reaction from any member of Scott's family.

Scott never turned toward us. He never once looked at us. I think he believed he was going to get away with it.

I turned to Brent and put my arms around him. We held onto each other and sobbed.

It was done.

Afterward, we went upstairs to the special overflow room, which was packed with family, friends, members from the DA's office and MPD, spouses of the prosecutors and detectives who'd worked the case, and some members of the San Mateo County Sheriff's Office. All had waited there through the reading of the verdict. Even some of the people we had met from Redwood City were present. We were all crying and hugging one another. The last two years had taken a toll on us and everyone involved in the case. We lost our daughter, but our family and friends and Laci's girlfriends had made our loss their loss, and they'd been with us every step of the way since December 24, 2002, when Scott had started this nightmare by calling to ask if Laci was with me. They'd been through so much, and been so supportive; they had been indispensable. I thanked God for all of them, and I thanked each one of them individually.

Then Al Brocchini walked in. I was right there in the doorway. We hugged and he started to sob.

"I thought you'd never speak to me again," he said, referring to his difficult time on the stand.

"You thought wrong," I said, and hugged him again.

Then Craig Grogan walked in. He grabbed me and we held onto each other and cried. We didn't speak; we didn't have to. Everyone in that room knew getting this verdict was going to be extremely difficult because all of the evidence was circumstantial. Most had lived and breathed the case 24/7 for two years; they'd cried buckets of tears; they'd sat up all night with me; they'd searched rivers, lakes, swamps, farmland, and gutters; they'd had nightmares; they'd worked so hard; they'd prayed; and they'd done it all for Laci.

Between tears and hugs, all of us said the same thing: Thank God the jury saw the facts and realized that Scott murdered Laci. Thank God there was justice.

That afternoon we spent time with family and friends, some of whom had been stuck in traffic on their way to the courthouse and listened to the verdict on the radio. We went to the Canyon Inn, whose owners shut down the restaurant so we could have private time together. We had met the owners, Tim and Stephanie, when we first came to Redwood City. They are wonderful people, along with so many others we had come to know, including Mary, Maria, Doug, Maryanne, Don, Cameron, and so many more. We invited all the prosecutors and detectives and their spouses.

Rather than a celebration, there was a tremendous feeling of relief, a collective exhale. For me, it was a chance to say thank you, which meant a lot to me, and a time for all of us, like survivors, to raise a glass, or a few glasses, and toast each other for having made it to land. Ron, Dennis, and I each said some words, but there were no words that could express what we felt in our hearts.

I knew the penalty phase was scheduled to start at the end of the month. As I told several of the attorneys that night, I wasn't interested. Once I heard the guilty verdict, the trial was over for me. I didn't want to go back in that courtroom again. I didn't need to know if he was getting life or death. I just needed to know that Scott Peterson was guilty.

Chapter Thirty-one

After several delays, the penalty phase of the trial began on November 30, a Tuesday. Judge Delucchi's packed courtroom included Jackie and Lee Peterson, Geragos, and, of course, Scott, looking no worse since he had received the guilty verdicts. In a calm, unhurried voice, Dave Harris began the state's argument for giving Scott the death penalty over life in prison, explaining to jurors that they were going to hear Brent, Amy, Ron, and me tell them about Laci's life and the impact of her loss. As the DA made clear, this portion of the trial wasn't about who murdered Laci; it was about the effect of the crime, which he compared to "ripples on the water."

"When the defendant dumped the bodies of his wife and unborn child into the bay, those ripples spread out," Dave continued. "They touched many, many lives." That statement struck me as so true. Those ripples had inspired hundreds of strangers to help search for Laci, women to leave abusive relationships, and even soldiers fighting a war on the other side of the world to send e-mails. For Laci's family and friends, those ripples signified a very personal loss. Whether it was the lost chance to get another a phone call from Laci, the lost opportunity to meet our grandson and watch him grow, or the loss of our faith and innocence, something was gone in us forever, and that's what Ron, Brent, Amy, Dennis, and I were going to talk about.

The court had to decide whether Scott was going to get life in prison or death, but we wanted to keep the focus on Laci. This was our chance to tell the court about Laci's life and our loss in ways we couldn't the last time we were on the stand.

Taking the stand first, Amy said that our holidays would never be the same without Laci as the ringleader. Next was Brent, who described being irreparably crushed that his children wouldn't grow up with cousins. He also told of missing his sister. "I try to remember the good memories we have with each other, but they're overshadowed all the time by what happened to her," he said. "I miss her terribly." Then Ron reminisced about her as a fun little girl with a perpetually bright smile. "I wish I could be the one gone and not her," he said. "Part of my heart is gone."

I was last, and as I walked up to the stand, I didn't know if I was going to be able to speak. I'd gotten sick over the weekend and started to lose my voice. It bothered me. I feared I wasn't going to have a voice when my turn came to testify, and I'd miss the opportunity.

On Monday afternoon, though, I had gone to the cemetery to visit Laci and had felt a calm come over me. It was strange, and yet the change in my mood was undeniable. I realized it was pointless to worry about my voice. If I couldn't speak on Tuesday, it would be because Laci felt like I'd already said enough. And if I could speak, it was because she wanted me to.

"Tell us about Laci," Dave opened.

"Laci was just somebody that people gravitated to," I said. "She had a personality that made people feel comfortable. She was an upbeat person. She was more of a leader than a follower. She was involved. She followed her heart. She would fight for her beliefs, and when she wanted something, she went after it. She was a strong-willed person. . . ."

I didn't know exactly what Dave was going to ask, and something odd happened as I answered his questions. I was transported back in time to December 24, to the day and the hour that Laci had disappeared. I wasn't there physically, I was in that devastating moment emotionally, and I felt raw, vulnerable, and overwhelmingly sad.

As I spoke, I looked at Dave. I glanced at Scott but he didn't look back at me. There I was falling apart, and he purposefully ignored me. When Dave paused in his questioning to retrieve some photos from the clerk, I stared directly at Scott. He and Geragos were laughing. I was incredulous; *they were smiling and laughing together.* I was talking about how much I missed Laci, how she shouldn't have been murdered. How dare they!

Dave put up a photo of my mom, Laci, and me from a Mother's Day party in 2002, a week after Laci's birthday. The party had been at Laci's house. Jackie had been there, too. Then Dave asked how I'd celebrated the last Mother's Day.

"I laid on the floor and cried most of the day because she should have been there," I said. "She should have been a mother also, and that was taken away from her." I looked directly at Scott again and heard my voice grow louder, stronger, and angrier. "She wanted to be a mother!" Scott, looking indifferent, still ignored me. The anger I felt a second earlier turned to unbridled rage. I felt myself rise slightly out of my chair, and then I was yelling, "Divorce is always an option, not murder!" Later I heard that outburst caused the whole courtroom to sit up. I didn't realize I had shouted it. I hadn't planned on saying that, either. I simply spoke the words as they formed in my aching heart.

"Laci always got motion sickness and you knew that and that's the place you took her and you put her in the bay and you knew that she would be sick for eternity, and you did that to her anyway."

I described the way I said good-bye to Laci at the funeral home. "I knew she was in the casket and I knew the baby was there and I knew she didn't have arms to hold him, either. She should have had her arms and her head, her entire body.

"Every morning when I get up, I cry. It takes me a long time just to be able to get out of the house. I keep thinking, Why did this happen? I wanted to know my grandson. I wanted Laci to be a mother. I wanted to hear her called Mom. . . . I think about her all the time. . . . Laci didn't deserve to die!"

I remember at one point feeling as if I didn't have the strength to say one more word, yet I pushed myself because I wanted everyone to feel the last moment she spent with Scott Peterson. "I just hope she didn't know what was happening."

I finished at the end of the day. By the time I got home, my voice was totally gone and I was ready to collapse. I went straight to bed, but

I didn't rest. I felt terribly guilty, almost ashamed by my testimony in court, for having talked so intimately about Laci, especially about the condition of her body. Even though those details had been discussed in the trial and printed in newspapers, I felt like I'd betrayed her, like I had revealed too much that was private.

Kim Petersen heard me crying, came in, and sat on the bed. She thought I was being too hard on myself.

"Don't you realize that wasn't you talking?" she said. "It was Laci. Think about it. You told me that if she wanted you to say more, she would make sure you still had a voice today so you could speak. Did you have a voice? Were you able to speak?"

I nodded.

"See, that was Laci speaking, not you," she continued. "Laci wanted Scott to hear her words. She wanted the jury to know what he did to her. Laci wanted her side of the story told, and she made sure you could do it."

That made sense to me and eased some of my guilt.

Geragos called on Scott's parents and friends to present his better side, but their words and anecdotes were about a Scott that didn't exist anymore, not the Scott Peterson who sat in the courtroom. On December 9, 2004, Dave Harris delivered his closing arguments. Earlier, I reminded him that it was two years ago to the day that Scott had bought a boat and told Amber he had lost his wife. When he brought that up in court, Scott seemed bothered and looked as though he hadn't realized the significance of the date. But once his other attorney, Pat Harris, started with the defense's final words, Scott retreated back into his shell, and he was gone again.

On December 13, the jury came back with a verdict. Ron and I were at a store in Redwood City when Mark Smith of the Modesto DA's office called my cell phone to tell me the jury had made a decision, and the judge was going to announce it after lunch.

That afternoon, the clerk read the verdict. "We the jury in the above titled cause fix the penalty at death."

One thing Judge Delucchi said in particular moved me more than

I can say. In summarizing the case, the judge brought attention to Conner: "The young boy Conner wasn't even permitted to take a breath of air on this earth."

As I've said, the trial ended for me when Scott was found guilty. His life was over whether he got life in prison or death. As the decision was read, Scott sat with a blank look on his face. He didn't look scared or horrified. To me, he just didn't seem to care. He didn't look like it was a big deal to him. From what I saw, Scott's parents didn't react, either. Maybe they felt the way I did, or maybe they were still convinced he was innocent and would continue to fight. I couldn't imagine myself in their place. I felt bad for them.

That is, until Ron turned to Lee and said, "I'm sorry," and Lee responded by saying, "Fuck you."

Afterward, the jury met for several hours with the press, and we wanted to meet them as well, but to do so required walking through the media; none of us were up to being in the public eye at that time. I wasn't ready to make any statements. I didn't want to submit my family or myself to a battery of personal questions. I hadn't processed the whole emotional ordeal for myself. Instead I released a statement by e-mail and posted it on our Web site:

> Today is not a joyous day. It is just another sad reminder of WHOM we have lost, our Laci and Conner; a reminder of WHAT we have lost, a huge part of our family, and, our lives, as we once knew them.
>
> There are no winners in a case like this one. We are families who are suffering horrendous losses.

As for the jurors, we finally met them on January 15 at the Canyon Inn in Redwood City. The private gathering was oddly therapeutic. All of us were eager to meet, and I couldn't tell who needed it more, them or us.

Every one of them had a personal story about sacrifices they had made being on the jury and devoting six months of their lives to this trial. I marveled at the courage some of them showed in overcoming their own personal tragedies including children who had died and husbands who had been killed. It's amazing how much we shared in such a short time.

One woman gasped as she overheard Dave Harris retelling me the ladybug story. She said she'd been on a walk one day and saw a ladybug stuck to her shirt. She had tried shooing it away, but it wouldn't budge. The next day she was picked for jury duty. She said she had always felt that the ladybug had some significance.

The jury foreman was impressive in his knowledge of the details from the case. In fact, all of them were. Juror 1 discussed how the experience had changed him. It was a memorable, emotion-charged day—all of us strangers who'd gone through an extraordinary event together without knowing anything about each other until that January day.

All of us had tears in our eyes at one time or another when we spoke. Some of them explained how they'd reached their decision, citing Scott's lies, his lack of emotion, and his calls with Amber. They didn't see any alternative suspects, they didn't have any concerns or second thoughts about the way they'd voted, they understood the case as well if not better than anyone, and in the end, they all agreed Scott had murdered Laci.

Thirteen of the jurors were so committed to seeing the trial through to the end that they also attended the March 16 hearing where Delucchi upheld Scott's death sentence. Scott wore a suit, but his hands were shackled around his waist. In contrast to the way I broke down when I saw him chained at his arraignment, I was now beyond feeling sorry for him. On this exact date two years before, I'd followed a psychic's directives to the Berkeley Marina and the Albany Bulb, knowing Laci was somewhere in the water.

She'd turned up near there less than a month later.

No, I didn't feel sorry for Scott. I was numb. I was tired of being in court. I prayed this was the last time.

The hearing was our chance to address Scott directly through our Victim's Impact Statement. Brent went first and was immediately interrupted by Scott's mother, when she said, "That's not true, Brent." Then Lee Peterson cut him off, shouting, "You're a liar." I was incensed. We'd waited two years for this chance to confront Scott. They had no right to talk. I was ready to say something if Delucchi didn't, but fortunately he issued a warning: "I don't care who you are, if you interrupt the proceedings, you're going to be removed from the courtroom, all right?"—after which Lee stormed out of the courtroom. Jackie followed a few moments later after a bailiff said something to her. They missed Brent's shocking admission—that he'd bought a gun intending to kill Scott. "[But] I chose not to kill you myself for one reason," he said. "So you would have to sweat it out and not take the easy way out."

Rose expressed her disgust for once letting Scott touch her pregnant stomach, then Amy shared similar feelings of revulsion and anger. Dennis called Scott a "piece of shit" and said he "was going to burn in hell for this." Ron was equally blunt.

Through it all, Scott talked to Geragos or leafed through papers. But I was next, and I wanted him to pay attention to me. I'd worked on my statement since February 2003, more than two years, and I wanted him to hear every word. It wasn't just me talking to him. It was also Laci.

"There is unbelievable sadness in my heart for the loss of what was and what should have been," I said.

"On December 24, 2002, the Scott Peterson I had known for more than eight years ceased to exist. The Scott I knew was the one Laci loved so much. He was the center of her world. I entrusted him with her, to love and protect her.

"Scott, you made a conscious decision to murder Laci and Conner—"

At that point, I saw him shake his head in disagreement.

"Yes, you did," I snapped. "You planned and executed their murders. You decided to throw Laci and Conner away, dispose of them as though they were just a piece of garbage. You thought, after a few weeks, we would stop looking for Laci and then just forget about her, as though she never existed.

"Your arrogance led you to believe you are more intelligent than everyone else; that you would be able to manipulate the entire situation so you would never be suspected of any wrongdoing. This was easy for you to believe because you killed Laci long before you murdered her.

"You were wrong, *dead* wrong. You aren't intelligent at all. You are stupid. Stupid to believe you could get away with murder. Stupid to believe murder was your only way out of marriage. Stupid to believe we would forget about Laci. You equated a small town with small minds.

"On December 14, 2002, you told Laci you had to meet a business associate in San Francisco and would have to spend the night there. You told her you wouldn't be able to attend the Christmas party with her that evening. On December 15, 2002, we had dinner with you and Laci at your home.

"I didn't know, at that time, that you didn't go to San Francisco; instead you attended a Christmas party with your lover and then spent the night with her. You attended a Christmas party with your girlfriend while your unsuspecting seven-and-a-half-month-pregnant wife attended her Christmas party *alone*.

"It makes me ill knowing, at the very time we were having dinner with you and Laci that evening, you had already set your plan in motion to murder her. There was no way for me to know December 15, 2002, would be the last time I would ever see Laci alive. BUT YOU KNEW IT!

"You are selfish, heartless, spoiled, self-centered, and *you are a coward*. But above all, you are an evil murderer.

"You murdered my beautiful Laci and her precious baby, Conner, my grandson. You murdered your *own* baby. *YOU ARE A BABY KILLER!!!!!!* Not even Satan will claim to have a part in your making. You were man-made, a product of the environment you were raised in.

"You could have chosen to change your path and distance yourself from evil. Unfortunately, you didn't. You, Scott, are proof that evil can lurk anywhere. You don't have to *look* evil to *be* evil.

"You wanted to eliminate Laci from your life. The logical solution would be divorce. However, typical of your selfish, cowardly way, you chose what you thought would be the easiest way for *you*. You *murdered* her. WHY? WHY, SCOTT, DID YOU MURDER HER? The fact you no longer wanted Laci did NOT give you the right to murder her. She was not a possession to rid yourself of. HOW DARE YOU MURDER HER!!!! She was MY baby. I *always* wanted Laci, and I *will* for the rest of my life. I trusted you. Laci loved you with all her heart, unconditionally. You lied to her over and over again, and when she was most vulnerable, you selfishly cheated on her and then you murdered her.

"You hide behind a façade and pretend to be someone you are not. I now know you are nothing but an empty, hollow shell. You have no love, no feelings, no compassion, no heart, and you have NO soul. You have no remorse for murdering your wife and your baby.

"Laci was only five feet tall, Scott. She didn't stand a chance to physically protect herself from you. It was easy for you to overpower and, then, murder her and your own innocent baby boy. How did that make you feel, Scott? Were you proud of yourself? Did you feel a sense of accomplishment? Did you feel relief?

"Your selfish act of murdering Laci has caused unbearable pain and heartache. You took a beautiful life, and her precious baby, away from us. There is a huge hole in my heart that will never heal. I grieve every single day for Laci and Conner. I miss Laci so much; I miss having a daughter, our friendship, our talks, our laughter. I miss making plans with her, our shopping excursions, our lunches together. I miss teasing her, hearing her giggle, watching her mature. I miss her telling me about the plants she purchased for her yard and the new recipe she is going to try tonight. I miss listening to her talk about her baby and her plans for the future. I miss her asking me for advice or for my opinion. I miss being my daughter's mother. I will never have the opportunity to see her become a mother.

"I will never meet my grandson. I'm left only to wonder what color would his hair and eyes be. Would he look like Laci? Would he have her long dark eyelashes? Would he have her dimples? Would he have her upbeat personality? Would he have her laugh? What would his interests be? What kind of person would he be? Would he like school? Would he like sports? What costume would Laci have him wear for his first Halloween? Would he cry when he has his picture taken with Santa? What would be in his Easter basket?

"I will never have the opportunity to know—because his father murdered him.

"I wasn't there to protect Laci, to protect her from you, her husband, the man she loved and thought loved her, the last person she should *need* to be protected from. Laci didn't know the Scott that sits in this courtroom. She would never put her life, or the life of her baby, in jeopardy by living with a murderer. She loved you but she didn't NEED you, Scott. Laci would have survived a divorce and learned to live without you had she been given the opportunity.

"I find solace in the irony that you sentenced *yourself* to death when you murdered Laci. You were afforded something that Laci was not— an opportunity to plead your case in an attempt to avoid a death sentence. You were given a trial, an attorney, a judge, and a jury. Laci wasn't that fortunate. You took it upon yourself to be her attorney, her judge, and her jury. You took it upon yourself to sentence her to death and be her executioner.

"Tell me, Scott, before you murdered Laci, did you *ask* her if she wanted to *die*? Did you *ask* her if she wanted to *live*? NO, you didn't! I could ask you, 'Do *you* want to die? Do *you* want to live?' But I won't ask because *I* don't care what *you want*. I only care that you get what you *deserve*, DEATH.

"What you didn't count on was Laci's spirit and her love for her family, friends, and her baby were more powerful than your evilness. Laci tried her best to protect her baby. She kept him inside her body right up until the very end. It is truly a miracle, and I thank God, that both Laci and our baby Conner were found. They are together again, and will remain together for all eternity.

"We had to bury Laci without her arms to hold her baby in and without her head to see and hear and smell and kiss her sweet little baby Conner with. There was a time when I couldn't bear to look at a picture of Laci, because each time I did I envisioned her this way. You have no idea what the very thought of this does to my soul.

"I finally convinced myself to see her body as she was, not as she is. Now, what I see when I look at her pictures is her beautiful smile, her contagious giggle, her happy heart, her love of life, her great expectations of becoming a mother, her generous soul, her knowing how much I love her, and me knowing how much she loves me.

"I am haunted every single day with visions of you murdering Laci. Did she know you were killing her? Did she look at you? Did you look into her eyes while you were killing her? Was she alive when you put her in the water, struggling to free herself from the weights you put on her? I *know* she was terrified, and I wasn't there to save her life.

"Nothing will ever undo your evil act. However, it's time for you to take responsibility for murdering Laci and Conner, *your son, your own flesh and blood.* You deserve to be put to death as soon as possible.

"I want to know, Scott, what were you *thinking* as you were killing Laci and Conner? What do you think *Laci* was thinking as you, her beloved husband, was killing her and your son? I'll tell you what *I* think they were thinking and I hope these words haunt you every second of every minute of every hour for the rest of your life!

"Laci was thinking: SCOTT!! WHAT ARE YOU DOING? WHY ARE YOU KILLING ME? YOU KNOW HOW MUCH I LOVE YOU. I BELIEVED IN YOU. YOU PROMISED TO TAKE CARE OF ME AND PROTECT ME. YOU'RE MY LOVER, MY PARTNER, AND MY BEST FRIEND. I WANT TO BE YOUR WIFE AND THE MOTHER OF YOUR BABY. YOU TOLD ME YOU WANTED THAT, TOO. SCOTT, I WANT TO LIVE. I DON'T WANT TO DIE. I DON'T UN-DERSTAND WHY YOU'RE KILLING US. PLEASE STOP. I DON'T WANT TO DIE!! I DON'T WANT TO DIE!

"Conner was thinking: DADDY!! WHY ARE YOU KILLING MOMMY AND ME? I HAVEN'T MET YOU YET, BUT I LOVE YOU. IF YOU LET US LIVE LONG ENOUGH FOR YOU TO MEET ME, I KNOW YOU WILL LOVE ME, TOO. DADDY, PLEASE, PLEASE DON'T KILL US. I WANT TO

LIVE. MOMMY HAS ENOUGH LOVE FOR BOTH OF US. I PROMISE I WON'T TAKE HER AWAY FROM YOU. DADDY, WHY ARE YOU KILLING US? PLEASE, PLEASE STOP. WE DON'T WANT TO DIE. WE DON'T WANT TO DIE!

"And now, Scott Peterson, I am saying this to you: YOU DESERVE TO BURN IN HELL FOR ALL ETERNITY!"

When I sat down, everyone was in tears—except for Scott, his lawyers, and his family. I didn't care. I was done with him, done with the trial, just done. Scott declined Judge Delucchi's offer to make a statement. Then Delucchi announced he was officially upholding the death sentence, calling the murders "cruel, uncaring, heartless, and callous."

At 3:10 a.m. the next morning, Scott was removed from San Mateo County Jail, wearing an orange prison outfit, shackles, and a bulletproof vest. He was put in a white van and driven to San Quentin State Prison, overlooking the bay where he'd disposed of Laci, and where he became the six hundred and forty-fourth prisoner on death row. The trial may have been behind us, but we still felt Laci's absence, and we always will. We'd always have questions, we'll always cry, and our hearts will always ache.

So different had our lives become, Scott's and ours, and yet we'd always share Laci, each in different ways. For me, the ringing phone would never be Laci. Christmas would never feel like a celebration. I'd always remember her birthday without her. I'd never turn down her street and see her. I'd never know my grandson. I'd never hear him talk.

God, how I miss her. How I will always miss her . . .

Chapter Thirty-two

R on and I were with friends on a houseboat in the bay, under the Bay Bridge in fact, when my father was killed in a car accident. It was August 1981. He was fifty, still young.

Ron got a phone call, then waited until we got home to tell me. When he turned to me and said, "I have some bad news," I felt my legs go weak and I had to sit down. I could barely breathe, but I asked, "Has something happened to Laci?" Then he told me it was my dad. I headed out the door to go to my parents' home. Ron filled me in on the way there. But after my father's funeral, life gradually returned to normal. I'm not sure why or exactly how it happened, but I think it may have had something to do with the fact that my dad was older than me and his death, while still an unexpected tragedy, followed a natural order. I know it was hard for my mom, but after the first crushing days and months, I began to accept the loss.

I can't accept Laci's murder. I just can't. There's nothing as devastating as the death of a child, and there's nothing as unacceptable as murder. Together, the two are an unimaginable horror. December 24, 2002, is the day the sky crashed down on our lives. Time stopped.

Laci's been gone almost three years as I write this sentence and the wounds have yet to heal. I measure life from that call—things happened either before or after. Life has gone on, but in increments of pain, anger, and grief. From what I know, that's how it is for families of murder victims. It's certainly that way for me. The trial seems surreal, almost like it didn't happen. I'm glad Scott received the punishment he deserved, but I can't say I derived any satisfaction from it. There definitely hasn't been any closure.

Other than the steel doors in Scott's jail cell clanking shut every night, what's closed? The hole in my heart hasn't closed. Laci's still gone.

What happened is just sad. Laci, at twenty-seven years old, seven and a half months pregnant, exuberant, generous, full of life, and excited about the future, was murdered. The person responsible was the man she trusted more than anyone.

Our lives shouldn't be like this at all. Not Laci's, not Scott's, not ours, or the Petersons'. I'm heartsick for all of us. I still want to know what possessed him to do it. I want to know what he did. I want to know what happened to Laci. I want to know what made him think he could get away with it. So many questions unanswered.

And then, there was one brief, wonderful, peaceful moment when she came back. It was mid-June 2005, and I was asleep, dreaming about Laci—something I've rarely done. As it happened, I was also able to watch it from afar, two distinct vantage points, allowing me to remember the details with unusual clarity.

In the dream, the day was bright, warm, and sunny, and I felt the way I did before Laci was murdered, happy, content, and hopeful, like maybe something good was going to happen. Then I saw my dad, who's buried in the same cemetery as Laci, lead my daughter, whole and beautiful, out from her grave. My father knew how much I needed to see her. Holding her hand, he brought her home to me. Then he disappeared, leaving the two of us alone.

Laci and I were in the backyard, where we sat beneath the fruitless plum tree. I sat cross-legged and she laid on her right side with her cheek on my thigh. She was wearing the same bathrobe she'd worn as a little girl. I took my fingers and brushed her bangs to one side, stroked her cheek, and marveled that she always had the softest complexion.

Laci said something to me, and her voice was raspy from not

speaking for two years. It felt wonderful to have her back. I was able to touch her again. She looked up at me and smiled, the same way she did as a little girl, the same way she did as a teenager, the same way she did the last time we were together and I put my hand on her pregnant belly.

I was at peace. All was calm.

As she talked, Laci extended her left arm in the air, waving it around for emphasis. She always gestured as she talked. I used to say she talked with her hands, just as I did. We were alike in so many ways, close in so many ways. I stared at her beautiful little hand, adoring her long, slender fingers and soft skin. I saw her fingernails were polished.

"Is that Dutch Tulips?" I asked, remembering the name of the color both of us liked.

"Yes," she said with a giggle.

Then, she said something else. "Mom, why did Scott want to kill me?" she asked.

"I don't know, honey," I said.

"I didn't want to die," she said. "Why did this happen?"

"I don't know, honey," I repeated.

"Mom, I came to tell you that I'm okay," she said. "I wanted you to know that we're at peace. And I love you."

The last thing I remember is saying, "I love you, too." And I did. And I do. And I always will.

Acknowledgments

There are so many people to acknowledge and thank for their work, help, support, friendship, concern, prayers, and love. I'm obviously talking about more than this book, but this book wouldn't have been possible if I hadn't made it through this ordeal, and, although it sounds cliché, you can't possibly survive anything like this alone, and I was never alone.

Every day since December 24, 2002, I have stood in the center of a circle of love and derived the strength to face each obstacle from so many people, beginning with my family, Brent and Rose Rocha; Amy Rocha; my mother, Elta Anderson; my sister, Susie Aquino, and her husband, Gil; my cousin Gwen Kemple and her husband, Harvey; and, of course, my rock and my love Ron Grantski. They are my life support and helped me get through my darkest hours. Our lives have been changed and will never be the same.

The line separating family from friends disappeared that very first day when they left their dinners, canceled their plans, and came to help search for Laci. Many of us have been together every day ever since, and as a result, I no longer differentiate between family and friendship when it comes to Terri Western, Sandy Rickard, Lissa McElroy, Lin Pereira, and Patty Amador. They went far beyond friendship and provided more than anyone could possibly expect. Likewise, I could not feel any closer to or prouder of Laci's girlfriends Stacey Boyers, Lori

Ellsworth, Rene Tomlinson, Renee Garza, Kim Tyler, and Kim Mc-Neely. When I'm with them I feel as though I'm with Laci.

There are special people in this world who leave a lasting impression on you. Kim Petersen, Shelly Streeter, and Betty Williams, the staff at the Carole Sund/Carrington Foundation, and the foundation itself, have done just that. They gave of themselves far beyond the scope of their jobs.

As I've said, I didn't plan to write a book, but once I decided to do it I was helped by a first rate team of professionals. Todd Gold sat with me as I went through the devastating process of reliving this nightmare, and he delivered on his promise to ensure the words remained my own. My editor at Crown, Luke Dempsey, really connected with the material and with me personally, and he made sure I was satisfied with every page. Lindsey Moore, assistant to the editor, did a tremendous amount of work and a great job of sorting through and keeping track of the mess that was handed to her. I also appreciated the sage counsel of my agents, Endeavor's Brian Lipson and Dan Strone of Trident Media Group.

I want to thank my aunt Ruby and her husband, Ron, for their support and love and for attending the trial almost every day; Heather Smith, for helping me get through the worst times; Shawn Rocha, for establishing the Laci and Conner Memorial Bike Ride; Rita Keller and Bonnie Hearst, for coming back into my life; Don and Addie Hansberry, for your support and your love for Laci. Some things would have never happened without the special efforts of special people, including Lacipeterson.com webmaster Jonathan Smith; Candy Ballard, who also tended the Web site; our attorney Adam Stewart; the Red Lion Hotel and its management; all the wonderful people who set up and worked at the volunteer center; the selfless people who volunteered their time and efforts in the search for Laci; Donna, Don, and Don, MPD Police Chaplains and First Baptist Church for orchestrating the beautiful memorial service for Laci; Don and Maryanne, who generously gave us their home in Redwood City; Blake and Rita, who opened their home to our family; Bob and Larry, for donating an apartment for our use; Tim and Stephanie, the gracious owners of the

Canyon Inn; and, the very special individuals still wishing to remain anonymous who provided funds for the reward.

On January 7, 2005, the $50,000 reward was paid to the people who found Laci and Conner. They didn't attend the press conference, but I thanked them from the bottom of my heart. They could have kept walking and ignored what they found, but they didn't and we are eternally grateful to them.

It's still difficult to come to terms with the fact our lives will never be the way they once were, and I have realized that neither will the lives of so many of the dedicated professionals who worked on the case. It was never just a job to detectives Craig Grogan, Al Brocchini, and John Buehler or the prosecutors, Rick Distaso, Dave Harris, and Birgit Fladager. They lived the case day and night, and through their expertise, dedication, commitment, and humanity they encouraged me to have faith at a time when I could have easily lost it forever.

I want to say the same for Modesto Police Chief Roy Wasden, Stanislaus County District Attorney Jim Brazelton, D.A. criminal investigators Mark Smith and Kevin Bertalotto, Det. Phil Owen, Sgt. Doug Ridenour, Sgt. Ron Cloward, Alex Loya of the D.A.'s victim's services, Laurie Smandra of the FBI's victim services, and Mary Ganley of the San Mateo County Sheriff's Department. As I say in the book, the divers who searched the frigid bay waters for Laci moved me to tears, and I remain grateful.

After Scott was sentenced, the detectives and prosecutors who worked on the case took off extra time. All of them needed to regroup and be with their families again. Most of them had been on the case for more than two years, much of that time was around the clock, and it had a profound effect on their lives.

Our District Attorney, Jim Brazelton, has since retired, and Birgit Fladager is running for that office. Rick Distaso is now a judge; Dave Harris was promoted to Chief Deputy District Attorney. And Craig Grogan is still a detective with the Modesto Police Department. All of us stay in touch with one another..

One thing I want to emphasize: The leading cause of death among pregnant women is murder, and the father of the baby commits the overwhelming majority of those murders. Those are startling and sad facts, and it must stop. We need to impress upon our children—our future adults—that violence is not an alternative, and it should never be acceptable.

I will always speak for Laci and I will, forever, be her voice.

Index

If you would like to make a contribution to the Laci and Conner Search and Rescue Fund, please send your tax-deductible contribution to

The Laci and Conner Search and Rescue Fund
Administered by the Carole Sund/Carrington Foundation
PO Box 4113
Modesto, CA 95352-4113